D1447434

NEW PRAGMATISTS

New Pragmatists

Edited by
CHERYL MISAK

CLARENDON PRESS · OXFORD

OXFORD
UNIVERSITY PRESS

Great Clarendon Street, Oxford OX2 6DP

Oxford University Press is a department of the University of Oxford.
It furthers the University's objective of excellence in research, scholarship,
and education by publishing worldwide in

Oxford New York

Auckland Cape Town Dar es Salaam Hong Kong Karachi
Kuala Lumpur Madrid Melbourne Mexico City Nairobi
New Delhi Shanghai Taipei Toronto

With offices in

Argentina Austria Brazil Chile Czech Republic France Greece
Guatemala Hungary Italy Japan Poland Portugal Singapore
South Korea Switzerland Thailand Turkey Ukraine Vietnam

Oxford is a registered trade mark of Oxford University Press
in the UK and in certain other countries

Published in the United States
by Oxford University Press Inc., New York

British Library Cataloguing in Publication Data

Data available

Library of Congress Cataloging in Publication Data

Data available

Typeset by Laserwords Private Limited, Chennai, India
Printed in Great Britain
on acid-free paper by
Biddles Ltd, King's Lynn, Norfolk

ISBN 978–0–19–927997–5

1 3 5 7 9 10 8 6 4 2

Contents

List of Contributors

David Bakhurst is Professor of Philosophy at Queen's University, Kingston, Canada. His areas of expertise include ethics, epistemology, and Russian philosophy and psychology. In addition to many articles in books and journals, he is the author of *Consciousness and Revolution in Soviet Philosophy* (Cambridge University Press, 1991) and co-editor (with Christine Sypnowich) of *The Social Self* (Sage, 1995) and (with Stuart Shanker) of *Jerome Bruner: Language, Culture, Self* (Sage, 2001).

Arthur Fine is Professor of Philosophy and Adjunct Professor of Physics and of History at the University of Washington. Past President of the Philosophy of Science Association and of the Central Division of the American Philosophical Association, his research concentrates on the foundations of quantum physics and interpretative issues relating to the development of the natural and social sciences. His works include *The Shaky Game: Einstein, Realism and the Quantum Theory* (University of Chicago Press, 1996).

Ian Hacking is Professor of Philosophy and History of Scientific Concepts at the Collège de France, author of numerous books on probability, experimental science, the philosophy of language, and psychiatric disorders. His most recent books are *The Social Construction of What?* (Harvard University Press, 1999) and *Historical Ontology* (Harvard University Press, 2002).

David Macarthur is a Lecturer in the Philosophy Department at the University of Sydney. His interests include scepticism, pragmatism, philosophy of psychology, history of modern philosophy, Wittgenstein, and aesthetics. He co-edited (with Mario De Caro) *Naturalism in Question* (Harvard University Press, 2006).

Danielle Macbeth is Professor of Philosophy at Haverford College in Pennsylvania. She is the author of *Frege's Logic* (Harvard University Press, 2005), and has also written on issues in the philosophy of language, the philosophy of mind, and the history and philosophy of mathematics. Her current major project is 'The Metaphysics of Judgment: Truth and Knowledge in the Exact Sciences'.

Cheryl Misak is Professor of Philosophy at the University of Toronto. She is the author of *Truth and the End of Inquiry: A Peircean Account of Truth* (Clarendon Press, 1991 and 2004), *Verificationism: Its History and Prospects* (Routledge, 1995), and *Truth, Politics, Morality: Pragmatism and Deliberation* (Routledge, 2000).

Terry Pinkard is University Professor at Georgetown University. He is the author of *Hegel's Phenomenology: The Sociality of Reason* (Cambridge University Press, 1994), *Hegel: A Biography* (Cambridge University Press, 2000) and *German Philosophy 1760–1860: The Legacy of Idealism* (Cambridge University Press, 2002).

Huw Price is Federation Fellow and Challis Professor of Philosophy at the University of Sydney, where he heads the Centre for Time in the Department of Philosophy. He was formerly Professor of Logic and Metaphysics at the University of Edinburgh. His publications include *Facts and the Function of Truth* (Blackwell, 1988), *Time's Arrow and Archimedes' Point* (Oxford University Press, 1996), and a range of articles in journals such as *Journal of Philosophy*, *Mind*, *British Journal of Philosophy of Science*, and *Nature*.

Jeffrey Stout is a member of the Department of Religion at Princeton, where he is also associated with the departments of Philosophy and Politics, the Center for Human Values, and the Center for the Study of Religion. His most recent book is *Democracy and Tradition* (Princeton University Press, 2004).

Introduction

As Robert Westbrook, our best intellectual historian of pragmatism, notes, pragmatists have always disagreed amongst themselves about the content of the position. Charles Sanders Peirce, the founder of the doctrine,

> quickly denied paternity of the child James had adopted and announced he would henceforth refer to his own doctrine as 'pragmaticism', a word 'ugly enough to be safe from kidnappers'. John Dewey, though deeply indebted to James's thinking, nonetheless took care to distinguish his own 'instrumentalism' from what he took to be James's more tender-minded efforts to use pragmatism to secure religious belief. Peirce, in turn, responded to Dewey's praise of his essay on 'What Pragmatism Is' (1905) with a puzzled letter noting that Dewey's instrumental logic 'forbids all such researches as those which I have been absorbed in for the last eighteen years'. (Westbrook 2005: 1)

New Pragmatists can be seen as the latest contribution to this long-standing set of debates. Some of the papers in this volume explicitly try to reclaim the label 'pragmatism' from a particular interpretation of it—from Richard Rorty's view that there is no truth or objectivity to be had, only solidarity, or agreement within a community, or what our peers will let us get away with saying. But all the papers—even those with no mention of Rorty—are united in their efforts to articulate a position that tries to do justice to the objective dimension of *human* inquiry.

Ian Hacking calls Rorty's view 'neo-pragmatism' to distinguish it from classical pragmatism. I'm happy enough to put up with the infelicity and distinguish Rorty's neo-pragmatism from what I am calling 'new pragmatism'. Jeffrey Stout's terminology for the view which interests us here is the 'revisionist movement in contemporary pragmatism'. Whatever we call it, this kind of position is emerging from a variety of sources—such as the work of Simon Blackburn, Robert Brandom, Donald Davidson, John McDowell, and Crispin Wright. It is not of much concern in this volume whether these philosophers have in fact been influenced by the classical pragmatists or whether they see themselves as part of the pragmatist tradition. What matters is that the best of Peirce, James, and Dewey has resurfaced in deep, interesting, and fruitful ways. Hacking's riff on James's *Pragmatism: A New Way for Some Old Ways of Thinking* is apt: *Pragmatism: An Old Name for Some Ways of Thinking a Century Later*. The essays in this volume give us a multi-faceted snapshot of these now popular ways of thinking.

Danielle Macbeth, for instance, begins with a contrast between, on the one hand, Sellars and Peirce, who take the pragmatist conception of meaning to contribute to an adequate account of truth, and on the other, James, Dewey, and Rorty, who take that same conception of meaning to foreclose the possibility of such an account of truth. Her aim is to explain both why there is the latter position and how we might go forward in the spirit of the former.

One of the pillars of the new pragmatism is the thought that standards of objectivity come into being and evolve over time, but that being historically situated in this way does not detract from their objectivity. The trail of the human serpent is over everything, as James said, but this does not toss us into the sea of post-modern arbitrariness, where truth varies from person to person and culture to culture. As Hacking puts it:

We discovered how to make proofs in mathematics . . . discovered the laboratory style of reasoning, in which one manufactures apparatus to purify and even to create phenomena, and thereby generates new ways to be truthful about unobservable structures that underlie experience. The fact, that the methods of argument we now regard as canonical have a history, and once did not exist even for the wisest of the ancients, does not make them any the less the objective standards.

Stout also puts the point nicely: 'Philosophers who believe that classical pragmatism was on to something important . . . have recently renewed the effort to provide accounts of inquiry that are both recognizably pragmatic in orientation and demonstrably hospitable to the cognitive aspiration to get one's subject matter right.' Arthur Fine and David Macarther and Huw Price join forces with Hacking, Stout, and Macbeth to give us deep accounts of how the pragmatist might pull this off.

Another pillar of the new pragmatism (and of classical pragmatism as well) is that knowledge has no certain foundations. All beliefs, no matter how strongly held, are fallible. Hacking notes that some will trace this thought to Hegel, and Terry Pinkard, Macbeth, and Stout give us a sense of how the connection between pragmatism and Hegel can be made. Macbeth argues that science is an ongoing, so historical, enterprise which involves fundamental transformations in our being in the world as it progresses through various stages. She argues that the pragmatist conception of meaning applies only to modern mathematical concepts, and that the capacity to have such concepts essentially depends on our first having a natural language. She sketches a story about how we begin as mere animals, become rational animals through acculturation into natural language, and then become moderns through our development and use of a symbolic language.

Stout and Pinkard focus on the issue of normative authority as the link between pragmatism and Hegel. Pinkard examines Hegel's thought that we can be subject only to those norms of which we can regard ourselves as the authors. He says, getting at the very heart of Hegel and of the new pragmatism:

On the one hand, from the normative point of view, there is no 'outside'; wherever we stand, we are always, to use a Sellarsian turn of phrase, inside the practice of giving and asking for reasons. Yet it is also quite clear that we can take an 'outside' point of view on our own reasons, and, still standing within the space of reasons, look at our own and others' claims as the products of class, history, self-deception . . . and so on.

Stout takes up the idea that 'To be a subject in this (Hegelian) sense is . . . to be a constrained doer, a user of norms, a locus of responsibility, and thus someone fit to be held responsible by others and by oneself to obey those norms that prove capable of critical questioning'.

Indeed, you will find in these essays a sustained interest in norms. We are in the position, says Fine, of Kuhn's revolutionary scientist 'who must choose how to project the values of established practice into new terrain and, at the very same time, must oversee how things go and adjust accordingly'.

That is, as Peirce and Dewey stressed, we are always immersed in a context of inquiry, where the decision to be made is a decision about what to believe from here, not what to believe were we able to start from scratch—from certain infallible foundations. We do not go forward arbitrarily. That would be a relativism of the 'silly' or 'idiot' kind, in Fine's view, not the sophisticated relativism/pragmatism that he offers. The central question for Fine—and for all pragmatists—is the question of how we should go from present practice to a future practice, where our very standards themselves may be thrown into question. He argues that our judgements about how to go on are *judgements*, not 'arbitrary whims'—they depend on reasons, ideas, experience, goals, interests, and on 'cooperation with the natural world'. Science is a 'rational enterprise without foundations'.

Macbeth argues that logic is in the same boat, not only for Peirce but also for Frege, and Stout argues that morals and politics are in it as well. The practice of ethics has us following norms which require resistance to the selfishness and self-delusion of the ego and disciplined attention to the actual merits, needs, and suffering of others. The practice of democratic social criticism has us following norms which require attention to the condition of the least well-off and suspicion of the self-justifying stories that societies tell of themselves.

In the practice of science, the norms require us to observe objects. As Stout says: 'The norms in each case are embedded in social practices. But [they] orient one's attention to objects (that is, persons and things) that are distinct from the inquiring subject and distinct also from any consensus that may have been reached among inquiring subjects.' Stout puts the new pragmatist thought nicely and attributes this version of it to Brandom: 'Apart from such practices, there is no such thing as getting something right or wrong. But in trying to correct and replace previous descriptions of something . . . what we are doing is holding our descriptions of the things *answerable* to the thing.'

The 'boat' metaphor here is of course apt—Fine quite rightly aligns Neurath with pragmatism. Neurath's image of having to rebuild our boat of knowledge plank by plank while at sea might well be thought of as the insight at the heart of Peirce, James, and Dewey. Peirce's own metaphor is strikingly similar: science 'is not standing upon the bedrock of fact. It is walking upon a bog, and can only say, this ground seems to hold for the present. Here I will stay until it begins to give way' (*CP* 5. 589).

There is one further pillar of pragmatism, again shared (at least in theory) by all versions of pragmatism. That is the commitment to 'taking a look', as Hacking calls it—to keeping philosophy connected to first-order inquiry, to real examples, to real-life expertise. Peirce's pragmatic maxim, which is designed to capture not a full account of meaning, but rather, an important aspect of meaning, is that to understand a concept, we need to explore its relationship with practical endeavours.

Rorty claims to be doing just this when he 'finds' that the concept of truth plays no role in our inquiries. But as Price shows so nicely in 'Truth as Convenient Friction' (2003), had Rorty taken a more careful look, he would have found that truth is indeed necessary for our debates and inquiries. Without it, there could be no disagreement and no conversation at all. Getting something right, as Stout argues, 'turns out to be among the human interests that need to be taken into account in an acceptably anthropocentric conception of inquiry as a social practice'.

In my own contribution to this volume, I take a look at how the concept of truth plays a role in human life and inquiry. Truth, I argue, is the aim of inquiry. But truth here is truth as Peirce saw it—belief that would be indefeasible or not defeated by evidence and argument. The pragmatist account of truth, I claim, captures the naturalist spirit of certain deflationist accounts of truth, yet is robust enough to explain why truth is important to us.

Macarthur and Price also argue that we must focus on the function or use of the concept of truth. If natural creatures in our circumstances come to speak in certain ways, there is no further puzzle to be worked through. In both my paper and in theirs, one will find an argument that the pragmatist conception of truth, *contra* Wright and Blackburn, cannot merely hold locally (in ethics, for instance), but must hold everywhere—it must be a global account.

Continuing in the vein of taking a look at our practices of investigating, Fine examines the practice of science, and David Bakhurst examines the practice of ethics. Bakhurst sets the pragmatist epistemology going in the language of Sellars and McDowell. The space of moral reasons is real, but it can be inhabited only by beings that can occupy the moral point of view. We cannot step outside of ethical thought and practice and view our practices 'sideways on'. He goes on to argue that rationality and consistency cannot be fully explained in terms of adherence to a set of rules or principles. Rather, moral judgement demands sensitivity to the salient moral dimensions of particular cases. The new pragmatist will 'elucidate moral concepts by a detailed exploration of their role in our lives. The task will be to see what is actually going on when people engage in moral evaluation, deliberate about what to do, justify their decisions, praise and blame others, and so on'.

As Macarthur and Price argue, 'The pragmatist we have in mind wants to dismiss or demote . . . metaphysical puzzles in favour of more practical questions, about the roles and functions of the matters in question in human life.' This is indeed what lies at the heart of pragmatism and the hope is that the new pragmatists can connect our philosophical concepts of truth, rationality, and norms to the practices which are so central to human life—science, ethics, and politics. If the essays in this volume elucidate some of those connections, then something substantial will have been done for pragmatism's good name.

BIBLIOGRAPHY

Peirce, C. S., *Collected Papers of Charles Sanders Peirce*, i–vi, ed. C. Hartshorne and P. Weiss (1931–5); vii and viii, ed. A. Burks (1958) Cambridge, Mass.: Belknap Press; abbreviated *CP*.

Price, H. (2003) 'Truth as Convenient Friction'. *Journal of Philosophy*, 100: 167–90.

Westbrook, Robert (2005) *Democratic Hope: Pragmatism and the Politics of Truth*. Ithaca, NY: Cornell University Press.

1

On Our Interest in Getting Things Right: Pragmatism without Narcissism

Jeffrey Stout

The trail of the human serpent is . . . over everything.

—William James, 'What Pragmatism Means' (1991: 31)

The critics of pragmatism have long charged that it fails to do justice to the objective dimension of human inquiry. Philosophers who believe that classical pragmatism was on to something important, but that it requires careful reformulation if it is to meet the objections that have been raised against it, have recently renewed the effort to provide accounts of inquiry that are both recognizably pragmatic in orientation and demonstrably hospitable to the cognitive aspiration to get one's subject matter right. One example of such an account can be found in Robert Brandom's massive book *Making It Explicit* (1994: esp. ch. 8, sect. IV). One of Bjørn Ramberg's recent papers (2000), though hardly as elaborate, also aims to provide such an account. Both of these philosophers explicate cognitive aspirations and conceptual norms pragmatically—as artifacts arising in human discursive practices of a certain kind. In framing their explications, they rigorously avoid resorting to metaphysical talk about correspondence to the real. But they also want to be able, at the end of the day, to affirm coherently that inquiry is an *objective* affair, that it is *successful by its own lights* only to the extent that it *correctly* characterizes the subject matter it has taken up—a cognitive achievement of which neither the individuals nor the communities engaged in inquiry can ever be perfectly certain. Even though inquiry is best conceived as an essentially social activity, whether what we say is correct in this objective sense is not to be understood as conforming to social consensus, for all of us could be wrong about the topic being discussed.

By emphasizing objectivity and the possibility of collective error in this way, Brandom and Ramberg are trying to supply something they find lacking in the work of Richard Rorty, a philosopher they both greatly admire. My books *Ethics after Babel* and *Democracy and Tradition* belong to the same revisionist movement in contemporary pragmatism and exhibit a similarly selective appropriation of Rorty's writings.[1] In this paper I assess Rorty's response to the interest his revisionist friends have shown in correcting his pronouncements and in rehabilitating 'the rhetoric of "objectivity" ' (Rorty 2003: 6). With one crucial exception, which emerges in the final pages of *Rorty and his Critics* (2000a), Rorty's response has been to warn his fellow pragmatists against backsliding. But the exception complicates things considerably, as we shall see.

Rorty's worry is that the new pragmatists are undermining a crucial insight expressed in William James's famous dictum about the trail of the human serpent. Either the trail of the serpent is over *everything*, or it isn't. To imply that it isn't, for Rorty, is to go over to the other side. The attempt to rehabilitate the rhetoric of objectivity within the context of a pragmatic philosophy actually gives away the store. Rorty's point is not, of course, that pragmatism has an essence and that anyone who wants to be called a pragmatist must endorse it. His point is that the most interesting and liberating thing in pragmatism is the boldly thorough character of its anthropocentrism. To compromise its anthropocentric account of inquiry—as a set of human activities answerable only to human interests—is to deprive pragmatism of its radical challenge to the received philosophical tradition and to the culture in which ideas from that tradition circulate.

Brandom and Ramberg are both trying to develop a kind of prag-matism that avoids what Mark Johnston calls narcissism (1993b).[2] It goes without saying that all pragmatic accounts of inquiry accord some kind of philosophical priority to human practices, and thus involve

---

[1] Ch. 11 of *Ethics after Babel*, expanded edn. (Stout 2001) criticizes Rorty's 'pithy little formulae' at some length. Ch. 3 of *Democracy and Tradition* (Stout 2004) criticizes his secularist political theory for violating his own ideal of 'conversation'. Part 3 of the latter book does not discuss Rorty at any length, but one of its purposes is to outline a version of pragmatism that can inherit the strengths but not the weaknesses in Rorty's various formulations.

[2] Johnston (1993a) is another important attempt to formulate a revisionist pragmatism.

some kind of anthropocentrism. The question is whether pragmatic anthropocentrism can be formulated in a way that makes sense of the ways in which inquirers show concern for things distinct from themselves and from the practices in which they are engaged. 'Narcissism' in Johnston's sense—the sense at issue in *Democracy and Tradition* and in this paper—simply refers to anthropocentrism of a sort that loses sight of the objective dimension of inquiry. As Rorty sees it, however, the point of pragmatism is 'precisely to encourage narcissism':

> What Stout calls narcissism, I would call self-reliance. As I see it, the whole point of pragmatism is to insist that we human beings are answerable only to one another. We are answerable only to those who answer to us—only to conversation partners. We are not responsible either to the atoms or to God, at least not until they start conversing with us. (2003: 6)

'Narcissism', Rorty thinks, is simply a pejorative label for the original Jamesian claim that the trail of the human serpent is indeed over *everything*. A pragmatist who abandons this claim is, in Rorty's eyes, about as interesting as a libertarian who favours the Patriot Act or a Marxist who doesn't believe in revolution.

When Rorty declares that he is a narcissist and proud of it, he addresses us as the radical herald of a future in which people will no longer concern themselves with truth and objectivity, thus freeing them up to embrace self-reliance shamelessly. This is Rorty's prophetic persona, which he adopts whenever he wants to emphasise his distance from both the received philosophical tradition and the intuitions that it appeals to for support. The dramatic mask he wears at these moments bears the image of Friedrich Nietzsche—Nietzsche as Rorty imagines him, not, say, as Bernard Williams (2002) did. As Rorty put it more than two decades ago, 'there is nothing deep down inside us except what we have put there ourselves, no criterion that we have not created in the course of creating a practice, no standard of rationality that is not an appeal to such a criterion, no rigorous argumentation that is not obedience to our own conventions' (1982: p. xlii). His utopia is a 'post-Philosophical culture' (1982: p. xlii) in which thoroughgoing self-reliance would replace authoritarianism as the common sense of the age. His 'preferred narrative is a story of human beings as having recently gotten out from under the thought of, and the need for, authority' (1995: 71).

The persona of the Nietzschean prophet is also the one Rorty adopts when expressing the view that truth and objectivity are nothing 'more than what our peers will, *ceteris paribus*, let us get away with saying' (1979: 176). This view reduces inquiry of all kinds to cultural politics. 'Those who wish to ground solidarity in objectivity—call them "realists"—have to construe truth as correspondence to reality,' Rorty says. 'By contrast, those who wish *to reduce objectivity to solidarity*—call them "pragmatists"—do not require either a metaphysics or an epistemology.... For pragmatists, the desire for objectivity is not the desire to escape the limitations of one's community, but simply the desire for as much intersubjective agreement as possible, the desire to extend the reference of "us" as far as we can' (1991: n. 22; italics added). In passages like these, Rorty appears to commit himself to reducing truth and objectivity to matters of social fact—in short, to a kind of anti-realism. While this commitment would lend support to the idea that junking the rhetoric of objectivity completely (in favour of an idiom of social consensus) is both possible and advisable, it is not the only view Rorty has expressed, and it seems not to be his considered opinion.

Let us therefore consider Rorty's other personae. He sometimes styles himself as a therapeutic thinker, who sets out not to reform ordinary uses of 'true' by redefining truth sociologically, but rather to help us recognize and resist the philosophical temptation that repeatedly emerges in their vicinity. In Ludwig Wittgenstein's terms, this is the temptation to assert philosophical theses, either realist or anti-realist in content, about what truth is. In Donald Davidson's terms, it is the temptation of defining truth. When arguing along these lines, Rorty at one point says that pragmatism, in the sense that both James and Davidson are pragmatists, 'offers no "theory of truth."' All it gives us is an explanation of why, in this area, less is more—of why therapy is better than system-building' (1991: 128). The therapy is directed against the compulsion to take sides in an endless and fruitless metaphysical debate between those who define truth as correspondence to reality and those who define it in terms of either idealist metaphysics or sociology. The therapeutic Rorty carefully backs away from his own anti-realist definitions of truth, and instead reinforces the idea that nonphilosophical uses of 'true'—whether they appear in scientific, moral, aesthetic, or religious contexts—are perfectly in order.

Of course, a strictly therapeutic philosophical persona is ill-suited to prophecy. In his prophetic mode, Rorty asserts what appear to be rather sweeping philosophical theses, which take the form of a utopian vision of post-Philosophical culture and a corresponding meta-narrative about the overcoming of authoritarianism. While Rorty seems inclined in his more scrupulous moods to stand clear of both realist and anti-realist theories of truth, thereby confining himself to a therapeutic stance on this particular philosophical issue, he does not in fact restrict himself to writing patiently therapeutic Wittgensteinian diagnoses. In a paper on John McDowell, he writes:

Like me, McDowell regards himself as a therapeutic philosopher. He hopes, as I do, to create a 'frame of mind in which we would no longer seem to be faced with problems that call on philosophy to bring subject and object back together again.' We both want to 'achieve an intellectual right to shrug our shoulders at skeptical questions' and to 'disown an obligation to try to answer the characteristic questions of modern philosophy'. (1998: 142)

But Rorty quickly shifts into a prophetic mode that is entirely lacking in McDowell's more consistently therapeutic writing:

I take the linguistic turn in philosophy . . . to be a turn away from the very idea of human answerability to the world. I agree with Heidegger that there is a straight line between the Cartesian quest for certainty and the Nietzschean will to power. So I think that modern European philosophy amounts to an attempt by human beings to wrest power from God—or, more placidly put, to dispense with the idea of human answerability to something nonhuman. . . . I regard the need for world-directedness as a relic of the need for authoritarian guidance, the need against which Nietzsche and his fellow pragmatists revolted. (1998: 142–3)

In Rorty's work therapeutic diagnosis becomes a means for advancing an assertively prophetic vision that is not content to leave everything as it is.

The implications of this stance for modern philosophy are not immediately clear. On the one hand, 'the characteristic questions of modern philosophy' are to remain unanswered. We are meant to shrug them off, and to seek therapy whenever this proves difficult. On the other hand, the modern philosophical 'attempt by human beings to . . . dispense with the idea of human answerability to something nonhuman' is to be accepted. This latter claim calls to mind Robert Pippin's *Modernism as a Philosophical Problem* (1999), which argues that the central question of modern philosophy is whether the quest for self-reliance or autonomy can be realized in acceptable terms. Rorty implicitly grants that modern philosophy, construed as a quest for self-reliance, is the very tradition to which he pledges allegiance. This is the tradition that his pragmatism strives to complete. The modern philosophical questions that Rorty hopes to shrug off are the ones that derive principally from Cartesian representationalism. These are the questions that have for too long burdened the modernist quest for self-reliance with metaphysical and epistemological concerns about the gap between subject and object. As long as the quest for self-reliance is carried out and evaluated in terms of subject–object dualism, Rorty thinks it is bound to seem an essentially *subjective aspiration* in need of *objective authorization*. Viewed in this light, Rorty's work does not prophesy the advent of a culture that has no use for philosophy. Rather, it aims to disentangle two equally ambitious philosophical projects from each other in the hope of fostering the one he favours. The contribution he hopes to make to modernism involves rescuing the project of self-reliance from the clutches of representationalism.

If Rorty were a strictly therapeutic pragmatist (in the sense that entails being a theoretical quietist), he would need to argue that concerns about subjectivity and objectivity and about the nature of truth are the product of a metaphysical picture that philosophers have wrongly been tempted to read into ordinary language. Whereas this seems to be the tack he takes in his remarks about the nonphilosophical uses of 'true', he is generally reluctant to place much weight on the line between the ordinary and the philosophical. He has recently dissociated himself from philosophers who place 'emphasis on the Ordinary and on the need to avoid putting forward theses in philosophy. . . . The Ordinary strikes me as just the latest disguise of the *ontos on*' (2000c: 90). He rejects the 'wholesale quietistic impulse. I am anxious to give the peace of the grave to lots of worn-out old philosophical problems . . . but I have no doubt that every attempt to get rid of old problems by revisionary attempts to break free of old inferential connections will itself generate unexpected new inferential connections, new paradoxes, and (eventually) new "problems of philosophy" for the textbooks to mummify' (2000d: 348). Rorty's pragmatism is just such a revisionary project. Its exercises in therapeutic analysis are instrumental to his larger prophetic purpose, which Pippin identifies as the project of modernism in philosophy. Any intuitions or features of ordinary usage that stand in the way of this project are to be discarded. Rorty attributes no authority to them at all.

When writing in praise of therapeutic philosophy and against system building, Rorty seems to rule out endorsement of any full-blown philosophy as a successor to the representationalism of the Cartesian era. But there are other passages in which he seems to imply that Davidson has developed a systematic philosophy of language and mind that he is prepared to accept, at least in outline. Given that Davidson favoured the concise, free-standing essay to the treatise as a mode of expression, Rorty even occasionally volunteers his services as an expositor of the interconnections among his most important claims. Those claims add up to 'a picture of the relations between the human self and the world which, though "naturalized" through and through, excludes nothing'. Rorty goes on to declare Davidson's work 'the culmination of a line of thought in American philosophy which aims at being naturalistic without being reductionist' (1991: 113). When he criticizes Davidson, it is mainly for failing to recognize the true import of Davidsonian philosophy. For in Rorty's view, Davidson, by eschewing the concept of representation and related notions, worked out a philosophical vocabulary in which the problems characteristic of representationalism do not arise. It is therefore a vocabulary that assists the pragmatic revisionist in articulating the aspirations of self-reliant human practices without appearing to succumb to any sort of subjectivism.

Davidson's is not the only such vocabulary. Nietzsche's French followers, such as Michel Foucault and Jacques Derrida, have produced others. Much of Rorty's writing is designed to display the advantages which these various vocabularies possess and to correct their deficiencies. The advantages all have to do with their utility as vehicles of self-reliance. The deficiencies fall into three distinct categories. The first category includes conceptual commitments that, from Rorty's point of view, reflect excessive deference to the intuitions and concepts accorded priority in representationalism. The second category includes neglect of the political and cultural projects of self-reliance manifested in the institutions and practices of liberal democracy. The third category includes outright antipathy for those institutions and practices. The problems that Rorty identifies in Nietzsche's French followers fall mainly into the third category. Rorty traces Davidson's neglect of liberal democracy to the scientism he inherited from his analytic teachers. The remedy for such neglect is the same as the remedy for the hatred of liberal democracy expressed by the Nietzscheans—namely, the example of John Dewey.

Davidson's vocabulary does not help the friends of self-reliance fight their political or cultural battles in any direct way. What it does help with is the articulation of an acceptable form of naturalism. Naturalism is a vehicle for the expression of self-reliance, according to Rorty, insofar as it displaces the urge to surrender cognitive authority to the allegedly supernatural source of all things. But so long as naturalism remains trapped within a representationalist dualism of subject and object, its account of inquiry must tilt toward either subjectivism or objectivism. If it tilts in the former direction, it will make inquiry seem to be cut off from the nonhuman world of which human beings seek knowledge. If it tilts in the latter direction, it will make inquiry answerable to the nonhuman world in a way that compromises self-reliance. The former option leaves us trapped in our own subjectivity. The latter essentially abandons the self-reliance that the Enlightenment thought it had gained in overcoming authoritarian supernaturalism. Davidson's achievement, as Rorty sees it, is to slip between the horns of this dilemma by reformulating naturalism in a nonrepresentationalist idiom. To the extent that the resulting form of naturalism is also nonreductive—insofar as it precludes, say, the reduction of talk about human intentions to talk about microphysical entities—it also opens up plenty of space for the vocabularies in which we express Romantic aspirations of personal self-trust and collective self-determination. It is by opening up this space that it provides indirect support for the political and cultural projects of self-reliance. Even so, according to Rorty, Davidsonian naturalism needs some fine-tuning, because Davidson was at some points insufficiently radical in describing what he was doing.

Ramberg (2000: n. 352) takes Rorty to have been especially troubled in the 1990s by Davidson's insistence on attributing philosophical importance to two topics, one of which is the concept of truth. In the first chapter of *Truth and Progress* (1998: 19–42) Rorty approves of Davidson's refusal to define truth, but criticizes his equally adamant refusal to endorse a deflationary attitude toward this topic. Rorty recognises that Davidson makes essential use of the concept of truth in constructing his accounts of belief and meaning. All this shows, to Rorty's mind, is that among the perfectly innocuous uses of the term 'true' is the disquotational one that Davidson's theorizing exploits. This is one of the uses that Rorty catalogues in his earlier interpretation of Davidsonian pragmatism (1991: 128). Rorty holds that Davidson exaggerates the significance of the concept by taking what is best described as a 'theory of complex behavior' and labelling it misleadingly as a theory of truth (Ramberg 2000: 353). That the theory employs the concept of truth does not make it a theory of truth. Davidson responds by arguing that insofar as his theory succeeds in explaining complex human behavior, the essential use which his theory makes of the concept of truth reveals that without this concept 'we would not be thinking creatures, nor would we understand what it is for someone else to be a thinking creature' (2000: 72).

This dispute might seem to be a minor terminological quarrel, but for Rorty it was not minor at all. Representationalism makes everything seem to hang on the concept of truth. Overemphasizing this concept's importance while distancing himself from pragmatic deflationism led Davidson to say, for example, that 'truth depends on how the world is' (2000: 73) and thus to create 'new pseudo-problems in the course of dissolving old ones' (Rorty 2000*b*: 78). Such remarks are regressive, Rorty thinks, because they threaten to obscure the significance of Davidson's rejection of representationalism. Rorty's project of self-reliance demands a clean break with the preoccupations and categories of representationalism. The remark that 'truth depends on how the world is' almost begs for explication in representationalist terms—as a relation of correspondence between representation and represented. This remark is a prime example of what Rorty means by the rhetoric of objectivity.

The second issue to which Ramberg calls attention concerns Davidson's claim that interpretation is indeterminate, which Rorty had declared a regrettable holdover from Quine's scientism. Even if we knew all of the physical facts, according to Davidson, this would not settle which interpretation of a person's verbal and nonverbal behavior we should accept. In Quine's work, this thesis does serve a philosophical program that places scientific explanation on a firmer ontological footing than the interpretation of human agency—the former being a realm of 'fact', whereas the latter is not. Ramberg argues, however, that Davidson succeeded in disentangling this thesis entirely from its original Quinean context and, at least in his later work, had no interest in ranking vocabularies according to their respective abilities to state facts. In Davidson's 'deontologized version' of indeterminacy, Ramberg argues, what we have is 'simply a way of putting the point that one vocabulary is not reducible to the other' (2000: 356). This point is essential to a sort of nonreductive naturalism that lends indirect support to the political and cultural projects of self-reliance.[3] But that is not the point's sole significance. For once the irreducibility of the vocabulary of agency is raised to awareness in this way, the next thing that comes into view is the same vocabulary's indispensability to any enterprise, including any form of scientific inquiry, that concerns itself with applying the norms of rationality and objectivity or with the difference between true and false beliefs. According to Davidson, our use of the scientific vocabulary

---

[3] This is a topic on which Ramberg writes with eloquence (2000: 356, 364–7).

of prediction and control requires, as its essential background, a community of agents 'engaged in the project of describing their world and interpreting each other's descriptions of it' (Ramberg 2000: 362). Only because we actually employ the vocabulary of agency and invoke the norms implicit in that vocabulary when communicating with one another are we able to engage in anything worth calling inquiry.

When Davidson said, 'There is no going outside this standard to check whether we have things right' (Ramberg 2000: 361, quoting Davidson) he was making a claim fully in keeping with Rorty's commitment to self-reliance. But, as Ramberg rightly argues, this claim goes hand in hand with Davidson's claims about the norms of rationality and about the need for charitable interpretation of others. The self-reliant inquirer is also inescapably a member of an interpretive community, an invoker of norms involving the notion of rationality, and a person constantly engaged in distinguishing truth from error on a retail basis. The concern with truth expressed in the process of repeatedly drawing this distinction with respect to particular beliefs and statements does not involve treating truth as the overarching goal of inquiry, as distinct from other human interests. Nor does it involve treating 'reality as it is in itself' as a nonhuman source of authority. But it does involve an attempt—indeed, a largely successful attempt, if Davidson was right—to offer descriptions of the specific subject matter being discussed in one's community at any given moment, to interpret what the descriptions being offered by others mean, and to evaluate those descriptions (under an interpretation) as correct or incorrect. As Ramberg writes:

The possibility of *error*, generalised in the notion of inappropriateness with respect to purpose, goal, or end, takes the form in (assertively-used) language of the possibility of a failure of a claim to be in accord with what it says something about. That possibility is inseparable from the capacity of redescription to affect our *dispositions*, because it reflects the fact that utterances are utterances—uses of language—just in so far as they link particular occasions of utterance with other possible or actual occasions or situations. (2000: 363; italics in original)

The best reason for describing Davidson's theory of complex behavior as a theory of *truth* is that the notion of a descriptive claim's *being in accord with what it says something about* is, according to theory, essential to human inquiry, language use, and, for that matter, agency in general.

Rorty responds to Ramberg not by issuing the expected warning about the dangers of rehabilitating the rhetoric of objectivity, but rather, remarkably, by declaring him correct on both points. First, Ramberg succeeds in showing how Davidson's doctrine of the indeterminacy of interpretation can be dissociated from the Quinean project of scientistic ontology and induced to lend support to the Rortian project of pragmatic self-reliance. In showing this, he persuades Rorty that the vocabulary of agency is privileged in the sense of being inescapable. 'We cannot stop prescribing, and *just* describe, because the describing counts *as* describing only if rule-governed, only if conducted by people who talk about each other [and to each other] in the vocabulary of agency' (2000*a*: 372; italics in original).[4] Second, Ramberg is correct in holding that Rorty had made a mistake in going 'from criticism of attempts to define truth as accurate representation of the intrinsic nature of reality to a denial that true statements get things right'. And from this it follows, says Rorty, that 'true' and 'refers' do name word–world relations, albeit noncausal ones, after all. Thus Rorty shall no longer 'be able to say that *all* our relations to the world are causal relations'. He is quick to add that he is not here reinstating the notion of 'reality as it is in itself'. What a true descriptive claim about the whiteness of snow is true *of* is not reality as it is in itself—an adventitious representationalist notion—but rather *snow*, an entity referred to by the relevant descriptive expression, an entity we pick out by employing that expression. 'No snow, no truth about snow, because nothing to get right.' We talk about snow because it serves our interests to do so, interests that cannot be reduced to an interest in truth as accurate representation. This, Rorty says, is the truth in pragmatism. '*What is true in realism*', however, '*is that most of what you talk about you get right*' (2000*a*: 374; italics in original).

These lines from Rorty's response to Ramberg comprise the most startling passage in *Rorty and his Critics* and one as surprising as any in the entirety of Rorty's published writings. Rorty is not usually in the business of explaining how to combine what is true in pragmatism with what is true in realism. I am tempted to sum up what he is doing in this passage by saying that he is trying to formulate a non-narcissistic pragmatism, a pragmatism that can do justice to the objective dimension of inquiry. For he is describing inquiry as a human practice that answers to human interests, but also as portraying *as an expression of human interests* the distinction between getting one's subject matter right and merely holding beliefs about that subject matter (or holding beliefs that one's peers would let one get away with holding). The norms we are

---

4 The point I have inserted in brackets is made on p. 373.

guided by in this practice, however fallibly, are norms of the people, by the people, and for the people participating in the practice. But those norms have to do with getting things right in a sense of 'right' that cannot be reduced to communal agreement.

The philosophers I am calling revisionist pragmatists are all trying to get both of these points adequately stated in a single account of inquiry. However self-reliant the practice of inquiry may be, they are saying, there need be nothing narcissistic about it, for it essentially involves an attempt to do descriptive justice to the subject matter being discussed. It is therefore crucial not only to avoid the metaphysical quagmire caused by viewing truth as a substantial something capable of definition, but also to avoid reducing objectivity to solidarity, understood as a sociological fact. Getting one's subject matter right is not the same thing as achieving agreement with one's fellow inquirers. For even if we could not all be wrong about most things, as Davidson and Rorty have claimed, we could still all be wrong about anything in particular. The idea of *getting one's subject matter right* that Rorty embraces at Ramberg's urging does not boil down to the idea of getting 'as much intersubjective agreement as possible' (Rorty 1991: 23). Accepting the former idea involves adopting a normative stance that can achieve expression only in the vocabulary of agency, whereas accepting the latter idea does not. Losing sight of this distinction—or, worse still, deliberately trying to efface it—is what turns pragmatic self-reliance into narcissism, because it leaves us able to focus only on facts about ourselves as a community of inquiry while eliminating the normative notion of objectivity that our community requires us to employ. (A further extreme would be solipsism, by which Rorty is not similarly tempted.) Ramberg's affirmation of the inescapability and irreducibility of an essentially normative vocabulary of agency, as an essential background to the enterprise of descriptive inquiry, helps keep the distinction in view.

Getting something right, in short, turns out to be among the human interests that need to be taken into account in an acceptably anthropocentric conception of inquiry as a social practice. If inquiry is to be understood pragmatically, as a set of human activities answerable only to human interests, and we grant that getting something right is among the human interests implicitly at work in these very activities, then we can have our pragmatism and our objectivity too—that is to say, pragmatism without narcissism. This, I believe, is the point that revisionists have been trying to make all along. It is important, in making this point, to avoid interpreting the notion of getting something right as either an explanation of what truth is or as an idea that requires explication in terms of a metaphysical dualism (between our verbiage, inscriptions, and attitudes, on one side, and reality or the world as it is in itself, on the other). The notion of getting something right cannot be an explanation of what truth is, because truth, for a Davidsonian pragmatist, remains an unexplained primitive—one of the basic concepts assumed by any subsequent explanatory activities. The Davidsonian's approach to truth is 'to trace its connections to other concepts' that are equally basic, not to define it. The definitions offered so far all turn out on examination to be either 'empty' or implicated in an untenable dualism of some sort (Davidson 2000: 72–3). Rorty's way of combining Ramberg's Davidsonian emphasis on getting something right with Rorty's long-standing endorsement of Davidsonian scruples about untenable dualisms is to say: 'There is no such thing as Reality to be gotten right—only snow, fog, Olympian deities, relative aesthetic worth, the elementary particles, human rights, the divine right of kings, the Trinity, and the like' (2000*a*: 375).

Hence, (1) we inquirers have an interest in getting things right; (2) this interest needs to be understood in the context of the social practices in which it is expressed; and (3) it need not be seen as implicated in a pseudo-explanatory conception of correspondence to the real. If these are three core commitments of a pragmatism that steers clear of narcissism, what becomes of Rorty's oft-repeated claim that truth is not a goal of inquiry? By conceding (1) to Ramberg, and thus apparently joining forces with the revisionists, has he implicitly granted that *having true beliefs* about some things is one of our goals after all? In his essay 'Is Truth a Goal of Inquiry: Donald Davidson versus Crispin Wright' Rorty argued:

The need to justify our beliefs and desires to ourselves and to our fellow agents subjects us to norms, and obedience to these norms produces a behavioural pattern that we must detect in others before confidently attributing beliefs to them. But there seems no occasion to look for obedience to an *additional* norm—the commandment to seek the truth. For . . . obedience to that commandment will produce no behavior not produced by the need to offer justification. (1998: 26)

I assume that Rorty has in mind something like the following argument. Seeking anything is an activity, and what one does in seeking something is necessarily done from a first-person point of view in the present moment. Whatever I am seeking when I am engaged in inquiry is sought from this point of view. From that point of view, seeking to hold true beliefs about something and seeking to hold beliefs about it that I would be justified in holding involve doing exactly the same things. As an inquirer, I am never in a position to compare my beliefs with reality as it is in itself. All I can do is whatever it takes to live up to my epistemic responsibilities as someone who aims to be entitled to the beliefs I hold. If there is no practical difference between aiming to hold true beliefs about something and aiming to be justified in holding whatever beliefs I hold about that topic, it makes no sense to speak of truth as a goal of inquiry. The idea of truth as a goal of inquiry introduces a conceptual difference that makes no practical difference—the kind of difference that pragmatists are committed to junking. Thus, discovering the truth about something, and in that sense getting something right, should not be said to be one's aim as an inquirer, apart from the aim to have beliefs one is entitled to have about that topic.

What are we to make of this argument? Consider an Olympian athlete who takes pride in her excellence as an archer. Aiming to hit the bull's-eye and aiming to live up to her discipline's standards of athletic excellence lead her to do exactly the same things: to release the tension from her body, focus her attention, adopt the appropriate stance, draw her bow in a certain way, and so on. But why would it follow that it makes no sense to say that hitting the target is one of her goals? Suppose the woman shoots her arrow with this goal in mind. She adopts the proper stance, draws her bow perfectly, and otherwise does what an excellent archer is supposed to do. Unfortunately, a gust of wind blows her arrow to the left of the bull's-eye. Will she not be disappointed? Will not one of her goals remain unmet? It seems that it does make sense, then, to speak of my having two distinct goals even if I do exactly the same things in trying to accomplish them.

It may be true, nonetheless, that the goal of getting something right should not be considered *apart* from—in complete abstraction from—the goal of holding beliefs one is entitled to hold. Return to the case of the archer. Surely somewhere in the list of things she is expected to do, if she is to count as an excellent archer, is take dead aim at her target. This aim is embedded, so to speak, in the standards of competence and excellence that have arisen in the practice of archery. Trying to shoot well involves adopting this aim. Archers who generally fail to take dead aim, who do not have hitting the bull's-eye as one of their goals, are not excellent archers. But putting the point in this way allows us to see how important it is to continue referring to this goal if we want to capture the target-directedness of the practice. If we let this goal slip out of the picture, we are bound to lose track of one dimension of success and failure that matters to anyone actually participating in the activity.

The grain of truth in Rorty's argument is that our interest in truth as distinct from justified belief does not arise mainly in contexts where we are limited to first-person, present-tense uses of 'is true' and 'is justified in believing'. At any given moment, the beliefs I count myself as entitled to accept and the beliefs I count as true are, to the extent that I am living up to the best available norms of belief formation, the same beliefs. But inquiry is a *social* practice, and it takes place in *time*. We need the distinction between truth and justification largely because we have an interest in assessing the success of our own beliefs over time and because, to have beliefs at all, we are necessarily caught up in communicative interactions with others, interactions that require us to assess, as well as interpret, what those others say and believe. Both of these forms of interpretive assessment involve departures from first-person, present-tense uses of the relevant expressions. And they both involve a distinction between two sorts of cognitive propriety: the kind that a person exhibits by believing responsibly, given the epistemic circumstances, and the kind that a belief (or the corresponding assertion) exhibits by getting the subject matter right.

The distinction between these two sorts of propriety allows me to say of someone (in the third person) or to someone (in the second person) that he or she is now epistemically entitled to believe something I take to be false. By the same token, the same distinction allows me to say that while I was once epistemically entitled to believe that *p*, given the evidence and styles of reasoning then available to me, *what* I then believed failed to get the subject matter right. Once I get this far, however, I can easily speculate about the possibility that what I now believe about something fails to get the subject matter right, even if I happen to be epistemically entitled to believe it, given our current epistemic circumstances. This thought raises the possibility that a lone dissenter could be getting the subject matter right even though everybody else is getting it wrong, as well as the possibility that we could all be doing our best as inquirers and still all be wrong about something in particular. But if I can get this far, thanks to the introduction of a distinction between two sorts of propriety involved in the social and temporal practice of inquiry, I am also in a position to express my *hope* or *desire* to get my subject matter right—and not mean by this simply that I shall some day have achieved a condition of perfect conformity to the epistemic norms of responsible believing currently accepted in my community. It therefore makes sense to take an *interest* in getting something right, in a sense that involves treating truth as a distinguishable *goal* of inquiry. Still, the second point I made about the archer also applies here. Discovering the truth is a distinguishable goal of inquiry, but this goal arises in the context of a social practice in which aiming at truth is among the things a practitioner is supposed to do. An inquirer who lacks this goal is like an archer who fails to take dead aim. Having the goal is part of what it takes to be a competent practitioner. But achieving the goal involves more than simply displaying the virtues recognized within the practice—something like actually hitting the target.[5]

Much of the ground I have just been covering is treated in somewhat different terms in Brandom's *Making It Explicit*, but understanding his terms requires some stage-setting. Brandom's way of affirming the inescapability and irreducibility of normativity is to make what he calls 'normative pragmatics' prior to semantics in his account of conceptual content. This move, which reverses the explanatory relation that representationalism establishes between semantics and pragmatics, postpones the account of semantic content until after the more basic notions of commitment, entitlement, and normative attitude have been introduced. Semantic content is to be understood ultimately in pragmatic terms, as a matter of what human beings do, which in turn is seen as normative all the way down—a matter of deontic statuses and attitudes that are initially implicit in the social practice of giving and asking for reasons, but can in principle be made explicit by means of the expressive rationality epitomised in Socratic method.

When Brandom says, 'One of the central challenges of an account of conceptual norms as implicit in social practice is . . . to make sense of the emergence of. . . an *objective* notion of correctness or appropriateness' (1994: 594; italics in original), he is committing himself to the project of formulating a pragmatism untainted by narcissism. It makes sense to refer to Brandom's work as pragmatic because he asserts the priority of the practical over the objective and the subjective in an acceptable account of conceptual norms and of their use in practical deliberation

---

[5] Of course, the interest that pragmatism advises us to take in getting something right is, even so, 'a practically constrained interest, an interest restricted in principle to accessible truth (at least to this and probably to something more practically accessible)' (Johnston 1993a: 112). As Johnston argues, this practical restriction 'has a powerful anti-speculative bite, at least as powerful as that of Verificationism', but does not itself depend on the latter doctrine.

and theoretical inquiry. He finds this reordering already in Kant, and credits Hegel with the insight that the practical sphere here being accorded priority needs to be understood in social terms. But it is crucial, according to Brandom, that this affirmation of the priority of the social-practical *not* be viewed as a plea for the elimination of talk about subjectivity and objectivity. The social-practical sphere is that in which human *subjects* are shaped into beings constrained by norms, and thus into beings who are free in the sense of being fit to be held responsible for their judgments and actions. It is also the sphere in which *constraints of objectivity* are placed on subjects insofar as they are engaged in inquiry. To be a subject in this (Hegelian) sense is not to be in possession of a Cartesian glassy essence; it is, rather, to be a constrained doer, a user of norms, a locus of responsibility, and thus someone fit to be held responsible by others and by oneself to obey those norms that prove capable of surviving critical questioning.[6]

In the practices of moral education and ethical self-cultivation, the norms require resistance to the selfishness and self-delusion of the ego and disciplined attention to the actual merits, needs, and suffering of others. In the practice of democratic social criticism, the norms require attention to the condition of the least well-off and suspicion of the self-justifying stories that societies tell about themselves. In the practice of natural science, the norms require certain forms of close observation of objects and use of a vocabulary that lends itself to 'objectifying' descriptions. The norms in each case are embedded in social practices. But the ones I have just mentioned orient one's attention to objects (that is, persons and things) that are distinct from the inquiring subject and distinct also from any consensus that may have been reached among inquiring subjects. Following these norms involves checking 'subjective' tendencies like wishful thinking and rationalization. Implicit in them is a distinction between behaving responsibly as an inquirer and actually getting one's subject matter right—between being justified in believing

---

[6] To be a fully self-conscious subject (again in a sense derived from Hegel) is to do all of these things (and various others) while identifying with a community of subjects who mutually recognise one another as answerable to one another. According to Hegel, this social-practical dimension of mutual recognition is an essential condition of the distinction that human inquirers draw between subject and object. But full awareness of the priority of the social-practical necessarily emerges long after the distinction between subject and object is already in use. This is the key to understanding why Hegelian pragmatism, as the raising to self-consciousness of the social-practical, must make its way against an already entrenched array of philosophies caught up in a subject–object dualism.

something and having a true belief. In each of these areas, *getting something right* is a crucial normative notion, and in none of them should it be conflated with the factual notion of merely being in conformity with one's peers. The normative notion of objective correctness arises in discursive social practices. Apart from such practices, there is no such thing as getting something right or wrong. But in trying to correct and replace previous descriptions of something, according to Brandom, what we are doing is holding our descriptions of the thing *answerable* to the thing.[7] The point of non-narcissistic pragmatism, when expressed in this way, is to keep answerability to one's subject matter—'objectivity', for short—from being reduced to social agreement.

In an attempt to clarify this notion Brandom embarks on an elaborate discussion of the social interaction that occurs when different individuals keep track, normatively and interpretively, of each other's discursive commitments and entitlements while giving and asking for reasons.[8] Brandom emphasizes that the process of keeping track, which he calls 'deontic scorekeeping', is carried out by each participant in the social practice from the perspective of his or her own theoretical and practical commitments. Concepts, he says, 'are essentially perspectival' (1994: 594) in the sense that their content can be specified only from one perspective or another, against the background of an individual's beliefs and intentions. But the scorekeeping perspective of anyone engaged in inquiry, in the socially articulated attempt to apply concepts *correctly*, includes 'the distinction between claims or applications of concepts that are objectively correct and those that are merely taken to be correct' (1994: 595). This distinction, Brandom explains, is implicit in each scorekeeper's ability to specify the conceptual content of other people's commitments in both *de re* and *de dicto* form: '*S* claims *of y* that *y* is . . .' as well as '*S* claims that *y* is . . .'. Individuals keeping track of each other's commitments in terms of this distinction focus on 'the relation between the commitments *undertaken* by a scorekeeper interpreting others and the commitments *attributed* by that scorekeeper to others' (1994: 599). Each individual does this in relation to each other, each of them drawing the distinction for themselves from their own point of view.

[7] John McDowell speaks of answerability in a similar way in his book *Mind and World*, paperback edn. (1996: esp. pp. xi–xii). Rorty criticizes McDowell (1998: 138–52).
[8] I have discussed Brandom's account of objectivity at length elsewhere. In addition to *Democracy and Tradition* (2004: ch. 12), see Stout 2002.

The form of sociality on display here is dialogical, not conformist. Each perspective 'is at most *locally* privileged in that it incorporates a structural distinction between objectively correct applications of concepts and applications that are merely subjectively taken to be correct' (Brandom 1994: 600). I keep track of your commitments and those of our fellows in terms of this distinction. You keep track of my commitments and those of our fellows in terms of the same distinction. Everyone else does the same, applying the distinction from his or her point of view. The mistake to be avoided by the pragmatic analyst is that of taking the community as a whole to possess a globally privileged perspective, to which individuals are uniformly obliged to conform if they wish their cognitive commitments to be correct. This is precisely the mistake that Rorty makes when he defines objectivity as solidarity, thereby eliminating both the possibility of everybody being wrong about something in particular and the *normative* notion of getting something right. The irony is that this mistake is itself an especially dangerous form of authoritarianism, because it collapses objective norms into group conformity. Given that collective narcissism is a type of authoritarianism, self-reliance must take measures to protect itself against it.

There is no point in striving to escape 'the thought of, and the need for, authority' as such. All discursive social practices involve structures of responsibility and authority, and Brandom is wise to make the elucidation of these structures a central feature of his pragmatism. He is also wise to interpret Rorty's attitude toward authority charitably, by taking it to be not a dismissal of authority as such, but rather the claim that 'any normative matter of epistemic authority or privilege—even the sort of authority exercised on what we say by what we talk about—is ultimately intelligible only in terms of social practices that involve implicitly recognizing or acknowledging such authority' (2000: 159). The best way to express commitment to the project of self-reliant inquiry is to claim the norms generated by and administered in our social practices as *our* responsibility while also emphasizing that they include a norm of objective correctness. The social practices conspire with natural forces to make us who we are. The norms we employ arise in the context of our interactions with one another. It is our responsibility to administer, criticize, and revise those norms while also acknowledging the (defeasible and contingent) authority they have accrued over time by serving our purposes well. Insofar as they are objective norms, however, they do not require us to agree with our peers on any topic in particular. Their authority derives not from a privileged communal perspective, but rather from the history of a many-sided conversation that repeatedly reveals the need to break from an extant consensus on this or that particular.

I do not think Brandom is abandoning something essential to pragmatism when he tells his Hegel–Heidegger–Sellars story about the precipitation of objective norms out of social practices. What he is doing, it seems to me, is marking the point at which his kind of pragmatism diverges from what Rorty sometimes says when he adopts his prophetic persona and dismisses both authority and objectivity as such. Brandom is also distancing himself implicitly from all forms of postmodernism that proclaim the disappearance of the subject and the tyranny of the objective. What needs to be avoided, Brandom implies, is not our normatively charged talk of truth and objectivity in the contexts of science, ethics, and politics, but rather objectivist philosophical accounts of that talk, on the one hand, and postmodernist rejections of that talk, on the other. Once we slip between these false alternatives, he thinks, we are in a position to mean something coherent and nonmetaphysical by saying that our claims 'answer normatively' to whatever it is that our claims are about (2000: 166). Rorty, however, maintains that Brandom's idiom of 'answerability to the facts' spoils everything by going objectivist. 'My fear', he writes in response to Brandom in *Rorty and his Critics*, 'is that countenancing these dangerous idioms will be taken as a concession by the bad guys' (2000*e*: 187).

I, for one, have trouble seeing a difference that makes a difference between Brandom's talk about answerability to the facts and Rorty's startling admission, in response to Ramberg, that 'true statements get things right'. Brandom and Ramberg, as far as I can tell, are making the same point in slightly different terms. Rorty worries that the notion of a fact carries the implication that the world comes already divided, so to speak, at the joints. But what the term 'fact' means in Brandom's philosophy is to be determined by the inferential connections he weaves between it and the other terms he employs. He takes pains to deprive it of connections that would require him to take back his previous assertion of the priority of the social-practical over the subjective and the objective. This is part of a broadly Hegelian strategy of showing how the same locutions can mean one thing in the context of the subject–object dualism and something else—neither objectivist nor subjectivist in its implications—when absorbed into the context in which pragmatic philosophy achieves awareness of the priority of the essentially normative (*geistig*) social-practical sphere. Still, if the term 'fact' gets in the way, we can easily put the point Brandon wants to make about objective correctness a bit differently.

The vocabularies in which we claim this or that about something or other—thus raising to salience the things, properties, events, and relations with which we have come to be concerned—are products of our social practices. Change the vocabularies enough by using terms differently, and you will end up talking about somewhat different things, properties, events, and relations. As a result, you will be entertaining somewhat different candidates for truth and falsity, and using those conceptual vehicles to make different claims. For a descriptive act, an application of a concept, to succeed in answering to what is being talked about, for it to have conceptual content at all, it needs to have a place in a broader, socially interactive activity in which individuals give and ask for reasons and keep track of commitments and entitlements. No such social practice, then no conceptual content, no conceptual norms, no subjects holding each other responsible, no objectivity. Nonetheless, even if our planet had never become hospitable to talkative creatures like ourselves, even if no planet had done so, there might well have been things, properties, events, and relations that *could have been discussed by language users had they come to exist.* In making reference here to things, properties, events, and relations in a neighbouring possible world, I am of course implicitly relying on one of our social practices in the actual world. I am using one of our vocabularies to talk about the counterfactual possibility of a world that lacks the likes of us. As long as we are mindful of this reliance, there is no paradox in speaking in this way. By the same token, our present social practices also equip us to say of the actual past that our planet existed millions of years ago, before there were language users to express this truth by applying concepts of the requisite sort. Our planet did exist way back then. Equivalently: *it is true* that our planet existed way back then. Again equivalently: that our planet existed way back then *is a fact.* We, however, did not exist way back then. Hence, there is at least one fact (in the sense that Brandom is trying to explicate) that obtained before there were talkative beings to render it salient in speech. And it would be easy for us, thanks to the conceptual richness of our discursive social practices, to name many others. But if the term 'fact' bothers you, feel free to ignore the last five sentences in this paragraph, for the main claim I am making on Brandom's behalf does not depend on them.

So much for the notion of a fact. What, then, about the notion of answerability? I have already quoted Rorty's prophetic declaration that we should dispense with the idea that we are answerable to anyone or anything other than our fellow language users. Brandom would agree that our fellow speakers are the ones to whom we owe answers when the propriety of our acts and judgments is called in question. We language users are the only ones who are fit to be held responsible, and the only ones who are conceptually equipped to hold one another responsible. As participants in the relevant social practices, we alone are responsible, as individuals and as a group, for what Brandom calls the grooming and upkeep of the norms being applied. None of these points is at issue. When we are investigating earthworms or distant galaxies, our subject matter cannot *answer back* or *hold us answerable* for the concepts we have applied to it. But as responsible inquiring minds, we do have a grip on a distinction between applying a concept and applying a concept rightly—between undertaking a cognitive commitment and undertaking a true cognitive commitment. Whether our cognitive commitments about earthworms and distant galaxies are true is not up to us; that depends on how it is with the earthworms and the distant galaxies. This is what Brandom is getting at by speaking of a claim's answerability to the facts. It appears to be the same thing as Ramberg is getting at by speaking of a claim's being in accord with what it says something about and what Rorty is getting at by speaking of a statement's getting something right. So again, if one is worried that Brandom's use of the term 'answerability' *seems* to imply that earthworms and distant galaxies *demand* to be described in a certain way, as only a person can demand something of someone, one can easily replace the troublesome locution.

Davidson once wrote, 'Correspondence, while it is empty as a definition, does capture the thought that truth depends on how the world is . . .' (2000: 71). What Brandom is saying would turn into a correspondence theory if he treated successful answering to the facts as an explanation of that in which truth consists. But Brandom does not make such a move, any more than Rorty (or Ramberg) treats getting something right (or getting what is said into accord with what is being talked about) as an explanation of that in which truth consists. Revisionist pragmatists all try to walk a fine line between correspondence theory and the old Rortian rhetoric that entails reducing inquiry to an exercise in social conformity—collective narcissism. If Rorty is serious about getting right the idea of getting something right within the context of a pragmatic account of inquiry, then he is trying to walk the same line. Of course, walking fine lines is not what prophets are all about; neither is consistency their primary virtue. So it should perhaps not be surprising to find Rorty criticizing Brandom for revisionist backsliding and endorsing Ramberg's revisionist pragmatism in the same volume in 2000, or to find him singing the praises of 'narcissism' three years later. The confusion generated by Rorty's recent writings appears to result from the difficulty he has walking Ramberg's Apollonian fine line while also dancing the prophetic dance of Nietzschean self-reliance. His Apollonian and Dionysian performances appeal to somewhat different audiences, but when taken together they leave his considered views unclear.

If 'pragmatism' ceases to be the name of an active philosophical movement, it will probably be because the term comes to stand for a form of collective narcissism, according to which the only intelligible sense of 'getting something right' has nothing to do with *the subject matter being talked about*. Young people who are seeking the excitement of membership in an outrageously bold intellectual vanguard will opt for a rhetoric of self-reliance that is more extravagant than anything to be found in the general vicinity of William James and John Dewey.[9] They will quickly skip over Rorty's pragmatism and give their hearts to Nietzsche and his French followers. Meanwhile, young people who are attracted to the quite different sense of empowerment that comes from learning how to draw careful distinctions will be reluctant to collapse truth into social agreement. If what they end up calling 'pragmatism' appears to eliminate this distinction, they will find some other 'ism' to endorse. Rorty's rejection of the rhetoric of objectivity, his endorsement of narcissism, will repel them. They will never get to the fine print about getting something right.

In the end, the ism-mongering matters little. What does matter is the attempt to do justice simultaneously to the objective and social-practical dimensions of inquiry. This is something well worth getting right. 'Pragmatism' remains an apt name for a tradition trying to tell a story about the emergence of objective norms in the context of social practices, a story that can help us take responsibility for those norms in a spirit of self-reliance. The question is whether this story can be told

---

[9] I do not mention C. S. Peirce in this context because Rorty does not elevate him to the heroic status he assigns to Dewey and James. Some latter-day pragmatists would argue that Peirce had already achieved a perfectly acceptable 'pragmatism without narcissism', and that Rorty's neglect of Peirce is exactly what gets him into trouble in the first place. In this paper, I sidestep the interpretation of the classical pragmatists entirely. Generally, I am less interested in getting the classical pragmatists right than in getting right certain topics that the classical pragmatists were addressing.

without collapsing the normative notion of 'getting something right', a notion pertaining to cognitive *success*, into a sociological fact. The answer, according to both Brandom and Ramberg, is yes, provided that we own up to the normative commitments being expressed (as well as being talked about) in the story being told. The story employs the normatively charged vocabulary of agency to make sense of the normatively charged notion of objectivity. But that is because our social practices, including pragmatic philosophy, the practice of bringing our practices to reflective self-consciousness, are normative all the way down. We cannot talk about our practices without relying on them. To take part in any form of inquiry is to adopt and express a committed stance in a community of normatively committed subjects.

Self-reliance is largely a matter of fully acknowledging the responsibility this stance entails and then acting accordingly. Our norms are our doing. Each time we apply a concept we contribute something to the evolution of our norms—all the more so when this involves explicitly stating those norms philosophically. As subjects, we are products of the norms as they currently stand, just as our norms are products of the social practice in which our predecessors carried out their cognitive projects by applying concepts to things they considered worth talking about. The inheritance now rests in our hands. Only we can administer its norms. What becomes of them is up to us. But whether we succeed in applying concepts correctly, relative to our norms, is not entirely up to us. Why? Because those very norms, once made explicit, make us mindful that all of us might be wrong about various things that are worth caring about. At any moment, the opinion of our peers might be leading us astray.

BIBLIOGRAPHY

Brandom, R. B. (1994) *Making It Explicit: Reasoning, Representing, and Discursive Commitment.* Cambridge, Mass.: Harvard University Press.
——— (2000) 'Vocabularies of Pragmatism: Synthesizing Naturalism and Historicism'. In R. B. Brandom (ed.), *Rorty and his Critics*, 156–83. Oxford: Blackwell.
Davidson, D. (2000) 'Truth Rehabilitated'. In R. B. Brandom (ed.), *Rorty and his Critics*, 65–74. Oxford: Blackwell.
James, W. (1991) *Pragmatism*. Buffalo: Prometheus Books.
Johnston, M. (1993*a*) 'Objectivity Refigured: Pragmatism without Verificationism'. In J. Haldane and C. Wright (eds.), *Reality, Representation, and Projection*, 85–129. New York and Oxford: Oxford University Press.

_____ (1993*b*) 'Verificationism as Philosophical Narcissism'. *Philosophical Perspectives*, 7: 307–30.

McDowell, J. (1996) *Mind and World*, paperback edn. Cambridge, Mass.: Harvard University Press.

Pippin, R. B. (1999) *Modernism as a Philosophical Problem: On the Dissatisfactions of European High Culture*, 2nd edn. Oxford: Blackwell.

Ramberg, B. (2000) 'Post-ontological Philosophy of Mind: Rorty versus Davidson'. In R. B. Brandom (ed.), *Rorty and his Critics*, 351–69. Oxford: Blackwell.

Rorty, R. (1979) *Philosophy and the Mirror of Nature*. Princeton: Princeton University Press.

_____ (1982) *Consequences of Pragmatism*. Cambridge: Cambridge University Press.

_____ (1991) *Objectivity, Relativism, and Truth*. Cambridge: Cambridge University Press.

_____ (1995) 'Response to Bernstein'. In H. J. Saatkamp, jun. (ed.), *Rorty and Pragmatism: The Philosopher Responds to his Critics*, 68–71. Nashville and London: Vanderbilt University Press.

_____ (1998) *Truth and Progress*. Cambridge: Cambridge University Press.

_____ (2000*a*) 'Response to Bjørn Ramberg'. In R. B. Brandom (ed.), *Rorty and his Critics*, 370–7. Oxford: Blackwell.

_____ (2000*b*) 'Response to Donald Davidson'. In R. B. Brandom (ed.), *Rorty and his Critics*, 74–80. Oxford: Blackwell.

_____ (2000*c*) 'Response to Hilary Putnam'. In R. B. Brandom (ed.), *Rorty and his Critics*, 87–90. Oxford: Blackwell.

_____ (2000*d*) 'Response to James Conant'. In R. B. Brandom (ed.), *Rorty and his Critics*, 342–50. Oxford: Blackwell.

_____ (2000*e*) 'Response to Brandom'. In R. B. Brandom (ed.), *Rorty and his Critics*, 183–90. Oxford: Blackwell.

_____ (2003) 'Comments on Jeffrey Stout's *Democracy and Tradition*'. Paper delivered at the Annual Meeting of the American Academy of Religion, Atlanta, 23 November 2003.

Stout, J. (2001) *Ethics after Babel*. Princeton: Princeton University Press.

_____ (2002) 'Radical Interpretation and Pragmatism: Davidson, Rorty, and Brandom on Truth'. In N. Frankenberry (ed.), *Radical Interpretation in Religion*, 25–52. Cambridge: Cambridge University Press.

_____ (2004) *Democracy and Tradition*. Princeton: Princeton University Press.

Williams, Bernard (2002) *Truth and Truthfulness*. Princeton: Princeton University Press.

2

On Not Being a Pragmatist: Eight Reasons and a Cause

Ian Hacking

Nothing is easier than to familiarise one's self with the mammalian brain. Get a sheep's head, a small saw, chisel, scalpel and forceps (all three can best be had from a surgical instrument maker), and unravel its parts either by the aid of a human-dissecting book, such as Holden's 'Manual of Anatomy,' or by the specific directions ad hoc given in such books as Foster and Langley's 'Practical Psychology' (Macmillan) or Morrell's 'Comparative Anatomy and Dissection of Mammalia' (Longman's).

James 1890: i. 11 n.

Of course pragmatism is true; the trouble is that it doesn't work.[1]

One of the few domains in which I am a consistent pragmatist is pragmatism itself: use it when it is useful, but don't when it isn't.

Hacking 1998: 93

Our editor Cheryl Misak has long been asking me to contribute to this collection, which is to illustrate the extent to which contemporary philosophers have become, or simply are, pragmatists. I have long been resisting, because I do not think of myself as a pragmatist, or identify my ways of doing philosophy with pragmatist ways.

---

[1] '[A] famous and deep joke attributed to Sidney Morgenbesser' (Williams 2002: n. 14).

I have no problem with a number of pragmatist attitudes. Some of the theses favoured by pragmatists, by neo-pragmatists in the style of Richard Rorty, or by the new pragmatists whose essays are included in this book, arise from and seem natural in many other contemporary perspectives: my own, for example. This would not have troubled William James very much. In 1907 he called his classic exposition *Pragmatism: A New Name for Some Old Ways of Thinking.* He would have been happy with a book that one could amuse oneself by writing today, *Pragmatism: An Old Name for Some Ways of Thinking a Century Later.*

But one cannot just foist a name on an unwilling recipient. There is the problem that Misak mentions in her introduction: it is not so clear what pragmatism is. We have the three canonical forebears. We have Rorty, whom I lamely call 'neo-pragmatist'—a label modelled on what in the nineteenth century was called 'neo-Kantianism'. Rorty avows his pragmatism: quite a number of his sentences used to begin, 'We pragmatists'. He has admired John Dewey in print, but I cannot see Peirce having had much sympathy for Rortyian conversation as the terminus for philosophy—hence my prefix 'neo-'.

Presumably most contributors to this collection are content to be called pragmatists. I have to be the odd man out. One might adopt this convention: a philosopher is a pragmatist only if he or she says so. I will not say 'if and only if', because self-enrolment should not suffice. But if one denies being a pragmatist, establishes that one has been little influenced by the classical pragmatists, and shows that one's ideas arise naturally from other traditions, is that not prima facie evidence that one is not a pragmatist?

Who cares about a label? The personal remarks that follow are of no general interest, except to illustrate several ways in which a philosopher can be led to express pragmatist-sounding ideas without feeling any sense of commonality with self-identified pragmatists. They may, however, suggest that some or even many of the doctrines that our editor would claim as pragmatist are not peculiarly so.

0 THE CAUSAL OR HISTORICAL EXPLANATION

I identify myself as an analytic philosopher, knowing full well that I practise analysis in my own idiosyncratic ways. When in public debate someone wants to pin some other label on me, I may get annoyed and say I am Leibnizian. On two occasions, both a very long time ago, being asked to describe my philosophical position in French company, I said: 'I am both a positivist and an anarchist at the same time.' But I have never called myself a pragmatist. The closest I got was in the third epigraph above.

Things might have been different had I begun my formal study of philosophy in the United States. Instead, I began at Cambridge University, where I did a two-year B.A. in moral sciences after studying mathematics and physics in Canada. America would have been a different experience. But not because I would have learned about pragmatism: on the contrary, because I would have been educated in the shadow of logical positivism. Hence I would have discovered pragmatism as rebellious liberation, or if I did not do so myself, I would have been liberated by Rorty's lovely book *Philosophy and the Mirror of Nature*.

I had a wholly eccentric education centred on Frege, Moore, and Russell. Wittgenstein had recently died. One absorbed a good deal of the man, and had the incomparable advantage of never attending a lecture in which his name was mentioned. Instead, he was internalised, and remains one of the two most profound influences on the ways in which I do philosophy.

The most original philosopher in Britain at the time was J. L. Austin. I did go to Oxford to attend his last course of lectures. I acquired a rather ascetic sense of moral philosophy not from the usual run of writers on ethics, but indirectly from F. R. Leavis. I never went to his lectures, but I spent late nights hanging out with Leavites. That was the most absolutist ethics imaginable, derived from an intense reading of novels in what Leavis called 'The Great Tradition'. Pragmatism, not. It did encourage a strong taste for what Philipa Foot and Bernard Williams were later to call 'thick' moral concepts, 'rude' over 'bad', 'treachery' over lying. Although Leavis's classic book *The Great Tradition* was conspicuously non-pluralist, it did create the sense that morality is historically situated, without inviting simplistic relativism. For me (but not for Leavites in general) it fostered a way of thinking that Bernard Williams was to articulate in *Ethics and the Limits of Philosophy*, a work resolutely opposed to neo-pragmatism. I acquired something like what Williams (2005) later called 'Left Wittgensteininism'.

I read Carnap's *Logical Syntax of Language* in my first term as an undergraduate in moral science, largely to show off. Yes, I could read things that were (in the context of that time and place) totally out of the way and bizarre. That is still one of my character defects. In an evening discussion group run by a young research fellow (post-doc), I pompously declared that we had to distinguish syntax from semantics. 'And what exactly do you mean by semantics?', I was asked. With an education like that, who needs pragmatism? Not pragmatism as prophylactic, anyway. When Rorty's *Mirror* was published, I was asked to be one of the commentators on the book at the Eastern meeting of the American Philosophical Association. It is obvious from what I said, even that late in the day, that I had no idea why so many young American philosophers found the book so exciting (1980*a*).

1 ON NOT NEEDING PRAGMATISM FOR FALLIBILISM

One thesis now strongly associated with pragmatism is that knowledge has no foundations, and that all beliefs, no matter how strongly held, are fallible. I am of that party. If I needed a twentieth-century philosopher to choose as role model here, it would be Karl Popper. He had little use for pragmatism. Once in a while I tauntingly declare that I am the last living Popperian. I would never, ever, call myself Peircian, living or dead.

I absorbed Popper rather late, largely thanks to another *émigré* from *Mitteleuropa*: namely, Imre Lakatos. I got to know him as soon as he arrived in Cambridge. I needed only Lakatos's name, 'fallibilist', to become one, and that was years before discovering that Peirce had taught a similar lesson, and that both men claimed that methods of the sciences had the unusual virtue of being intrinsically self-correcting. Authors whom I really did admire, most notably F. P. Ramsey, taught the virtues of pragmatism for their generation, but they did not speak to me or mine in the same way.

It never occurred to me that all knowledge needed foundations, so I did not well understand what Popper opposed. I did indeed know pretty much by heart Frege's *Foundations of Arithmetic*, as translated by J. L. Austin. But I did not think of it as providing 'foundations' in any literal sense. It offered a brilliant analysis of the concept of number. From the start I never thought of it as discovering what the numbers 'really are'. Instead, it brought into being a whole new way of comprehending the numbers, which calibrated well with, and made sense out of, less sharp perceptions.

Frege had a dream of understanding a pre-given truth that made arithmetic certain, but I never caught the dream. Russell, once my hero, really did seek certainty in mathematical logic. When I was a student, the search for certainty seemed as dated as Edwardian clothing, soon to be favoured by Teddy boys. The ambitions of Frege and Russell were picked up and continued in a noble way by some members of the Vienna and Berlin Circles. They were then transported wholesale to the United States—like so many other of the best aspects of German-language culture, civilisation, and learning. Philosophy had been in the doldrums in the United States, and in my opinion the imports had wholly salutary effects. They passed me by. I was educated in another milieu, which was in many ways vastly inferior. Nevertheless, it served me, personally, well.

When I became interested in probability, I of course learned Carnap's confirmation theory, but it had lost all connection with human reasoning. It was not just sterile; it was dead. The attempts by J. M. Keynes and Harold Jeffreys to develop a logic of probable reasoning had been full of life, but already in 1926 F. P. Ramsey enunciated their death knell in the simplest and truest words imaginable: 'But let us now return to a more fundamental criticism of Mr. Keynes' views, which is the obvious one that there really do not seem to be any such things as the probability relations he describes' (1926: 161). Carnap's confirmation functions were intended as the formal logic of Keynes's probability relations, and these functions do exist; but they are irrelevant to the probable inference that is the guide in life. Hence I turned away from Keynes and learned some thick statistical theory, and wrote *Logic of Statistical Inference* (1965). Note, not *the* logic. People asked me why not, and even then I could say that there is no such thing as *the* logic of anything.

2 TAKING A LOOK IS NO MORE CHARACTERISTIC OF NEO-PRAGMATISM THAN IT IS OF ANY OTHER CONTEMPORARY STYLE OF PHILOSOPHIZING

Thus I took a look at statistical inference, as it was understood in the 1960s. Ever since writing that first book, nearly all my work has turned to real life, real knowledge, real expertise. I have come to call that *taking a look*. For an illustration, let's use the most trivial example. For a note titled, 'Was there ever a Radical Mistranslation?' (1981),[2] I looked up

---

[2] Repr. with a few extra pieces of information in my *Historical Ontology* (2002: 152–9).

every example in the literature, of an alleged real radical mistranslation. I started with 'kangaroo', which I had myself used as an example of a radical malostension until Jack Smart put me right. I ended with *indri*, a Malagasy word for a type of lemur that is alas now very rare but once was common in Madagascar. In the course of a discussion with several other philosophers about naming, Quine had said that 'indri' was native for 'there he goes!' as the lemur scooted up a tree (Discussion 1974: 500). I gave good (but not conclusive) reason to think, contrary to the *OED*, that a word much like *indri* was an old word for a very specific type of lemur, in a very specific Malagasy dialect. This shows *nothing* about the a priori doctrine of indeterminacy of translation, but it suggests that one should, as I now like to put it, always 'Take a look'. It also encourages a reality check on more abstract doctrines about translation. At the very least, it forces one to acknowledge the immense breach between actual, rare-if-ever indeterminacy of translation, and logically possible indeterminacy, which is ubiquitous (and thereby boring?).

It would be mere equivocation to say that my insatiable need to take a look at real-life examples or real-life expertise proves that I am at heart a pragmatist. Perhaps mine is an attitude that could, by a stretch, be called pragmatism in sense 2 of *The American Heritage Dictionary*: 'A practical, matter-of-fact way of approaching or assessing situations or of solving problems'. But it has nothing to do with sense 1: '*Philosophy.* A movement consisting of varying but associated theories, originally developed by Charles S. Peirce and William James and distinguished by the doctrine that the meaning of an idea or a proposition lies in its observable practical consequences'.

Neo-pragmatists are no more given to asking for real-life examples or for mastering the rudiments of a branch of useful knowledge than so-called Wittgensteinians or those who admire Heidegger. Undoubtedly the first philosopher whom I came across who fostered this proclivity to take a look was J. L. Austin. I still regard it as a great misfortune that his *Sense and Sensibilia* is no longer read, while *How to do Things with Words* has been used and abused for all sorts of purposes. The former is a masterpiece of reflection on what is actually said in a certain sub-community of English-speaking people. It was combined with an inspired sensibility to detect what sounds right to those of us who inhabit that community. Austin may have been a pragmatist sense 2, but was definitely not a pragmatist sense 1.

The original Oxford school of ordinary language philosophy shared Austin's careful attention to linguistic detail. Even after Peter Hacker's demolition of the confusion, there is still a tendency abroad to speak of some 'linguistic philosophy' that covers both Wittgenstein and Oxford. Aside from the fact that the two detested and despised each other, their instincts with respect to reality are quite different. Wittgenstein did not care a fig what we say in ordinary literate Viennese or English, and built a philosophy around imaginary possibilities. I regard Wittgenstein as a primary source for my ways of thinking, but not for my superficial if pervasive habit of dwelling on thick descriptions of real cases.

It hardly needs saying that my later enthusiasm for the writing of Michel Foucault wholly reinforced my obsessive taking a look. Foucault is admired by no well-established pragmatist today, and is regarded by some of them as a deplorably evil influence. Foucault was a fact-lover: me too. I said above that Wittgenstein remains one of the two most profound influences on the ways in which I do philosophy—the second, of course, is Foucault.

3 ON DISAGREEING ABOUT TRUTH

Truth, in the saying so often attributed to William James, is what works. A coherence theory of truth is commonly taken to be a core doctrine of pragmatism. If I had to subscribe to a named theory of truth, it would be the redundancy theory introduced by F. P. Ramsey, with the rider that an affirmation of the form 'it is true that *p*' is used to say something about the assertion, conjecture, proposition, hypothesis, or whatever *p*, usually one already introduced into the discussion or conversation. Straight J. L. Austin, in short (1961: 94).[3] But I do not wholeheartedly agree even with that. When it is said that the concept of truth is necessary for any human communication, I reply that if so, it is a purely formal concept—which is a way to understand Tarski. Tarski did say that his semantic approach was consistent with any substantive theory of truth, which is part way to saying that it is about a formal rather than a substantive concept.

I have recently been deeply influenced by Bernard Williams's last book, *Truth and Truthfulness: An Essay in Genealogy* (2002). This has received a pretty lukewarm reception, like Colin McGinn's (2003). If we

---

[3] Austin is kinder to pragmatist theories of truth than one might expect (1961: 98 n. 1). He was not a 'correspondence theorist', as casual readers often imagine. He favoured a particular and detailed version of a 'correspondence' theory for *simple sentences*.

may take Richard Rorty's review (2002) as expressing the neo-pragmatist reaction, then this book shares almost nothing with pragmatism. In contrast, my public admiration (2004*b* and 2005) appears to know almost no bounds. Williams takes *truth* to be timeless, to have no history, to be part of the structure necessary for human linguistic communication. That, I say, is truth as formal concept. In contrast, Williams takes *truthfulness* about a subject matter to have a history and to have a beginning. He dates the beginning of historical truthfulness with Thucydides. He locates the possibility of authentic truth-telling about oneself in the eighteenth century. I used to think of the truth about a subject matter as coming into being, but I now see it as the possibility of truthfulness. I had the good luck to express the idea correctly in 1982: 'although whichever propositions are true depends on data, the fact that they are candidates for being true is a consequence of historical fact' (2002: 167).

This line of thought has to do with the evolution of standards of objectivity, of what feels like an inevitable, 'timeless canon of objectivity, a standard or model of what it is to be reasonable about this or that type of subject matter' (2002: 188). We discovered how to make proofs in mathematics, and brought into being new ways of being truthful. Human beings discovered the laboratory style of reasoning, in which one manufactures apparatus to purify and even to create phenomena, and thereby generates new ways to be truthful about unobservable structures that underlie experience. The fact, that the methods of argument we now regard as canonical have a history, and once did not exist even for the wisest of the ancients, does not make them any the less the objective standards.

These ideas of truth, truthfulness, and objectivity are foreign to neo-pragmatism. I (1996: 73) have even used the idea of scientific styles of reasoning to object to Richard Rorty's criticism of Bernard Williams's insistence on a distinction between scientific and moral reasoning, although that thought needs further development. Some will trace back to Hegel the notion that standards of objectivity evolve in history. Peirce grew up as something of a Hegelian, but so far as he was concerned, there were only three rather ahistorical methods of reasoning: deduction, induction, and the method of hypothesis (abduction). He did not reflect on the historicity of mathematical proof.[4] He did not see

---

[4] The invention of the deductive methods used in Euclidean geometry is elegantly investigated by Reviel Netz (1999).

that the method of hypothesis is not enough; the natural sciences require a rather late European invention: the laboratory and its apparatus for creating phenomena to study and measure.[5]

Our editor, in her Introduction, argues that a historical attitude to objectivity is part of the most recent pragmatist thinking. Excellent: this shows that the new pragmatism shares more than might have been expected with other contemporary strains of thought. It does not show that the current historicisms are pragmatist in nature, but rather that pragmatism has recently bought into some blend of historicism.

4 ON AGREEING, TO SOME EXTENT, ABOUT WHAT'S REAL

My *Representing and Intervening* (1983) used the then current debates about scientific realism as a wedge to introduce the serious study of experiment into the philosophy of the sciences, which at that time was wholly dominated by theory. The *Representing* part of the book (Part A: 21–128) is an introductory review of some debates, expressed in a way that I hoped would interest undergraduates, educate them, and induce a healthy scepticism. Page 2 warned that I did not care much about scientific realism. (Today I care still less.) Are questions about realism important, I asked? 'I doubt it,' I replied, and continued by saying that I was 'a realist on only the most pragmatic of grounds'. Not pragmatist grounds, but pragmatic ones. The first discussion of reality (pp. 32–3) recycles J. L. Austin's brilliant examination of uses of the word 'real', and thereby implies that 'realisms' of any philosophical sort are pretty numbing.

Representing has a long chapter (17 pages) on positivism—not the logical sort but the kind urged by Auguste Comte and Bas van Fraassen. That was the scientific anti-realism current in 1983. It is followed by a short chapter (6 pages) on pragmatism. It admires Peirce, and quotes at length his youthful statement about the real being what, sooner or later, information and reasoning would finally result in. I have never agreed with that, but have always been impressed by what he said in the same paragraph: that 'the very origin of the conception of reality involves

---

[5] One way to read Simon Schaffer and Steven Shapin (1985) is as the establishment of the laboratory style of reasoning. See my review of the book (1991).

the notion of a COMMUNITY without definite limits, and capable of a definite increase in knowledge' (quoted in Hacking 1983: 58).[6]

I picked up from Dewey the scathing phrase 'spectator theory of knowledge', which seemed to me to characterize most of the general philosophy of the sciences that was then being read and written (Popper, Carnap, Kuhn, Lakatos, Putnam, van Fraassen, the lot). 'My own view, that realism is more a matter of intervention in the world, than of representing it in words and thought, surely owes much to Dewey' (Hacking 1983: 62). *Owes*. Not in the sense that Dewey incited me to think that way, but in the sense that, when I looked back over the history of philosophy, I recognised that Dewey had been there before me. How did *I* get there? By talking to my scientific friends, especially the two I single out in the preface: Melissa Franklin, then of the Stanford Linear Accelerator, and Francis Everitt, of Gravity Probe B. In August 2005 I revisited Stanford on day 485 of the actual probe in space, watching and listening in the control room as the experimental observations were coming to an end. The liquid helium in the satellite is almost exhausted, and the next bit of fun, the data analysis, begins. By April 2007 we may have some results. 'In my opinion', I wrote in 1983, 'the right track in Dewey is the attempt to destroy the conception of knowledge and reality as a matter of thought and of representation. He should have turned the minds of philosophers to experimental science, but instead [Rorty's] philosophers praise talk' (1983: 63). (I had just unkindly said that 'Rorty's version of pragmatism is yet another language-based philosophy, which regards all our life as a matter of conversation'.)

In *Intervening* (Part B: 149–275) I tried to turn the minds of philosophers to experimental science such as is exemplified today by Gravity probe B. By a coincidence far better than anything I could have hoped for, similar trends were evolving in the history and in the sociology of the sciences. So an interest in experiment has taken root, but not as deeply as I would like. At the end of *Intervening* there is a brief return to the numbskull topic of scientific realism. 'Experimental work provides the strongest evidence for scientific realism. This is [. . .] because entities that in principle cannot be "observed" are regularly manipulated to produce new phenomena and to investigate other aspects of nature. They are tools, not for thinking but for doing' (1983: 262). That is surely in the spirit of pragmatism, but I know of no

[6] From Peirce's contribution to the 1868 *Journal of Speculative Philosophy*, 'Some Consequences of Four Incapacities'; repr. in Peirce 1968.

professed pragmatist who has even agreed with my criterion, let alone asserted it.

I am not 'against' theory, whatever that might mean; I wanted only to restore a Baconian enthusiasm for experiment. My current work in the philosophy of physics is about the intimate dynamics of interaction between theoretical modelling and the experimental creation of phenomena. My example is Bose–Einstein condensation, which had been on the theoretical drawing board since 1924, but was not realized until 1995.[7] That is a field in which, at present, no theoretical advance is possible without experiment, and no experimental inquiry is possible without theory. At the leading laboratories I have visited (which are all down in the basement to avoid vibration), they say: We are so lucky to have so-and-so (who leads a theory group on the fourth floor) who actually cares about what we are doing and can help us think about what to look for.

This example of ultra cold research—we are talking less than a nanokelvin above absolute zero—illustrates many aspects of physics. Soon after I came to Toronto, I organised a conference called 'Table-Top Experiments'.[8] The aim was to re-emphasize small experiments over large ones. So I am delighted that much of my new hobby really is conducted on table-tops, the laser table, and that the typical BEC lab consists of six people, a director, one or two post-docs, two or three grad students, and a lucky undergraduate or two.

I care about theory, but I am not, and was not, much interested in the reality of non-observable theoretical entities, which around 1980 was the philosophy-of-science flavour-of-the-year. Perhaps I have, and had, a pragmatist meta-sentiment, that it does not make the slightest difference to physics whether its theoretical entities are *in general* called real or not.

Perhaps it does matter to the funding of physics: It was once alleged in the journal *Nature* that the fallibilism or anti-realism of Popper, Kuhn, Lakatos, and Feyerabend caused Mrs Thatcher to put a spoke in the wheel of British physics. Actually it was her kind of pragmatism (sense 2 above, not pragmatism sense 1, the philosophy) that made Thatcher, the chemist turned Prime Minister, try to kill off fundamental physics, once a glory of the United Kingdom. She wanted cash value and saleable results.

---

[7] The manuscript of Einstein's 1925 paper turned up in Leiden just the other day, in August 2005. Bose–Einstein condensates were not produced until 1995, first by Karl Wieman and Eric Cornell in Boulder, and then by Wolfgang Ketterle at MIT.

[8] The papers were published much later in Buchwald 1995.

Of course it matters whether *particular* conjectured entities or quantities exist or not. Is there a positive electric dipole moment on the electron? Perhaps the fate of super-symmetry hangs in the balance. It certainly matters, in a very different way, whether proposed mental disorders are called real. Health insurance. Moral opprobrium or not. Self-esteem. I do not think 'real' is the most helpful word to use, but I was obliged to discuss such matters in *Rewriting the Soul* (1995) and *Mad Travelers* (1998). I did invoke Peirce at the last stages of my argument, but in an oddly non-pragmatist way (1998: 93).

5 ON READING PEIRCE, BUT NOT FOR PRAGMATICISM

Charles Sanders Peirce was the greatest philosopher of probability whom we have known. One example: He was the first philosopher to understand one of the two viable approaches to learning from experience using probabilities. The ideas had been intuited by Jacques Bernoulli and Laplace, but Peirce was the first to state the general mode of reasoning, and perhaps I myself finally caught on thanks to Peirce, though there were certainly others from whom I took similar ideas (Hacking 1980*b*). Learning from him about probability did not make me a pragmaticist.

Hilary Putnam (1994: 160–9) has drawn attention to Peirce's proposal that probable reasoning requires, among other things, altruism, in order to be sound. He rightly asserts that 'the problem Peirce raised [about probable inference] is so deep [. . .]', and he also drew attention to a letter from Peirce to James (Putnam 1994: 180 n. 36) emphasizing Buddhist virtues over banal charity. But even Putnam avoided detail. Advocating not only altruism as a logical foundation for science, Peirce invoked John the Evangelist's *three* cardinal virtues of faith, hope, and charity. 'Charity' here not the charitable donations to the poor that Peirce mocked, but the classic rendering of *caritas*, often translated as disinterested love. I used John's and Peirce's very profound trio as early as 1965 (p. 47), and in 2001 used the same passages to end my introductory text on probability and induction (pp. 265 f.). In a forthcoming book, 'The Tradition of Natural Kinds', I spend a little time explicating Peirce's use of the words of the Evangelist, as understood by Peirce and as understood by St John, in a way that might discomfit your average twenty-first century pragmatist, but not, I hope, Putnam.

It is an important fact that each of the three classical pragmatists was involved in practical endeavours. Peirce worked for years in the US Coast and Geodetic Survey, which is where he learned what the curve of error means. Amusingly, his classic example of the use of the method of hypothesis is taken from an experience when he went with the American expedition to Turkey to measure the transit of Venus. It involves a strange Turk arriving with four men carrying a canopy to shelter him from the sun: he must be the governor of the province. I can hardly accuse Peirce of not taking a look, both on and off the job!

I used Peirce as a 'witness' throughout *The Taming of Chance* (1990), as I had used Leibniz throughout *The Emergence of Probability* (1975). A long chapter on Peirce ended *Taming*, and I still hold it to be an important reading of Peirce. It emphasized his experience as a scientist, and gave some of the details which, curiously, few pragmatist commentators do. I also offered textual evidence (1990: 213) that Peirce well knew that his own account of truth in terms of the long run is circular. I know of no Peirce scholar who has paid any heed to the fact that Peirce blithely admitted (at least once) the circularity of his account of truth.

I said in section 0 above that, when annoyed, I call myself Leibnizian. I could never call myself Peircian. The two philosophers are similar, and both resemble a hardware store that I used when I first moved to Toronto. The shop had a vast inventory of all the objects that had been put into the century-old houses in my neighbourhood. So when some mysterious bit of plumbing or electricity or whatever went awry, I could take it to Luigi, and he would tell me exactly what it was and produce from one of his thousands of drawers a duplicate or surrogate. The shop finally went out of business from a surfeit of inventory. Just like Peirce and Leibniz—though their drawers were filled with the future, not the past. 'We should see [Peirce] as a wild man, one of the handful who understood the philosophical events of his century and set out to cast his stamp upon them. He did not succeed. He finished almost nothing, but he began almost everything' (Hacking 1983: 61).

Peirce had, in one respect, a character fundamentally different from that of Leibniz. Leibniz was content with almost any popularization or even bowdlerization of his ideas. Peirce thought there was one right exposition. Not Leibniz: he would have loved to have had a William James.

6 ON READING WILLIAM JAMES

I love reading James. When I was an honorary Leavite, I had to read all of his brother Henry. I am glad I did my duty, but I am a little relieved that I may never read much of him again. William, in contrast, is always a delight. He was a great stylist, with an enormous heart. In my forthcoming *The Tradition of Natural Kinds*, there is a chapter called 'The Joy of Kinds' which begins by quoting him, in part: 'Once we know that whatever is of a kind is also of that kind's kind, we can travel through the universe as if with seven-league boots'(1907: 179). How much more insightful than the turgid stuff about natural kinds one reads nowadays.

As I said, each classical pragmatist spent some time working in the real world. James's *Principles of Psychology* (1890) is a wonderful introduction to the psyche and its brain. I love that first footnote to the *Principles,* quoted as my first epigraph above. There is a philosopher who knew how to take a look!

7 ON NOT READING JOHN DEWEY

I once tried valiantly to read John Dewey, but it did not click. He goes on and on. He was a very important public figure in his day. Patrick Suppes told me that his seminars at Columbia were masterpieces of precision and concision, in great contrast to his books. My failed attempt at reading Dewey did, however, lead to that fine term of abuse 'spectator theory of knowledge'. What a splendid way to characterize all that is wrong with traditional epistemology! I always invoke it with admiration, but I have never given a page reference because I could not bring myself to actually reread some texts of Dewey to relocate the place he said it.

For me, Dewey does not mean New York but Chicago. The practical attempts at education, which meshed with the ambitions of the St Louis Hegelians: the Lab School. The emergence of successive Chicago Schools of sociology. For me, Erving Goffman was the greatest of sociologists (Hacking 2004*a*). Was he a product of pragmatist-oriented Chicago sociology? Of course. But I like the idea of his biographer, that the whole methodology of face-to-face interaction was something Goffman learned in his summer job while an undergraduate. He worked with the National Film Board of Canada at a time when it was making extraordinary face-to-face documentaries in sparse communities across the country (See Winkler 1999). Primed for pragmatist sociology, you might say, and he went off and wrote a Ph.D. doing face-to-face on an island in the Hebrides. He was taking a look, unlike so many sociologists who are content to crunch numbers.

8 ON LEARNING FROM NELSON GOODMAN

The name of Nelson Goodman is not one of the first to roll off the tongue when someone starts mentioning pragmatists or neo-pragmatists. He had the good fortune to be born too late to be a founding pragmatist, and too soon to be neo. He was a great nominalist, too much so, I think, to serve as a good role model for future pragmatists. I do think that his self-moniker, *irrealist*, is one that ought to enter the pragmatist lexicon.

I spent a long time worrying about the tradition of natural kinds from William Whewell and John Stuart Mill to now. In the end I had to conclude that for all its insights and inspirations over 160 years, the tradition has self-destructed (Hacking, forthcoming). Goodman got it right before anyone else saw the looming shipwreck. We should not, he argued, speak of natural kinds, but only of relevant kinds.

I say 'relevant' rather than 'natural' for two reasons: first, 'natural' is an inapt term to cover not only biological species but such artificial kinds as musical works, psychological experiments, and types of machinery; and second, 'natural' suggests some absolute categorical or psychological priority, while the kinds in question are rather habitual or traditional or devised for a new purpose. (1978: 10)

Relevant to whom? To us, or to you, or to them, to those who group items together, for this or that purpose. Relevance is all there is to be said, *in general*. Some philosophies take Goodman's relevance to be an expression of nihilism. It may, on the contrary, be close to bedrock, a word used more often in talk about Wittgenstein than Goodman.

Goodman is the only pragmatist from whom I ever learnt anything—that is, the only one who led me to think new thoughts or rethink old ones. Sidney Morgenbesser gets an assist, yes, the Sidney of all jokes, including the second epigraph above. The very first paper that I read in public, and which was later printed (1964), was a talk to the Aristotelian Society in 1962. There was this man in the back row looking wildly inappropriate for a covey of English dons of that time. He put up his hand, and out came the New York: 'Yeah, but what about grue?' Exactly. In *Logic of Statistical Inference* (1965) I wrote, alas without thanking Morgenbesser, that Goodman's riddles 'combine precision of statement, generality of application, and difficulty of solution to a degree greater than any other philosophical problem broached in this century'(p. 40). That endeared me to Nelson Goodman, who ever after ascribed greater philosophical insight to me than I merit. I have gnawed away at grue ever since.[9] Not because I want to solve the 'new riddle of induction', but because I think it is a deep *fact*. A bedrock fact. There is a 178-page bibliography of writing about 'grue'; the authors cited are of many persuasions, but card-carrying pragmatists are few among them (Stalker 1994: 280–457).

Partly thanks to his activities as an art dealer and patron, and partly thanks to his unusual contributions to aesthetics, Goodman is better known in quite a few American intellectual circles than any of his philosophical contemporaries, including Quine. It is characteristic that Mary Douglas, the great English cultural anthropologist, together with her then colleague at Northwestern, the pre-eminent philosopher of biology David Hull, should have put together a volume of essays (1992) inspired by and offered to Nelson Goodman. The title is *How Classification Works*, which well might serve as a title for a book in which to view pragmatism at work. Yet I would not readily identify any of its authors as a pragmatist. My own contribution, 'World-Making by Kind-Making' is an attempt to analyse a real case of kind-making—the making and moulding of the concept of child abuse. The evolving practices, value judgements, institutions, and laws connected with that appalling subject seem to me an exemplary case of world-making.

I don't know that Goodman much liked the paper. One piece of mine that he did recommend to many people was about Bruno Latour's *Laboratory Life* (Hacking 1988). That was written some time before people were taking Latour really seriously, either as potential ally or as ogre, the end of reason as we know it. My version of early Latour—not a faithful one, but a useful one—seemed to Goodman to be a right version of much scientific activity. That is a good point at which to end, by echoing a sentence from my second paragraph above: Some of the theses favoured by pragmatists, neo-pragmatists, or new pragmatists, arise from and seem natural in many other contemporary

---

[9] See Hacking 1994, 1993*a*, and 1993*c*. This material and more appears in one volume (Hacking 1993*b*).

perspectives: mine for example, or Bruno Latour's. But those selfsame perspectives do not owe much to pragmatism, and do not define one as a pragmatist unless one so chooses.

BIBLIOGRAPHY

Austin, J. L. (1961) 'Truth'. Repr. in *Philosophical Papers*, 85–101. Oxford: Clarendon Press.
Buchwald, J. Z. (1995) (ed.), *Scientific Practice: Theories and Stories of Doing Physics*. Chicago: University of Chicago Press.
Discussion (1974) 'First General Discussion Session'. *Synthese*, 27: 471–508.
Douglas, M., and Hull, D. (1992) (eds.), *How Classification Works: Nelson Goodman among the Social Sciences*. Edinburgh: Edinburgh University Press.
Goodman, N. (1978) *Ways of Worldmaking*. Indianapolis: Hackett.
Hacking, I. (1964) 'Guessing by Frequency'. *Proceedings of the Aristotelian Society*, 64: 55–70.
——(1965) *Logic of Statistical Inference*. Cambridge: Cambridge University Press.
——(1980*a*) 'Is the End in Sight for Epistemology?' *Journal of Philosophy*, 76: 579–88.
——(1980*b*) 'Neyman, Peirce and Braithwaite'. In D. H. Mellor (ed.), *Science, Belief and Behaviour*, 141–60. Cambridge: Cambridge University Press.
——(1981) 'Was there ever a Radical Mistranslation?' *Analysis*, 41: 171–6.
——(1983) *Representing and Intervening*. Cambridge: Cambridge University Press.
——(1988) 'The Participant Irrealist at Large in the Laboratory'. *British Journal for the Philosophy of Science*, 39: 277–94.
——(1990) *The Taming of Chance*. Cambridge: Cambridge University Press.
——(1991) 'Artificial Phenomena'. *British Journal for the History of Science*, 24: 235–41.
——(1992) 'World-making by Kind-making: Child Abuse for Example'. In Douglas and Hull 1992: 180–238.
——(1993*a*) 'Goodman's New Riddle is Pre-Humian'. *Revue internationale de philosophie*, 46: 229–43.
——(1993*b*) *Le Plus pur nominalisme. L'énigme de Goodman. «Vleu» et usages de «Vleu»*. Combas, France: Éditions de l'Éclat.
——(1993*c*) 'On Kripke's and Goodman's Uses of "Grue"'. *Philosophy*, 68: 269–95.
——(1994) 'Entrenchment'. In D. Stalker 1994: 183–224.
——(1995) *Rewriting the Soul*. Princeton: Princeton University Press.
——(1996) 'The Disunities of the Sciences'. In P. Galison and D. J. Stump (eds.), *The Disunity of Science. Boundaries, Contexts and Power*, 37–74. Stanford, Calif.: Stanford University Press.

_____ (1998) *Mad Travelers*. Charlottesville, Va.: University Press of Virginia.

_____ (2001) *Introduction to Probability and Inductive Logic*. Cambridge: Cambridge University Press.

_____ (2002) *Historical Ontology*. Cambridge, Mass.: Harvard University Press.

_____ (2004*a*) 'Between Michel Foucault and Erving Goffman: Between Discourse in the Abstract and Face-to-face Interaction'. *Economy and Society*, 33: 277–302.

_____ (2004*b*) 'Critical notice of Bernard Williams, *Truth and Truthfulness: An Essay in Genealogy*'. *Canadian Journal of Philosophy*, 34: 137–48.

_____ (2005) 'Truthfulness'. *Common Knowledge*, 11: 160–72.

_____ (forthcoming) 'Natural Kinds: Rosy Dawn, Scholastic twilight', in A. O'Hear (ed.), *Philosophy of Science*. Cambridge: Cambridge University Press.

James, W. (1890) *The Principles of Psychology*, 2 vols. London: Macmillan and Co.

_____ (1907) *Pragmatism: A New Name for Some Old Ways of Thinking*. New York: Longmans Green.

McGinn, C. (2003) 'Isn't it the Truth?' *New York Review of Books*, 10 April 2003.

Netz, R. (1999) *The Shaping of Deduction in Greek Mathematics: A Study in Cognitive History*. Cambridge: Cambridge University Press.

Peirce, C. S. (1968) 'Some Consequences of Four Incapacities'. In N. Houser and C. Kloesel (eds.), *Essential Peirce*, i: The Peirce Edition Project, Bloomington and Indianapolis: Indiana University Press.

Putnam, H. (1994) 'Pragmatism and Moral Objectivity'. In James Conant (ed.), *Hilary Putnam: Words and Life*, 151–81. Cambridge, Mass.: Harvard University Press.

Ramsey, F. P. (1926) 'Truth and Probability'. In *The Foundations of Mathematics and Other Logical Essays*, 156–98. London: Routledge & Kegan Paul Ltd.

Rorty, R. (2002) 'To the Sunlit Uplands'. *London Review of Books*, 31 October 2002.

Schaffer, S., and Shapin, S. (1985) *Leviathan and the Air Pump: Hobbes, Boyle and the Experimental Life*. Princeton: Princeton University Press.

Stalker, D. (1994) *GRUE*. La Salle, Ill: Open Court.

Williams, B. (2002) *Truth and Truthfulness*. Princeton: Princeton University Press.

_____ (2005) 'Pluralism, Liberalism, and Left Wittgensteinianism'. In *In the Beginning Was the Deed: Realism and Moralism in Political Argument*, 29–39. Princeton: Princeton University Press.

Winkin, Y. (1999) 'Erving Goffman: What is a Life? The Uneasy Making of an Intellectual Biography'. In G. Smith (ed.), *Goffman and Social Organisation, Studies in a Sociological Legacy*, 19–41. New York: Routledge.

3

Relativism, Pragmatism, and the Practice of Science

Arthur Fine

> But science in the making, science as an end to be pursued, is as subjective and psychologically conditioned as any other branch of human endeavor—so much so that the question, What is the purpose and meaning of science? receives quite different answers at different times and from different sorts of people. (Einstein 1934: 112)

Relativism is worrisome. Many regard it as a bad thing; a virus set to infect your whole way of thinking if your ideas seem to leave even a small opening for it. Others profess to believe that relativism is quite a good thing. Since no one knows exactly what relativism is, both camps could be right. Here I examine some non-idiotic forms of relativism whose 'dangers', I argue, amount to no more than an anti-foundationalism familiar from the pragmatic tradition. Seen pragmatically, relativism turns out to be robust with respect to standard anti-relativist arguments. Seen pragmatically, it might also help soothe the anxiety over nihilism or irrationality (or general chaos) that it triggers in some. For, as I suggest, pragmatic forms of relativism offer an appropriate setting for understanding good scientific practice.

I want to thank participants in the Ohio University Philosophy Forum and the Pacific Northwest Philosophy of Science Conference for responses to earlier versions of this paper. In addition, special thanks to Philip Ehrlich, Mathias Frisch, Roger Jones, William Talbot, and Philip Selznick for their help. (I know I have not satisfied you all.)

1. PARADOX AND ARGUMENT

'Everything is relative to everything.' All sides agree that this idiot form of relativism is silly and incoherent—and also that no one has ever held it. Opponents of relativism (including some whose ideas come uncomfortably close) charge that more sophisticated forms of relativism are also inconsistent, or otherwise conceptually defective. Their first line of attack usually develops some version of Plato's arguments in the *Theaetetus*, where Plato argues against Protagoras' saying, 'Man is the measure of all things, of those that are, that they are, and of those that are not, that they are not.' (Compare William James, 'The trail of the human serpent is thus over everything.') Suppose we call relativism about certain alleged universal concepts (or *universal relativism*) the doctrine according to which truths about those universals are relative.[1] (Ignore for a moment the question of relative to what and in what way.) Depending on the universals, this might yield relativism about reason or standards or values, or even about truth itself. Notice that the very idea that universals are relative sounds contradictory, and so (it is claimed) the argument will show. A typical version can go like this. Clearly universal relativism (truths about certain universals are relative), if it were true, would be about those universals and so would apply to itself. Thus it would follow that universal relativism, if true, is relative. But if it is relative, then it is not true in the intended sense. Hence, universal relativism is caught in a dilemma. It is not true, if it is true. Therefore, since it is also not true if it isn't, universal relativism is not true. Variants on this involve the idea that not many believe in universal relativism (alternatively, that some do not). So if the relativism in that doctrine makes truths about universals relative to what many believe (alternatively, to what some believe), then, by its own lights, it is not true. (This is a little closer to Plato in the *Theaetetus*.) Again, universal relativism if true is not true, and therefore universal relativism is not true.

---

[1] Here I formulate relativism metalinguistically: truths about universals are relative. That formulation suits the argument of this section. Later I descend to the object language where it is the universals themselves that are relative. The redundancy feature of truth allows this latitude, free of harm—at least I hope so.

The idea behind this Platonic line of argument is that relativism, when stated so broadly, is self-refuting. Charges of this sort appeal to philosophers, who have been trained to prosecute them (Putnam 1981: 119 and Boghossian 1996 are good examples of the genre). But, as Dewey reminds us, '[A]rguments and objections are but stimuli to induce somebody to try a certain experiment—to have recourse, that is, to a non-logical, non-intellectual affair' (*MW* x. 325 n. 1). So philosophers understand that proto-refutations, such as these, can be looked at instead as tools for adjusting the assumptions or presuppositions that engage the refuting arguments. They can help us, that is, realign our thoughts with the actions that prompt and test the thoughts. In the case of these Platonic arguments we can look at the assumption that if the truth of relativism is itself only relative, then relativism is not true as intended. This is a shaky assumption, since it is the relativist's actions that count here, and relativists are likely to show that they regard being relatively true as all the truth there is, and so true enough (see e.g. Meiland 1980). Faced with this relativist response, the critic of relativism may shift ground from logic to rhetoric (or marketing), moving from the claim that relativism is self-refuting to the claim that it is self-defeating. For suppose it suffices for universal relativism that it is true enough provided only that some believe it (whether one or many), then how could it be a doctrine that the relativist can advocate to non-believers (for whom it is already false!) in order to persuade them to change their minds? Indeed, what would be the point of having people change their minds? And if relativism is a doctrine that cannot be sold on its merits, then what merit does it really have?

The relativist could pursue a number of responses, but here I would emphasize only one. It is that universal relativism has its own appeal, and so perhaps it does not need much marketing in order to be sold. More fully, the charge that relativism is self-defeating is based on the idea that to persuade someone to adopt relativism requires theoretical advocacy, something like an argument in which I demonstrate to you the merits of relativism. But how can I persuade you that truths about certain universals are relative unless we share lots of ground in common, including lots of what we believe to be true about these very universals—as well as lots about logical inference and other universals. (This is the kernel of Davidson's (1984) attack on conceptual relativism, an attack that questions the very notion of a conceptual scheme.) So it looks as if we would need much that is not relative in order to be an advocate for relativism, and that may begin to look like needing too much. The relativist may well respond that perhaps we need not be an advocate in this sense, so perhaps we need nothing non-relativistic at all. For assuming that I want you to join in my relativism, why should I try to persuade you of it by an argument conceived of in this purely intellectual way? Conceived of pragmatically, however, as an inducement to try the 'experiment' of adopting universal relativism, perhaps all I need do is display it and invite you to examine it for yourself (see Goodman 1978: 22). This is a minimal but well-known pragmatic strategy ('Try it, you'll like it') and, given the apparent lure of relativism, it may be all the advocacy or argument the relativist needs.

In common with certain other sweeping philosophical doctrines (skepticism and solipsism come to mind), relativism has about it an air of self-referential paradox. From Plato's time to ours, the suspicion lingers that relativism is somehow inconsistent. It is self-refuting, or if not that, then self-defeating, or if not that, then in some other way it is conceptually flawed. The history of relativism, however, suggests the contrary conclusion. As above, relativism seems a robust doctrine, well able to survive despite all the arguments brought against it. If survival is a mark of fitness for ideas as well as for species, then relativism looks fit. If, further, fitness implies proliferation, then we see fitness confirmed by several contemporary movements that have taken a relativist turn. We need to look at this recent revival of relativism, but here I want to turn away from argument and paradox to look instead at some considerations that make relativism, however resilient, seem undesirable and even dangerous—a 'dictatorship' (Benedict XVI 2005) with 'pernicious consequences' (Boghossian 1996).

2. STANDARDS AND TRUTH

What are the relata of relativism? That is, to what are the universals relative? Candidates here include social relata such as individuals or groups. There are conceptual relata such as points of view, conceptual schemes, language games, or linguistic frameworks. Finally, there are very general relata that interweave these first two, such as practices or cultures or forms of life. All of the above might be indexed for time, and no doubt there can be other candidates as well. Suppose the universals are standards, and the relata are social practices. Then we get a characteristic relativism according to which standards are relative to social practices. Why should this be worrisome? In Carnapian terms the worry would not be over internal questions. To the extent to which the social practices are determinate, the standards will be fixed by the practice (even if they are not transparent to the practitioners). But if we are asked an external question, one about improving our practice or adopting better standards, then apparently our relativism leaves us with no place to go. In the end, all we can say is that this is how we do things and that is not. The spade turns here.

Thomas Kuhn's (1970) account of scientific development involves just such a relativism. For Kuhn, in the case of normal science, standards for the practice of science are internal to the paradigm that governs that practice. Thus when the buildup of anomalies leads to crisis, and revolution is in the offing, judgments about whether to change our practice, and how, have no home ground. It looks as though we have no resources to deal with choices involving revolutionary change. In fact, over the years, Kuhn had a great deal of practical advice to offer about how such choices are to be made. He says they are based on a number of criteria (or 'values'), including considerations of accuracy, consistency, scope, simplicity, and fruitfulness (1977: 322). But he emphasizes that, in the absence of a governing paradigm, the application of these criteria is not clear-cut. We have in effect to extend the notions of accuracy, consistency, and so forth, anew. In the eyes of his early critics (e.g. Shapere 1967 or Scheffler 1967), Kuhn's relativism leads to irrationality. It leads, that is, to there being no rational basis for revolutionary change. Kuhn and his supporters always resisted this charge. They were right to do so, since the posited criteria of choice certainly provide a rational basis (reasonable means toward reasonable ends) for judging newly proposed practices: a basis, that is, that (arguably) leads to reliable science. Indeed, these criteria, as Kuhn presents them, are even invariant, or absolute, over different sciences and epochs. It is just that the application of these criteria is not fixed by past practice. We have to extend the practice at the very same time that we determine what is scientifically simplest, most fruitful, and so on. The general point here should be familiar from Dewey's 'experimentalism': that we learn in inquiry itself how better to conduct it.

As I see it, then, the worry over a relativism that makes standards relative to practice is not properly speaking a worry about irrationality. Although the concern might be expressed in those terms, we can see from these reflections on Kuhn that there need be no issue of irrationality raised by this form of relativism. Rather, the worry is that if standards are made relative to practice, we have no substantive resource that determines how to respond when established practices are challenged. Just as with Kuhn's five criteria of choice, in a significant sense we help the criteria for change become substantive as we go. I believe that other sorts of relativism provoke the same worry.

Consider relativism over truth. Suppose we hold an acceptance theory of truth, so that something is true just in case the right people accept it under the right circumstances. This makes truth relative to acceptance behavior. One version of this might be a picture of truth as idealized rational acceptability. This is the picture that Hilary Putnam (1981) once promoted as central to his 'internal realism'.[2] There the right people are perfectly rational agents, and the right circumstances are those ideal for the acquisition of knowledge. Uncomfortable with all this idealization, and with the idea of this as a substantive 'theory' of truth, Richard Rorty suggests a more human reading where the right people are just us, and the right circumstances are when we are at our best (1993: 452). Elsewhere I have tried to show that, in general, this form of relativism is subject to a Platonic-style refutation; in effect, that on this relativistic conception, truth judgments become unintelligible (1989 and 1996: ch. 8). The argument, roughly, is that the grammar of truth leads to an infinite regress of conditions of acceptability. For if something is true, then it is true that it is true, and this can be repeated indefinitely. Thus, given the redundancy feature of truth (the equivalence of 'P' and 'it is true that P'), any seemingly simple judgment about the truth of an assertion, on this view, turns into an unintelligibly long jumble of judgments about acceptability conditions. This is a terrific argument. Indeed, it is close to one that Putnam himself formulates against relativism in general (1981: 119–24). But it can hardly be expected to put a stop to the game. For we really need to ask what it is that bothers us here, apart from grammar.

The answer, surely, is that acceptance, no matter how well dressed, is not truth. Unless we rig it so that 'the right people' accepting under 'the right circumstances' just amounts to accepting something when and only when it is true, no honest acceptance formula can be expected to capture truths and only truths. This is clear in Rorty's reading, where we want to ask whether, even at our best, couldn't we be wrong? What Rorty calls the 'cautionary' use of truth is just the use where we recognize that, yes indeed, of course we can be wrong—even at our best.

---

[2] See Mueller and Fine 2004 for the ins and outs of Putnam's treatment of realism and truth, and its relation to a consistent pragmatic core.

This cautionary feature of truth talk, however, might mislead some into forming a more substantial image of truth. This is the image of truth as a figure towering in the background of inquiry, guiding our efforts with a hidden but certain hand. Accordingly, when we speak of searching for the truth we expect our practices of acceptance to be constrained and guided by that hidden hand. But when truth is made relative to acceptance, our expectation is frustrated, for, made relative, truth can no longer provide a stable resource for reshaping practices of acceptance. It does not follow, that there is no truth. That could not follow, since, by virtue of redundancy, the concept of truth is available in every discourse or inquiry. Moreover, relativism about truth is about truth. It presupposes the concept of truth and otherwise makes no sense. The same holds for relativism about standards, or about other universals. Relativism is not nihilism. Rather, relativism puts us in the position of Kuhn's revolutionary scientist who must choose how to project the values (simplicity, fertility, and so forth) of established practice into new terrain and, at the very same time, must oversee how things go and adjust accordingly. What falls by the wayside in relativism is not truth itself but the substantial image, or idol, that some have made of it. That idol represents what Dewey calls a 'hankering for certainty', which 'has led to the idea that absence of immutably fixed and universally applicable ready-made principles is equivalent to . . . chaos' (*MW* xiv. 164). Chaos would mean that our choices for how to go on were simply arbitrary. They are not. They are guided, as Dewey would say, by intelligence, which continually looks ahead to the consequences of those choices and adjusts how criteria are applied, so as to further what look like the most promising results—insofar as one can tell.

3. WITHOUT RECOURSE

I have been trying to highlight a particular worry that is central to the distress that relativism can provoke. The worry is sometimes expressed by the claim that relativism leads to nihilism—chaos: no standards, no truth. Sometimes it is expressed by the claim that relativism leads to irrationality—chaos: no rational basis for going on. These are extreme claims and, in our brief examination of relativism over standards and relativism over truth, we can see that they are not correct. We can also see, however, that there is a worrisome core that lies behind the claims. It is that the universals that are being made relative (standards, truth, and so on) are just the things that are supposed to stand firm and guide the practice to which they are being made relative (social practices, acceptance behavior, and so forth). Thus relativism has the consequence that these universals cannot be called upon to guide practice when the question is raised about whether to alter the practice and, if so, how. So it is not that we lose truth or that we lose standards; it is just that we lose them as a reliable guide when it is a question of altering our practice. If there were no other guides, then indeed one might claim that we would have no rational basis for going on. But, as we have seen in the case of Kuhn's relativism, there may well be other values to guide us—even absolute values.

Of course this does not settle the matter, but simply shifts the worry to one about the character of these other values. Still, that is a progressive shift, for it is this worry, I would urge, that masquerades as a concern over nihilism or irrationality. The worry is that the values that rush in to fill the void left by relativism may not be up to the job of guiding us progressively from established practice to new practice. If we examine the values that Kuhn proposes, we can readily identify reasons for concern. Consider accuracy, which might seem straightforward, certainly more so than, for example, simplicity. By 'accuracy' Kuhn means that the results of observations and experiments should match what the theory implies. Of course Kuhn recognizes that a theory yields observational or experimental consequences only when supplemented by assumptions governing conditions of application, and he recognizes that various different assumptions may be reasonable in given circumstances. So what counts as a 'consequence' of a theory is inherently vague. For the same reason, what count as the 'results' of observation or experiment are similarly vague. Moreover, Kuhn realizes that we can only demand accuracy between theory and experiment within the proper domain of the theory. But what, exactly, is that, and how do we determine it? Finally, how are we to decide what degree of fit constitutes a 'match'? It emerges, then, that the injunction to choose accurate theories has little determinate content absent specific choices over theoretical consequences, empirical results, domains of validity, and degree of fitness. But what guides these choices except for another round of vaguely specified values, or the like?

Thus the worry is that relativism leaves us without recourse in moving from established practice to new practice. This does not mean that we are without any resources at all, but that the resources compatible with relativism are not firm enough. Our relativist guidebooks contain only incomplete sketches whose variables are themselves incomplete, and so on and so on. We are threatened by an indefinite regress. The implication is that relativism allows no foundations for science—or for knowledge, or for morality. There are no well-defined principles or norms (or whatever) that can always be counted on to guide us in moving from present practice to a future practice where the very norms or principles currently in play may no longer apply, or may not apply in the same way. To guide us we have only schema or rules of thumb that are incomplete and, apparently, incompleteable. The worry, in short, is that we have no (firm) leg to stand on. That worry is triggered by a correct perception about the consequences of relativism. Relativism is incompatible with foundationalism. But is this pernicious?

4. DO WE NEED A LEG TO STAND ON?

In 1905, his 'miracle year', Albert Einstein published several short papers that were instrumental in changing the practice of physics. It is only a slight exaggeration to say that physics has never been the same since. His paper on the photoelectric effect introduced the then revolutionary idea of the quantization of light, and later won him the Nobel prize. It was one of a series of papers in which Einstein developed many of the tools and ideas that culminated in the modern quantum theory. Two papers that he wrote on Brownian motion helped establish the reality of molecules. But the paper we remember most was the paper on the special theory of relativity. It was a rather off-beat piece of work, combining a little elementary philosophical analysis ('What is time?') with a heuristic derivation of known equations (the Lorentz transformations) for which hardly any experimental applications were discussed, and with no references at all to the literature. Much has been written about the background to that paper on relativity, and about Einstein's way of doing physics more generally. Of course Einstein was no nihilist or irrationalist, and in his own reflections about science Einstein was not a philosophical relativist either. (The name 'relativity' was given to Einstein's theory by Max Planck, and it stuck. Emphasizing what the Lorentz transformations leave fixed, like the spacetime interval, Einstein would have preferred to call his work 'the theory of invariants'.) Yet scholarship about Einstein's scientific work finds that it was also not foundational, in the sense of positing a firm ground for extending practice. Although he certainly valued unity and logical simplicity in his scientific work, these (and other values) were like Kuhn's criteria, needing to be re-situated with changing practice. As a leading scholar notes, one must view his work 'in context, taking into account both the inner logic...and the contemporary problematics' to which it was responding (Darrigol 2004: 618). No reputable scholar holds that Einstein worked from a set of ready-made principles that determined the outcome of his science.

Like Dewey and the pragmatic tradition, Einstein held that science was continuous with everyday thinking, not an esoteric field with arcane methods and practices all its own. He held, in particular, that the formation of everyday concepts, as well as the formation of concepts in science, was not determined by any logical means, no matter how 'inevitable' the concepts might seem to be or how close to 'pure' sense perception they appeared. Rather, he regarded scientific concepts as a free creation of the human mind.[3]

By 'free' he meant both that concepts are not innate and also that they are neither given in nor logically derived from experience. The only test for scientific concepts is whether they can be organized in a logically simple system that finds fruitful empirical applications. In framing new ideas in science and in changing how we practice science, nothing in past practice forces any particular movement into the future. That is not to say that how we go on is independent of what we have been doing. Certainly the course of science produces what Bruno Latour (1987) calls 'black boxes': that is, modules of theory, instrumentation, and experimental technique that support one another in ways that scientists rely on to do their daily work. But black boxes can be opened and tinkered with. In the history of science they are often discredited. Nothing in our current practice determines what attitude to take to our black boxes: which to accept and which to try to subvert. Further, nothing in our current practice determines whether we will succeed, either way, if we try. This again is Dewey's instrumentalism, or experimentalism. Doing science involves feedback from ongoing practice. We need to reflect on that practice and choose whether to proceed as usual or to try something new (if only we can come up with something new to try). We cannot operationalize those decisions. There are no fixed rules of practice that tell us to turn left if today's results are such-and-such, and to go straight ahead otherwise. Each such call is a judgment call, and,

---

[3] The expression 'free creation of the human mind' occurs in Dedekind 1888, who applies it to numerical concepts. Einstein read that work during his Bern years, and the expression seems to have made its mark (e.g. 1954: 291)

as Einstein suggests, these scientific judgments—like most everyday judgments—are not forced.

They are still judgments, however, and not arbitrary whims. They depend on reasons, ideas, experience, and skills; on interests and values; on goals and directions; on material, conceptual, and economic resources and rewards. They depend on the cooperation of the natural world. They also depend on our allies and on our adversaries. Everything that pertains to complex human action enters into judgments about how to practice science. Almost all the items that underwrite our judgments are also underspecified in some or other respects. Very often even our goals are not so clear and firm as we might like to imagine. Much less so are the ideas, interests, resources, and so on that enter into what we decide to do. As anyone who has practiced science knows, that includes our data and other experimental results, which are always subject to reinterpretation and re-evaluation. Usually we can rationalize whatever course of action emerges as a suitable modification of past practice. That is, we are able to show how it relates to judgments about goals and values and how it reflects appropriate means for attaining those goals while respecting those values. It is important to see that to behave rationally, in this sense, does not imply that the behavior is fixed by clear-cut rules or principles antecedent to the action itself. To behave rationally means only that we can rationalize our behavior in terms of suitable means, goals, and values that may themselves emerge only in the course of action.

This is the Einsteinian conception of the openness of science. It is a conception of science as a rational enterprise without foundations. I think it a realistic conception of how science works and, if you are a relativist about standards or the like, you will have to adopt something like it. If it is more or less on target as a description of ongoing science, then two things follow. One is that in doing science we do not, in fact, have a leg to stand on. The other is that we do not, in principle, need a leg to stand on. Unforced judgments that rely on underspecified constraints seem to be all the resources that science has, and all that science needs for its continued success and progress.

5. DEFUSING RELATIVISM?

Relativism, and the nonfoundational view of science that it implies, certainly allows for reasons, principles, and facts as integral components in the judgments that enter into scientific practice. What relativism goes against is the sort of foundationalism according to which these components are clear-cut and firm, and the judgments in which they issue inevitable. It is difficult to find support for such a foundationalism in the practice of science. There may appear to be abundant support, however, for the different idea that there is a foundation for the validation of scientific decisions after they have been made. Neo-positivism distinguished between the context of discovery and the context of justification, with the former defying strict logic and the latter exemplifying it. One tempting way of defusing the worry over relativism, then, would be to attach the concern about lack of foundations to the context of discovery, where it may seem unlikely to do any harm. The idea is that there may indeed be no strict scientific method that underwrites a logic of discovery, but once we have set off on a course of action, then, surely, there are strict principles for evaluating our new knowledge claims.

But this easy-sounding resolution is not correct. For the cognitive relativism we have been examining applies as well to the context of justification as to the context of discovery. Both are relative. Justification, no less than discovery, makes use of culturally bound and variable instruments of reason. The confidence intervals, correlation coefficients, and other statistical instruments of today's science are a product of nineteenth-century thought. Nothing of the sort was available to help Galileo interpret his data in Pisa. When Pasteur tells us that chance favours only the prepared mind, it was his own newly developed experimental methods that he was recommending, not Mill's methods, and certainly not Descartes's. Even the medical paradigm of placebo-controlled, double-blind trials has a history (why do you think it is 'double' blind?) and a shifting set of emendations (e.g. randomization) and learned limitations. These instruments of reason influence what principles are accepted, what facts are regarded as salient, and what reasons are given what weights. If this is so, then the best that could be said for justification is that it is determinate relative to such cultural instruments; i.e. relative to accepted practice. Part of the quest for certainty, as Dewey notes, tests ideas only against traditional, antecedent conditions. So, immersed as we are in current practice, it may well seem to us that validation is firmly rooted. That appearance, however, is a mirage. In fact, with regard to justification we are in no better position than before over the question about how to go on, about how to extend our practice into the future. To justify our choices, we need to make use of instruments of reason as they are reconfigured in the light of what we learn as a result of the very choices we are wanting to justify. Thus we cannot make the justification of scientific choices any more operational than we can make the discovery of those choices.

Otto Neurath was a pragmatist who resisted the distinction, drawn by some of his neo-positivist colleagues, between the context of discovery and the context of justification. His legacy contains a different image: that of having to rebuild our boat of science, plank by plank, while at sea. This is not a bad image for the nonfoundational approach to science that relativism implies.

6. SOCIAL CONSTRUCTIVISM

In more recent times, social constructivism has emerged as a significant nonfoundational approach to science. No doubt, part of why the 'great fear of relativism' (Hacking 1999: 4) has become a prominent cultural topic today is that social constructivists (along with some of their postmodern allies) feature relativism as one of their chief delights. They flaunt their relativism, which they regard as a virtue, and they actually promote it as an advance in our understanding of science. Indeed, different proponents of social constructivism may vie with one another over who is more relativistic than whom. It is with a certain enthusiasm, for example, that Andrew Pickering describes his account of science as a 'hyperrelativism' on 'the wild sides' of his constructivist colleagues (1995: 207–8). The issue for Pickering and those tamer relativisms is precisely the issue we have been treating: how to project established practice into the future.

A properly 'social' constructivist account would feature social factors as the primary determinants of what happens. This is the tack of the so-called strong program in the sociology of scientific knowledge. There one looks at established routines that can be socially inculcated, to the norm-building role of authority in a community, to social interests, and to shared goals as possible ways of explaining what causes beliefs to be held and what leads to the patterns of behavior that reflect these beliefs. The relativism of the strong program is marked by the assumption 'that all beliefs are on a par with one another with respect to the causes of their credibility' (Barnes and Bloor 1982: 23). This 'symmetry postulate' makes credibility relative to social factors, such as those cited above, and the constructivist part of this social constructivism makes validity (or justification) relative to credibility. Notice that this relativism has a causal-scientific flavour. According to the program, social factors cause certain beliefs to be held (or judged appropriate), and the task for the sociology of scientific knowledge is to find the causes. Despite this emphasis on social causes, the position of the strong program is not truly deterministic. Although at any given moment a particular constellation of social factors may determine what scientists do, that constellation itself is relative. It is a product of specific local circumstances that might well have been different. Thus, in spite of its emphasis on social factors, for the strong program there is no fixed foundation for changing practices. Its relativism functions to bring this out.

If one is skeptical about how much understanding of scientific belief can be had by looking only at social factors, then one might consider other strands in the constructivist movement, for not all constructivisms have an exclusively social flavor. Pickering (1995) gives a more balanced account, emphasizing both the role of the social and of the material world in the 'accommodations to resistance' that, for him, constitute scientific practice. He recognizes that independently of scientists' goals, plans, and interests, the material world also influences what scientists do. Pickering is shy about using the term 'constraint' here and saying simply that the material world constrains what we do. Pickering resists the language of constraints because of his pragmatic orientation. He wants to emphasize that the way the material world influences us is context-bound and emerges only as we act. That is, Pickering wants it to be clear that neither social not material factors are foundational in ongoing scientific practice. What he has against 'constraints' is that they sound too much like timeless foundations.

Bruno Latour's actor-network theory (1987) is yet another kind of 'social constructivism' that de-emphasizes the social (also the constructivism). Latour takes over from Michel Serres (1982) the notion of quasi-objects, hybrid entities that are neither social nor natural but share features of both. Latour calls them 'actants'. Those in the quantum business might describe an actant as an entity whose state of being is a superposition of the social and the natural. Tools and other artifacts would be primary examples of actants, but then so would corporations and virtually every other kind of thing that relates both to nature and to us. The point is that the concept of the social world and that of the natural world are each constructed in relation to one another—constructed, that is, from actants. Thus neither concept should be fundamental in understanding science. Like Pickering's, Latour's orientation is also pragmatic, with an emphasis not only on science in action, but also on relations as fundamental to science—just as in Dewey and James. Scientific practice is action made possible by temporarily stable networks of social-natural relations, and, at the same time, scientific practice is constituted by the work of extending and stabilizing these networks. Once again, the topic is how to extend present practice into the future, and the response of actor-network theory is that no foundational guides determine the extension.

If this brief survey is representative of the relativism to which social constructivists aspire, then it turns out to be something of a misnomer. For their relativism is primarily a commitment to a conception of scientific practice as open and nonfoundational. By advertising this commitment under the banner of relativism, they expose themselves to the hyper-charged armory of anti-relativist rhetoric, including the familiar charges of self-refutation and postmodern nihilism. Other vices are sometimes associated with constructivism—for instance, idealism or irrationalism—and it is questionable whether they too are actually to be found there. On the other side, one could question whether the primarily sociological tools that the constructivist movement brings to an analysis of scientific practice are up to the job. But, whatever may be the outcome of those other discussions, I must conclude here that what constructivists call relativism, if we bracket the misleading terminology, is just as they say it is; it is a virtue. In moving away from 'foundations' and 'scientific method', it constitutes an advance in our understanding of scientific practice.

7. CONCLUDING THOUGHTS

Relativism (idiot relativism excluded) is not paradoxical. Despite the clever work of a number of philosopher-prosecutors, we can dismiss their charges that relativism is self-refuting or self-defeating. Nor is relativism (even over standards or truth) dangerous. It does not lead to chaos. It does not imply nihilism or irrationality. To the contrary, insofar as it is concerned with standards, truth, and reason, it presupposes standards, truth, and reason. The false accusations are compounded from a correct perception and a mistake. The correct perception is that relativism is not compatible with firm and determinate foundations. The mistaken idea is that, without such foundations, what we do and value is arbitrary—anything goes. Again to the contrary, not anything goes without foundations. What does go, and goes well, however, is the particular institution of science itself. Thus the nonfoundational consequences of relativism seem to be a virtue, not a vice. While these considerations may rescue relativism from the false charges brought against it, they are not intended to vindicate relativism as a general doctrine. The extent to which a specific form of universal relativism is viable depends critically on the universals specific to that form, to what they are said to be relative, and how so. Relativism varies in kind and degree, as well as in plausibility. No one verdict is ready-made to fit all.

If relativism about truth takes the form of an acceptance theory of truth, for instance, then it is surely wrong. For truth is not acceptance, and any attempt to pin it down that way is bound to fail. If relativism about standards takes Kuhn's form, then its viability depends on whether Kuhn's account of scientific practice—in terms of paradigms, normal science, and his dynamics for revolutionary change—is viable overall. Some doubt that it is. If relativism adopts a version of the strong program and holds that justification in science is relative only to the interests and beliefs of particular communities of scientists, then this version would seem to leave out the role of the material world in scientific practice, and if that were actually left out, it would be going too far. Similarly off track would be a postmodern relativism claiming that validity (or justification) is relative only to such things as ideological correctness and political power, without regard to other desiderata, including truth, evidence, and reason.

If these last two instances of relativism seem not just wrong-headed but extreme, then we might recall that mainstream physics also contains some rather extreme relativisms. The debate that goes back to Newton and Leibniz over a substantival conception of space and time versus a purely relational conception is precisely a debate over whether the universals of space and time are relative or absolute with respect to material bodies. That debate in physics continues today, after Einstein, over the role of absolute structures in spacetime itself. Niels Bohr's Copenhagen interpretation of quantum mechanics, some version of which most contemporary physicists accept as the received view, involves a basic relativism about reality. This relativist understanding of the micro-world is also known as 'contextualism'—a handy pseudonym for relativism when you would rather keep a low profile. According to Bohr's doctrine of complementarity, basic physical properties of an atom—like its spatial location or its momentum—are relative to conditions of observation. Because position and momentum are not simultaneously observable, according to Heisenberg's famous Uncertainty Principle,

Bohr argues that one cannot 'define' these properties, and so ascribe them to an atomic object, except under specified conditions of observation. Thus a fundamental relativism (or contextualism) of properties in the micro-world becomes necessary, or so Bohr claims.

So, not only standards, truth, and reason, but also space, time, and even reality itself may be judged relative. But if we were to adopt relativism about the first trio of universals, then would it ever be possible to decide about the relativism (or not) of any of them?

The answer is that yes, if we work at it, most likely we will be able to grade relativisms into better and worse—because generally we do. But that sort of question, which seems inevitable in this context, brings us back again to the issue of foundations. It seems that to be human—in Descartes's terms, to be a thing that thinks—is to ask about ways to transcend the human condition. Not only the great religions, but also many of the myths and ideologies that run through different cultures, our own included, respond to that urge for transcendence. Like pragmatism, relativism responds as well. Like pragmatism, it responds in the negative. It rejects transcendence. The nonfoundationalism built into relativism says, pragmatically, that all that we have to count on is us. For some, that prospect seems too terrifying (or boring?) to live with. For others, it is just an invitation to roll up our sleeves and get to work. As Michel Serre says, for some it is

as though it were always a matter of constructing (or tearing down) a very solid edifice, whose peaks or foundation would organize all stability. It's possible to compose outside of solidity—in fuzziness and fluctuation. Nature itself does nothing else, or almost. (1995: 112)

BIBLIOGRAPHY

Barnes, B., and Bloor, D. (1982) 'Relativism, Rationalism and the Sociology of Knowledge'. In M. Hollis and S. Lukes (eds.), *Rationality and Relativism*, 21–47. Cambridge, Mass.: MIT Press.

Benedict XVI (2005) Homily at the mass for the election of the Roman pontiff, 18 April, 2005. Available on line at <www.weeklystandard.com/, Content/Public/Articles/000/000/005/513fkpya.asp?pg=2>.

Boghossian, P. A. (1996) 'What the Sokal Hoax Ought to Teach Us'. *Times Literary Supplement*, 13 December: 14–15.

Darrigol, O. (2004) 'The Mystery of the Einstein–Poincaré Connection'. *Isis*, 95: 614–26.

Davidson, D. (1984) 'On the Very Idea of a Conceptual Scheme'. In *Inquiries into Truth and Interpretation*, 183–93. Oxford: Clarendon Press.

Dedekind, R. (1888) 'Was sind und was sollen die Zahlen?'. Translated as "What Are Numbers and What Should They Be?", and edited by H. Pogorzelski, W. Ryan, and W. Snyder. Orono, Me.: Research Institute for Mathematics (RIM) Monographs in Mathematics, 1995.

Dewey, J. (1899–1924) *The Middle Works*, i–xv. Carbondale, Ill.: Southern Illinois University Press; Referred to as *MW*.

Einstein, A. (1934) *Essays in Science*. New York: Philosophical Library.

——(1954) *Ideas and Opinions*. New York: Bonanza Books.

Fine, A. (1989) 'Truthmongering: Less is True'. *Canadian Journal of Philosophy*, 19: 611–16.

——(1996) *The Shaky Game*, Einstein Realism and the Quantum Theory, 2nd edn. Chicago: University of Chicago Press.

Goodman, N. (1978) *Ways of Worldmaking*. Indianapolis: Hackett.

Hacking, I. (1999) *The Social Construction of What?* Cambridge, Mass.: Harvard University Press.

Kuhn, T. (1970) *The Structure of Scientific Revolutions*, 2nd edn. Chicago: University of Chicago Press.

——(1977) *The Essential Tension*. Chicago: University of Chicago Press.

Latour, B. (1987) *Science in Action*. Cambridge, Mass.: Harvard University Press.

Meiland, J. W. (1980) 'On the Paradox of Cognitive Relativism'. *Metaphilosophy*, 11: 115–26.

Mueller, A., and Fine, A. (2004) 'Realism, Beyond Miracles'. In Y. Ben-Menahim (ed.), *Contemporary Philosophy in Focus: Hilary Putnam*, 83–124. Cambridge: Cambridge University Press.

Pickering, A. (1995) *The Mangle of Practice*. Chicago: University of Chicago Press.

Putnam, H. (1981) *Reason, Truth and History*. Cambridge: Cambridge University Press.

Rorty, R. (1993) 'Putnam and the Relativist Menace'. *Journal of Philosophy*, 90: 443–61.

Scheffler, I. (1967) *Science and Subjectivity*. Indianapolis: Hackett.

Serres, M. (1982) *The Parasite*. Baltimore: Johns Hopkins University Press.

——(1995) *Conversations on Science, Culture and Time*, trans R. Lapidus. Ann Arbor: University of Michigan Press.

Shapere, D. (1967) 'Meaning and Scientific Change'. In R. G. Colodny (ed.), *Mind and Cosmos*, 41–85. Pittsburgh: University of Pittsburgh Press.

4

Pragmatism and Deflationism

Cheryl Misak

1. PEIRCE'S NATURALIST ACCOUNT OF TRUTH

C. S. Peirce, the founder of pragmatism, argued that a belief is true if it would be 'indefeasible', or would not be improved upon, or would never lead to disappointment, no matter how far we were to pursue our inquiries.[1] Although he occasionally articulated this view of truth in terms of a belief's being fated to be believed at the end of inquiry, on the whole he tried to stay away from unhelpful ideas such as the final end of inquiry, perfect evidence, and the like.[2]

He was also very careful to stay away from a reductive definition of truth: he did not want to *define* truth as that which satisfies our aims in inquiry. A dispute about definition is usually a 'profitless discussion' (*CP* 8. 100). Peirce's project is to try to get us to see the difference between two respectable tasks: providing an analytic definition of a concept like truth, which might be of use to someone who has never encountered the notion before, and providing a pragmatic elucidation of it—an account of the role the concept plays in practical endeavours. David Wiggins sees his point clearly:[3] 'To elucidate truth in its relations with the notion of inquiry, for instance, as the pragmatist does, need

This paper builds and is an improvement upon Misak 1998 and 2000: 57 ff. I've had many useful discussions with others about it—most importantly with Dorothy Grover and Joe Heath.

[1] See *CP* 6. 485, 5. 569. References to Peirce's *Collected Papers* (*CP*) are in standard form: volume number, followed by paragraph number. References to *Writings* (*W*) take the form: volume number, page number.

[2] See *CP* 5. 569, 6. 485, and Misak 2004: 35 ff.

[3] Sellars (1962: 29) did as well.

not . . . represent any concession at all to the idea that truth is *itself* an "epistemic notion" ' (2002: 318). When a concept is, as Wiggins (2002: 316) puts it, 'already fundamental to human thought and long since possessed of an autonomous interest', it is pointless to try to define it. Rather, we ought to attempt to get leverage on the concept, or a fix on it, by exploring its connections with practice.

This is the insight at the very heart of pragmatism. In Peirce's words: 'We must not begin by talking of pure ideas,—vagabond thoughts that tramp the public roads without any human habitation,—but must begin with men and their conversation' (*CP* 8. 112). In order to get a complete grasp of a concept, we must go beyond a 'nominal' definition and connect the concept to that with which we have 'dealings' (*CP* 5. 416).

Peirce argued that 'transcendental' accounts of truth, such as the correspondence theory, are examples of those 'vagabond thoughts'. They make truth 'the subject of metaphysics exclusively'. We would do better to illuminate truth by considering its linkages with assertion, belief, and inquiry. For those are the human dealings relevant to truth. When we assert, believe, or inquire, we take ourselves to be aiming at truth. We want to know, for instance, what methods might get us true belief; whether it is worth our time and energy to inquire into certain kinds of questions; whether a discourse such as moral discourse aims at truth, or whether it is a radically subjective matter, not at all suited for truth-value.

One link between truth, on the one hand, and assertion and inquiry, on the other, is as follows. There is an unseverable connection between making an assertion and claiming that it is true. What we do when we offer a justification of '*p* is true' is to offer a justification for the claim that *p*. If we want to know whether it is true that Toronto is north of Buffalo, there is nothing additional to check on ('a fact', 'a state of affairs')—nothing over and above our consulting maps, driving or walking north from Buffalo to see whether we get to Toronto, etc. The question of the *truth* of the statement does not involve anything more than investigating the matter in our usual ways. And were we to get a belief that would be forever assertible (a belief which would never lead to disappointment; a belief which would be indefeasible or not defeated were inquiry pursued as far as it could fruitfully go), then we would have a true belief. There would be nothing higher or better we could ask of it.

Peirce is thus wedded to something like Arthur Fine's (1986: 177) naturalism 'California Style'. We should not add anything philosophical to science, or to any other first-order inquiry—'no additives, please'. There is a point or an aim to any particular deliberation—to solve a problem, to build a better instrument, to decide what is just in the circumstances, or to confirm a hypothesis. When we inquire, we are wondering about those things, not about whether a statement or belief has the property of truth.

Fine himself infers that there is no one aim (truth) which all investigations have.[4] This inference is the hallmark of the deflationist position on truth. The deflationist holds (with Peirce) that what there is to say about truth is what there is to say about local inquiries, and (against Peirce) that it follows that we do not aim at truth or that there are no general features which true beliefs have in common. So Peirce, although he travels a fair distance along the same road as the deflationist, eventually parts company with the deflationist in that he thinks that he can say something about the property of truth, generally.

My argument shall be that Peirce, not the deflationist, arrives at the best expression of the naturalist rebellion against metaphysics. If we can wrench our gaze from the traditional correspondence view of truth, then the naturalist can and should take our investigations to aim at truth. If the naturalist follows Peirce in seeing truth as indefeasible belief, then it is unproblematic for the naturalist to say that we aim at truth. For 'truth' here is just a catch-all for the particular local aims of inquiry—empirical adequacy, predictive power, coherence with other beliefs, simplicity, elegance, explanatory power, getting a reliable guide to action, fruitfulness for other research, greater understanding of others, increased maturity, and the like. There is nothing over and above the fulfilment of those ends, nothing metaphysical, to which we aspire. The pragmatist steps away from metaphysically loaded accounts of truth and steps towards practice. A true belief is one which would be the upshot of our inquiries.

I shall suggest below that while the deflationist thinks that he too is stepping towards practice, he has an impoverished view of practice. The pragmatist of the Peircean stripe will argue that once we see that truth and assertion are intimately connected—once we see that to assert that *p* is true is to assert *p*—we can and must look to our practices of assertion and to the commitments incurred in them so as to say something more substantial about truth. Hard on the heels of the thought that truth is internally related to assertion comes the thought that truth is also internally related to inquiry, reasons, evidence, and standards of good

---

[4] See Fine 2001 and Ch.3, this volume, for Fine's current view.

belief. If we unpack the commitments we incur when we assert, we find that we have imported all these notions.

Consider the difference between the phrases 'I suspect that p' or 'It seems to me that p', on the one hand, and 'I assert that p' or 'I believe that p', on the other. What I do when I use the first two is distance myself from the obligations which come with assertion. Those obligations include committing myself to predicting that experience will fall in line with the belief, or, as Chris Hookway (2000: 65) nicely points out, with some successor of it.[5] I expect that the proposition will survive future inquiry.

I also commit myself to defending p; to arguing that I am, and others are, warranted in asserting and believing it. Of course, working out what it is to have warrant for a belief will be a difficult and controversial business, and no one can always live up to the commitment. But that does not interfere with the thought that to assert commits one to engage, if called upon, in the enterprise of justification. Failing to see that one incurs the commitment, failing to see that one is required to offer reasons for one's belief, results in the degradation of belief into something like prejudice or tenacity.[6] Truth, that is, is bound up with the practice of assertion, which then binds it further to expectations for experience, reasons, and inquiry.

With this snapshot of the pragmatist view in hand, let us turn to some varieties of deflationism to see just where the similarities and differences lie.

---

[5] Hookway shows that Peirce holds that when I assert that a statement is true, the content of what I commit myself to can be indeterminate (2000: 57). I hope that there will be a convergence and that convergence will be to a refined version of my current belief. What would prove to be defensible in the long run is some approximation of my current belief. So the connection between belief and assertion is not: to assert something is to assert it as true. An inquirer can successfully assert a proposition that she thinks is almost certainly not strictly true. This idea solves some pressing problems for Peirce. It explains how meaning can be preserved over time. And it explains how we can refer to individuals and to kinds when we don't fully understand their character. Changes in our view of x can be seen as moves or improvements within a general or vague picture. Indexical reference anchors our beliefs to the world: it explains how we can have beliefs and theories about x, despite the fact that we get much wrong.

[6] Brandom also argues that when we believe p, we commit ourselves to giving reasons. But he seems not to take this commitment to be a constitutive norm of belief or assertion, for he suggests that 'bare assertion' need not come with reasons. One can just think that people with beards are dangerous and be unprepared to give any grounds for this belief (1994: 228–30). He does, however, think that the practice of bare assertion is parasitic on the practice of assertion with commitment to give reasons. My point is a little more exacting. A belief, in order to be a belief, must come with a commitment to give reasons.

2. THE DISQUOTATIONALIST

Paul Horwich takes the infinite string of instances of the equivalence or disquotational schema (hereafter the DS) to entirely capture the content of 'is true.'[7] 'Snow is white' is true if and only if snow is white, 'Toronto is north of Buffalo' is true if and only if Toronto is north of Buffalo, and so on. There is no underlying nature of truth, no 'essence' of truth, no 'special quality which all truths supposedly have in common' (1990: 6). We can't say, that is, that truths are such that they get reality right or they would be warranted were inquiry to be pursued as far as it could fruitfully go. Horwich thinks that 'in fact nothing could be more mundane and less puzzling than the concept of truth' (1990: p. xi). We should not inquire into the 'typical manifestations' of true propositions (1990: 39), for believing that a theory is true is nothing but 'a trivial step beyond believing the theory' (1990: 60).

On Horwich's view, the only reason for holding on to the idea of truth is that it serves an important logical need. It is a useful device for infinite conjunction and disjunction and for expressing propositions which we cannot identify. This generalizing use is the *'raison d'etre* of the concept of truth'; 'the truth predicate exists solely for the sake of a certain logical need' (1990: 4, 2). Truth is a property, but there is nothing more to it than a generalizing function—it enables us to avoid cumbersome new forms of quantification (1990: 38). We are to hold on to the truth predicate for the sake of the logical need, but there is nothing to truth beyond its use in satisfying that need. The role of truth in our conceptual scheme, Horwich thinks, has now been explained (1990: 42, 36).

Horwich says that his view differs from pragmatism because he is not offering an eliminative analysis or an analytic definition of truth but, rather, an account of what a person understands when he understands claims about truth. He takes the pragmatist to offer an analytic definition of truth in terms of utility, presumably: '*p*' is true if and only if it is useful

---

[7] Thus, as David (1994: 66) notes, it does not seem possible to express the DS in ordinary terms, and it does not seem possible to elucidate it. Horwich says that the disquotationalist theory of truth can't be written down or fully articulated, for it has an infinite number of axioms (1990: 31). This is the theory's 'single unattractive feature' (1990: 42). We might import a thought of Sellars's here and think that disquotationalism is more like a telephone directory than a theory (1962: 33).

to believe *p* (1990: 34, 47). Horwich thinks that we ought, rather, to start from the idea that we must take practice or use seriously. If we do that, we shall see that 'no further fact about the truth predicate—nothing beyond our allegiance to the equivalence schema—is needed to explain *any* of our ways of using it' (2001: 150).

We have seen that the founder of pragmatism was explicit about not giving analytic equivalences, and he was not in the slightest tempted by the thought that a belief is true if it is useful. Perhaps Horwich has James in mind. It is pretty clear that the Peircean pragmatist is trying to do just what Horwich says that *he* is trying to do: offer an account (starting with practice and use) of what a person understands when he understands claims about truth.

If Horwich's objection to pragmatism should not be that pragmatism sets up an analytic definition of truth, perhaps he might then argue that the pragmatic elucidation which is offered is in some way spurious or metaphysical. But we must be careful not to slide with Horwich from a perfectly good thought about the mysteriousness of essences (there is no 'essence' of truth) to the thought that there can be no quality which truths have in common, or even typically. A theory of *x* which identifies characters or marks of *x*s can be perfectly respectable for someone wary of metaphysics. Everything, of course, depends on what characters are identified, and whether they are problematic. The offenders are suggestions that truths have the character of corresponding to states of affairs or facts, not the suggestions the pragmatist puts forward. We must not move seamlessly from the thought that the correspondence theory must be deflated to the thought that *any* theory of truth must be deflated.

What I think Horwich really finds objectionable in a view which goes beyond the DS is that the extra step offends against his sense that 'truth has a certain purity'. Our understanding of truth, he thinks, should be kept independent of other ideas—such as the ideas of verification, reference, meaning, success, or logical entailment (1990: 12).

But it turns out that Horwich thinks that one should call the DS the theory of truth *and then*, if one likes, go on to explain the relationships between truth and those other concepts. We are to get ourselves the most simple, pure, elegant, separate, theory of truth, and then we can 'conjoin that theory with assumptions from elsewhere' (1990: 26). In 'combination with theories of other phenomena', the DS will 'explain all the facts about truth' (1990: 26). There might be much that is right in another theory of truth; it is just that we are not to think of it as part of our *basic* theory of truth. It might be a 'legitimate extension' of the basic theory, but it should not be seen as a 'tempting alternative' to it (1990: 115).

Here we encounter a fundamental difference in philosophical temperament between the pragmatist and the deflationist. The pragmatist thinks that the deflationist's quest for purity will result in something rather empty and useless, for the important work is in spelling out the relationship between truth, on the one hand, and assertion, verification, success, etc., on the other. The way to deflate truth, the pragmatist argues, the way to make truth less metaphysical, is to link it with these other, more down-to-earth notions, not to claim independence from them. That is, the pragmatist, with Davidson, thinks that truth can only be illuminated by the connections between it and the 'human attitudes and acts that give it body'(Davidson 1996: 276).

Horwich says that he is also keen to explain our use of the truth predicate by an appeal to our practices. But he seems to think that we have two, and only two, ways of using 'is true': we use 'p is true' as a way to emphasize p and to say things that would otherwise cause problems for our logic. But once the truth predicate is retained in order to hold on to these uses, the door is flung open to others. The pragmatist wants to jam a foot in that door and keep it open. Yes, 'is true' has a role in amplifying what we assert and in making generalizations. But how could we possibly think that these are the only functions of 'is true' that we need to account for?

There are, on the surface, plenty of other ways we use the predicate. We take ourselves to be aiming at true beliefs when we assert or deliberate; we explain the improvement of our views by saying that we are getting closer to the truth or are exchanging a false belief for a true one; we distinguish between objective and non-objective discourses by distinguishing between those discourses which can aim at truth and those which cannot; many philosophers use the notion of truth to explain meaning, negation, logical consequence, why certain forms of sentences (such as ($p \rightarrow p$)) are always true and others forms always false,[8] etc.

---

[8] See Bar-On *et al.* 2000: 3 and Davidson 1996 for arguments about meaning, Dummett 1978 and O'Leary-Hawthorne and Oppy 1997: 184 f. for the argument about negation, Shapiro 1998 for the argument about logical consequence, Gupta 1993*a*, 1993*b* and Soames 1997 for the argument about $p \rightarrow p$. And see Price 2003 for the excellent argument that the role of truth is to make disagreements matter or to make sense of wanting to resolve disagreement.

In going beyond Horwich's two uses, we will give a better—i.e. more complete—account of how we use 'is true'.[9]

Those who want to be revisionist about any such usages of 'is true' must put forward an argument. They must show, for instance, that our grasp of logical laws, or of belief, or of the aim of assertion and inquiry does not turn on the idea of truth. It is not good enough to say that you are going to account for the uses of 'is true', home in on two uses, and then say that the other uses are illegitimate because they go beyond the two uses you favour. As Devitt (2001: 587) points out, there is nothing preventing an ordinary descriptive predicate from playing roles such as the generalizing role in logic. Or, as Dummett (2002) says, the generalizing role is just one face of the concept of truth. (He takes the other face to be an indispensable theoretical role in a theory of meaning.)

In deciding which temperament (pragmatist or deflationist) is most appropriate, we need to think about their motivations. Horwich's sense of purity, one surmises, is prompted by both a Quinean preference for simple desert landscapes and by the fact that the DS seems to be the only uncontroversial thing that we can say about truth (1990: 126). Here we ought to agree straightaway that claims about what arises from the DS—claims about what is involved in assertion and belief—are more controversial than the DS itself. The suggestions the pragmatist or anyone else offers are very much up for debate. But of course the fact that something is controversial says nothing at all about whether it is correct or important.

There is another problem with the deflationist's insistence on a simple, basic theory of truth. Given that Horwich sees that the relationship between truth and verification, success, and the like is not unimportant, it appears to be merely a matter of emphasis whether one calls the theory of truth that infinite string of equivalences, and then legitimately extends the theory, or whether one calls the DS-plus-extension the theory of truth. If that is the case, then the pragmatist seems the more reasonable of the two. For the pragmatist does not *deny* anything in the basic theory,[10] but turns his attention to the elucidation of it. The

---

[9] See Davidson 1996: 274 ff. and Jackson, Oppy, and Smith 1994: 294–5 for a similar point.

[10] Pragmatism is in step with the thought which underlies the disquotationalism—the idea that to assert that '*p*' is true is to assert *p*—but is very much out of step with the unrestricted application of this thought. The DS entails bivalence, and Peirce takes bivalence not to be a law of logic, but a regulative assumption of inquiry. Bivalence and the DS hold only when we are prepared to assert the statement or to think that it is a

deflationist, on the other hand, says that the pragmatist, the coherence theorist, the correspondence theorist—any truth *theorist*—has made a mistake in thinking that there is anything more to say about truth than what is expressed in the DS. But this claim is in tension with the thought that the DS gets the basic theory of truth right and there is then more to say about the connection between truth and other concepts. The pragmatist agrees with Horwich that 'is true' often expresses our inclination to accept instances of the DS. But that is the start of the conversation, not the end of it.

3. THE PROSENTENTIALIST

Dorothy Grover (2001, 2002) sees that pragmatism has affinities with deflationism. But she too objects to the thought that there is something general to be said about the nature of truth, and she objects to the thought that truth might have an explanatory role to play in philosophical questions about meaning, the status of science, realism, whether moral matters are objective, and so on (2001: 508).[11] In her view, 'is true', despite the fact that it looks like a predicate which describes a property, really functions as a prosentence, along the lines of a pronoun, to provide a way of naturally reading the anaphoric occurrences of propositions bound by quantifiers. Instead of saying 'For all *p*, if Icabod believes *p*, *p*', we can say the more natural 'Everything that Icabod believes is true'. And we use 'is true' to refer to a previously expressed sentence:

Bill: Did you hear that Icabod quit his job?

candidate for a truth-value. There are, that is, truth–value gaps. Note that the deflationist also has problems here. The Liar Paradox, for instance, prompts a bald announcement from Horwich that the statement 'This proposition is not true' must not be substituted for *p* in the DS: 'permissible instantiations of the equivalence schema are restricted in some way so as to avoid paradoxical results' (1990: 41).

[11] Horwich also thinks that truth is not a 'deep and vital element of philosophical theory'; for instance, the realism and anti-realism issue and related issues in the philosophy of science 'have nothing at all to do with truth' (1990: 54). It needs to be said that the pragmatist account of truth does not deliver answers to all of the big philosophical questions. Indeed, that account of truth is laudable because it does not straightaway close off certain answers to those questions —it does not, for instance, rule out moral judgements as candidates for truth-values; nor does it entail that moral judgements are truth-apt. Nonetheless, the concept of truth (as the pragmatist sees it) will be involved in settling these disputes.

Jim: If that's so, then he has more time to play tennis.
Sam: I believe that it's true—let's see if he can play this afternoon.

The prosententialist will say that just as we don't need a theory of 'so', likewise we don't need a theory of 'true'. Both are expressive mechanisms, used to take on inferential commitments. Again, we have the thought that the role of 'is true' in natural languages amounts to a convenient generalizing function (Grover 2001: 509). It is not a normally functioning predicate which describes a property. If we take 'is true' to play only a prosentential role, Grover thinks that we will get rid of the metaphysical mess which has traditionally surrounded the notion of truth.

The first thing the pragmatist ought to say to the prosententialist is that there is no reason to deny that our concept of truth has a prosentential role in natural language. Again, an ordinary property-expressing predicate can have roles like that articulated by Grover. But the pragmatist will hold that when we say 'That's so', or 'That's true', we carry a certain amount of essential baggage with us; we can't travel as lightly as the prosententialist suggests. We bring with us, for instance, the thought that we have good reasons for believing that Icabod has quit his job. We haven't simply guessed that he has quit it, dreamt that he has quit it, or hoped that he has quit it. 'That's so' or 'That's true' carry with them the thought that evidence does currently speak in favour of the statement asserted. And they carry with them the prediction that the evidence will continue to speak in favour of the statement asserted, or in favour of some close successor of it. That is, 'That's so' and 'That's true' play roles other than the grammatical role of generalizing and referring back to sentences.

My first attempt (Misak 1998) at arguing that the deflationist's neglect of the full range of roles played by 'is true' results in the loss of important issues and debates sparked a set of replies from Grover (2001, 2002). Deflationism, she says, might seem open to the charge that it can't deal with the important issues because its proponents have sometimes called it a 'theory of truth'. This has led to false expectations—to expectations that the theory must say something about the relationship between truth and things that are important to us. But deflationist theories, she maintains, are not theories of truth or theories of what truth is. They are theories of the truth predicate (Grover 2001: 505) or of the 'truth term' as Devitt (2001) calls it. They are theories which try to explain the role that 'true' plays in natural languages.

Grover argues that the deflationist can indeed explore the 'big' issues (2001: 510). Like Horwich, she thinks that the deflationist 'can articulate connections between truth and inquiry, assertion, and deliberation—should he or she want to do this' (2002: 124). A theory of the truth predicate says nothing about these connections, but one can move from a theory of the truth predicate to other kinds of theories.

We can move to theories of 'what-is-true' or theories of how the world is. These include 'science, creative endeavours, and value statements' (2001: 510). We ask questions, such as 'Are electrons basic units of the world?' or 'Do people act freely?', and the answers make no mention of the property of truth and its alleged bearers. Rather, there is talk of things in the world like electrons, people, actions, etc. The answers will be first-order, not philosophical. The prosententialist thinks that 'Our interest in truth amounts to no more and no less than our interest in knowing the way the world is' (2001: 512).

We are taken again to the naturalist thought, which we have seen is the pragmatist's guiding thought. There is nothing more to the concept of truth than what we can squeeze out of the concept of first-order inquiry. The pragmatist's account of truth can be captured in Grover's terminology by saying that were we to inquire into what-is-true, and were we to fulfil all of the aims which are bound up in such an inquiry, and were we to get a belief which could not be improved, we would have a true belief.

Grover also suggests that the deflationist can move, if she likes, to theories of theories of what-is-true. They tell us about the status of theories of what-is-true. They tell us, for instance, whether science or morals speaks to how the world is—whether science or morals in fact tell us what-is-true. Philosophy of science is full of such theories of theories of what-is-true, for it tries to identify the assumptions of inquiry and assess methods of inquiry.

Or perhaps, Grover says, under this rubric the deflationist will want to ask 'epistemic questions' of the sort 'Under what conditions would we know whether something is true?' Such questions will be read as: 'Under what conditions would we know whether electrons are the basic units of the physical universe?' and 'Under what conditions would we know whether people act freely?' (2002: 123). These, Grover says, are interesting, or big, questions, and the prosententialist can ask them.

The point she wants to make against the substantive-truth theorist is that 'whether a given linguistic item (as a bearer of truth) has the property truth, does not enter the picture' (2002: 123). On her deflationist view, the epistemic debates and the debates about theories of theories of what-is-true continue, and are facilitated by removing the 'digression' or 'detour' of asking what the property of truth is and what sort of thing bears that property. If we don't identify truth as a property, then those debates 'can proceed without the diversion that has been occasioned by the pursuit of the ever elusive truth property' (2002: 120).

But of course, the diversion through a truth property is a superfluous diversion only if the truth property which is sought is indeed elusive, such as correspondence with a fact or state of affairs. (It is the correspondence theory which Grover has in mind as the kind of substantive-truth theory which is bound to fail (2001: n. 8).) If truth is what satisfies our aims in first-order assertion and inquiry, then there is no search for an elusive property, or a metaphysical property, or a property which we cannot grasp. As Brandom, another prominent prosententialist, says, the deflationist approach 'is intended to be . . . *ontologically deflating*—or at least unexciting' (2002: 115). On the pragmatist's view, truth is deflated in this way—it is ontologically unexciting—it carries no commitments about what exists.

Indeed, Grover's explicit reason for ending the search for an elusive truth property sounds very much like Peirce's. Grover takes the merit of her position (i.e. not searching for a truth property) to be that 'theorizing about a truth property is irrelevant to inquiry' (2002: 120). Peirce takes the merit of his position (i.e. searching for a naturalized truth property) to be that only then will we get a concept of truth which is relevant to inquiry (see *CP* 1. 578, 5. 553, MS 684: 11).

Peirce, that is, agrees with Grover that we can explain our interest in truth by explaining our interest in what-is-true. We explain our interest in truth by sticking, as it were, to first-order inquiry and by staying away from metaphysical speculation about the nature of truth.

But the pragmatist will not agree with Grover that we merely have the option, to take up if we wish, of speaking to theories of theories of what-is-true. For one thing, the questions which get answered by going on to such matters are not bells and whistles. They are a vital part of what it is to think about what-is-true (or, in Peirce's terminology, about truth). You will find, for instance, people (in pubs, in undergraduate philosophy classes, in academic journals) who are keen to argue that there is no objectively right answer to a question such as 'Is female circumcision immoral?' You will find people arguing, that is, that we can't answer questions about what-is-true in the moral domain, because the best theory of theories of what-is-true has it that moral questions are not the sort of questions that have determinate answers. That is, Grover's three kinds of theory are inextricably tangled up with each other.

Grover sees that when philosophers with a focus on first order inquiry or when first-order inquirers (scientists and the like) engage in the further debates, they will appeal to things such as prediction, simplicity, and comprehensiveness, thus taking 'us a bit closer to the pragmatists' (2002: 129). They will appeal to the standards which govern our inquiries. She then asks: 'But then is their contribution really best understood in terms of providing an analysis of a truth property, or are they better represented as being concerned with acquiring knowledge of what-is-true?' The answer is that they are best understood as providing an elucidation (not an analysis) of the truth property, for they are concerned with articulating the characteristics shared by true beliefs or by what-is-true.

The dispute between deflationism and pragmatism looks more and more like a non-dispute. As soon as it is seen that the pragmatist's account of the property of truth is an account that is built from the ground up—from considering first-order inquiry (from considering whether p), then the deflationist can and should be happy with it.

4. THE SUPERASSERTIBILITY THEORIST

Crispin Wright does not aspire to be as purist as Horwich and Grover. Although his minimalist[12] position intends to retain the deflationist's aversion to thinking of truth as identifying 'some especially profound form of engagement between language, or thought, and reality' (1992: 72, 37), he nonetheless thinks that the deflationist has taken too much air out of the idea of truth. He suggests, with the deflationist (and, as we have seen, with Peirce), that 'p is true' amounts to the assertion that p. But against the deflationist (and again with Peirce), Wright finds something 'lurking behind the Disquotational Schema' (1992: 72). Our concept of the property truth incorporates the DS, but goes beyond it (2001: 751).

---

[12] Both Horwich and Wright call their position 'minimalist'. To avoid confusion, I reserve 'minimalism' for Wright's view.

Wright takes the point of the DS to be that to say that a sentence is true is to assert it, and to assert a sentence is to say that it is true. We must then ask what it is to assert or endorse a proposition. When we assert *p*, we approve it as meeting a certain standard or set of norms; we approve it as being in good shape, as far as the relevant norms are concerned (1999: 41 ff.). These norms govern both assertion and the use of the predicate 'is true': reason to regard a sentence as assertible is reason to regard it as true, and vice versa (1992: 16–18).

But Wright sees that one of the requirements on any conception of truth is that truth must come apart from warranted assertion—truth is not merely what passes for good belief. The achievement marked by 'is true' needs to be contrasted with the achievement marked by 'is warranted'[13] (1999: 45 ff.). He thinks that 'whether or not we can somehow eliminate or otherwise "deflate" the *word*, a corresponding property, and its contrast with assertibility, is part and parcel of assertoric content itself' (2001: 759). With respect to the dispute we have been tracking between the naturalist property theorist (for example, Peirce) and the naturalist non-property theorist (for example, Horwich and Grover), Wright comes down on the side of the former.

His position is even more closed aligned with Peirce's when he turns his attention to a truth predicate which he calls 'superassertibility', a special kind of warranted assertion:

A statement is superassertible . . . if and only if it is, or can be, warranted and some warrant for it would survive arbitrarily close scrutiny of its pedigree and arbitrarily extensive increments to or other forms of improvement of our information. (1992: 48)

This, of course, sounds very much like Peirce's thought that a belief is true if it would continue to survive inquiry were we to push inquiry as far as we fruitfully could.

Wright tries to put some distance between his view and Peirce's. He rejects the quest for a definition of truth, in favour of providing 'a body of conceptual truths that, without providing any reductive account, nevertheless collectively constrain and locate the target concept and sufficiently characterize some of its relations with other concepts and its role and purposes' (2001: 759).

---

[13] Wright takes the disquotationalist to think that truth must be *merely* good assertion. He then argues that truth cannot be so, that the extensions of the two concepts might well diverge (1992: 19, 49, 71). But the disquotationalist will want nothing to do with the claim imputed to him.

But he doesn't see that Peirce is in full agreement with him here. He takes Peirce to be offering a reductive definition of truth, as well as the implausible view that there is an ideal limit to our efforts at getting warranted beliefs—a point when all relevant empirical information would be in (1992: 46; 1999: 32). He takes it to be a 'key feature of the Peircean proposal' that 'some *single* set of "epistemically ideal conditions" would be apt for the appraisal of any statement whatever' (2001: 762). Moreover, he thinks that the Peircean view of truth requires that, were a person in such ideal conditions, she would know that she was; she would be in a position to acknowledge the fact[14] (1992: 46). Since an inquirer could never have an intimation that she had somehow managed to get to a state of comprehensive empirical information, the antecedent of the following conditional is 'conceptually impossible': were a subject to be in epistemically ideal conditions, and were she able to acknowledge that fact, she would believe *p*. Wright thinks this is very 'bad news for Peircean views of truth' (1992: 46).

This, of course, is an odd view of Peirce. He was very explicitly not interested in a reductive analysis of truth. And he was not focused on the ideas of total evidence, epistemically ideal conditions, and the solving of all questions.[15] Inquiry, he says, 'does not suppose that it can solve *all* questions', but 'it will at least never positively conclude any question to be absolutely insoluble' (*W* 3, 18). A regulative assumption of inquiry is that the question which we are investigating will have an answer. We must 'hope' that a settled answer would come to 'the particular questions with which our inquiries are busied' (*CP* 6. 610). But the fact that this assumption is indispensable to inquiry does not mean that we need to assert it. He says: 'I do not admit that indispensability is any ground of belief. It may be indispensable that I should have $500 in the bank—because I have given checks to that amount. But I have never found that the indispensability directly affected by balance, in the least' (*CP* 2. 113; see also 3. 432).

Inquiry, in the slogan 'Truth is what would be believed were we to inquire as far as we could', is not to be thought of as a completed inquiry, where every question is answered, including the question of whether

---

[14] His remarks in Wright 1992 are directed against Putnam as well as Peirce. See Misak 1992 for a similar objection to Putnam's pragmatism. In his 2001, Wright revises his view of Putnam and tries to stick the objection on Peirce alone.

[15] For a sustained argument for what follows, see Misak 2004: 149.

inquiry is complete. We are to focus on inquiry into a particular issue, and on whether our beliefs there are as good as they could be.

Peirce also never went anywhere near trying to spell out what epistemically ideal conditions might be, and he never went anywhere near the idea that an inquirer would know that she was in epistemically ideal conditions. In fact, his fallibilism explicitly has it that a person could never know that inquiry had been pursued as far as it could fruitfully go. Inquiry 'is not standing upon the bedrock of fact. It is walking upon a bog, and can only say, this ground seems to hold for the present. Here I will stay until it begins to give way' (*CP* 5.589). We might in fact believe all sorts of truths, but we cannot know when we are in such a position, precisely because we cannot know when we have a belief which would for ever satisfy our aims. (We of course can have good reason to think that current beliefs satisfy our aims better than previous beliefs.) This is good news for the pragmatist, for she will not be tempted to prematurely pronounce on what would be the upshot of inquiry.

Once we see how Wright's criticism of pragmatism is misdirected, the difference between his superassertibility predicate and the pragmatist account of truth appears to evaporate. Wright, like Peirce, thinks that truth is a property of beliefs. And both think that:

Rather than ask whether a statement would be justified at the limit of ideal empirical investigation, or under ideal empirical circumstances, whatever they are, we can ask whether an ordinary carefully controlled investigation, in advance of attaining any mythical limit, justifies the statement, and whether, once justified, that statement continues to be so no matter how much further information is accumulated. (1992: 47; see also 2001: 770 f.)

Peirce couldn't agree more. He argues that there is nothing higher or better we can ask of a belief than that it would for ever be assertible, by the standards which govern our practices of proper assertion. He insists that the truth theorist start with our current standards of inquiry and state of information, and characterize true belief as that which would be warranted, no matter how far those standards and that information were to be improved.[16] There is 'but one state of mind from which you can "set out", namely, the very state of mind in which you actually find yourself at the time you do "set out" ' (*CP* 5. 416).

---

16 See Misak 2004: 40 ff., 150 ff.

Peirce, that is, doesn't need to learn the lesson Wright thinks he
has to teach the pragmatists: 'For the purposes of pragmatism . . . the
crucial reflection is that superassertibility is . . . an *internal* property of
statements of a discourse'—a projection of the standards which actually
inform assertion within the discourse (2001: 781). Wright says that
the fact that 'superassertibility is fashioned from our actual practices
of assessment' makes it 'well equipped to express the aspiration for a
developed pragmatist conception of truth as any other candidate known
to me' (2001: 781). He is right to think that superassertibility is an
excellent candidate for a pragmatist conception of truth. What he fails
to see is that it is Peirce's pragmatist account of truth.

There is, however, one significant difference between Wright's view
and Peirce's. Wright's proposal is that we take as a truth predicate any
predicate which satisfies the DS and which takes truth to be distinct
from warranted assertibility. There may be more than one perfectly
good conception of truth.[17] He thinks that superassertibility is the truth
predicate of choice for certain discourses—discourses in which we think
that if *p* is true, then *p* is knowable (1992: 58, 75; 2001: 779 f.). Other
discourses have more robust truth predicates.

Part of Wright's project is a restructuring of the realist/anti-realist
debate. A discourse meeting only the minimal requirements for truth is
one about which we must take an anti-realist stance.[18] The realist must
show that the discourse in question does more than meet the minimum.
There *is* a basis for making a distinction between claims about the comic
and claims about material objects, for a discourse can go beyond the
minimum. One way of doing this is for a discourse to display what
Wright calls cognitive command. Here it is a priori that intractable
disagreements are due to one kind or another of cognitive shortcoming,
such as insufficient or divergent evidence, faulty reasoning, inattention,
oversight, or malfunction of equipment.[19]

---

[17] Wright 1992: 38. In his 1996 Wright does not foreclose on the possibility that
superassertibility holds everywhere—or at least, for every minimally truth-apt discourse.
If it turned out that Wright held the global thesis, one would have to see him
straightforwardly as a pragmatist. The global thesis, however, is in tension with the
direction of his argument in Wright 1992 and 2001.

[18] Wright 1992: 142, 174. This is a striking claim, as it is often held that disquotationalism captures, without mention of facts, states of affairs, and the like, the thought
at the heart of the correspondence theory.

[19] Wright 1992: 90 ff., 175, 222. Another way of showing that a discourse goes
beyond the minimum is to show that the discourse is such that we detect matters rather
than matters being dependent on how we judge them. Another is to show that appeals

Moral discourse, for instance, meets Wright's minimal requirements for a discourse which aims at truth—it is assertoric, it imposes a discipline on itself, and, we suppose, truth does not amount to warranted assertibility here and now. Morality satisfies the minimal platitudes about truth and does not need any 'metaphysical underpinnings' to show that it is up to the job (1992: 29, 204). Morality is minimally truth-apt—we can help ourselves to talk of truth for it (1992: 16, 28, 36, 178). But Wright does not think that a case can be made for moral discourse being governed by cognitive command. He has shown how the philosopher's debate about morals makes sense on his view, but he takes its resolution to lean in favour of the anti-realist.

What he wants to do here is to explain the difference between the realist and the anti-realist without suggesting that the anti-realist has to deny that the disputed statements aim at truth. We are all supposed to agree that any kind of assertible sentence enjoys minimal truth. And then we are supposed to go on to say how some discourses can be more objective than others. Those discourses will have a more robust truth predicate—more robust than minimal truth.

Wright worries that it will appear that his sympathies must lie with either of two unattractive options. One is a realism run rampant, where virtually every disciplined discourse is objective, and thus morality is objective. The other is a 'bloodless' quietism, where we 'simply have to settle for the bland perspective of a variety of assertoric "language games", each governed by its own internal standards of acceptability, each sustaining a metaphysically emasculated notion of truth, each unqualified for anything of more interest or importance' (1992: 76).

Wright directs two arguments towards these worries. First, not all discourses meet the minimal requirements. Wittgenstein's point about private language—for instance, one that is supposed to record sensations—is that such a language is not disciplined (1992: 141). But more importantly, the fact that truth predicates can exceed the minimum means that not all discourses are equally objective.

Wright's pluralism about truth predicates comes, however, at a heavy price. It comes at the price of some of the purported truth predicates being downgradable—not grade A robust truth, but grade B sustained warranted assertibility. Why call superassertibility a truth predicate when there are truth predicates around which make superassertibility, by

to facts have a wide explanatory role; that the subject-matter of the discourse figures in the explanations of other things.

contrast, look not up to scratch? Superassertibility or Peirce's predicate doesn't look like real truth, *if we have as a contrast something more robust*, something more like the truth predicate that the correspondence theorist has always sought. O'Leary-Hawthorne and Oppy direct a similar objection at Wright. It can't be that any predicate which has the formal properties of a truth predicate (in particular, satisfaction of the DS) deserves to be called a truth predicate: 'whether a predicate is a proper deserver of the name "truth" may depend upon whether that predicate picks up enough of the conceptual role of, and picks out a property sufficiently similar to that picked out by, the ordinary English "is true"' (1997: 190).

The problem for Wright is that it looks very much as if the minimal requirements are *not enough* to get us the full concept of truth. Just about every statement makes the minimal grade, and so that grade is indeed of little interest. It is not what we normally think of as truth—as what we aim at.

The fact that the Peircean pragmatist is not a pluralist about truth predicates does not entail that the differences between kinds of inquiry must be blurred. For Peirce would agree with Wright that the notion of superassertibility, or the pragmatist truth predicate, is 'relative to whatever notion of warranted assertion is in play in the particular discourse with which we may happen to be concerned' (2001: 771). The pragmatist will say that truth is proper assertion, but different discourses have different standards for proper assertion. Just think of how we justify '$1 + 10 = 11$', 'Lake Ontario is a salt-water lake', and 'It is unjust to put those with Arabic-sounding surnames through special searches at airports'. Different styles of reasoning and different standards of warrant will be appropriate for different discourses. Peirce uses the term 'sciences' to demarcate all discourses which aim at truth—all discourses which hope that experience and argument will eventually result in beliefs which could not be improved upon. With that bit of terminology in mind, here is his position:

Now the different sciences deal with different kinds of truth; mathematical truth is one thing, ethical truth is another, the actually existing state of the universe is a third; but all those different conceptions have in common something very marked and clear. We all hope that the different scientific inquiries in which we are severally engaged are going ultimately to lead to some definite established conclusion, which conclusion we endeavour to anticipate in some measure. Agreement with that ultimate proposition that we look forward to,—agreement with that, whatever it may turn out to be, is the scientific truth. (*CP* 7. 187)

It might be asked here, given that mathematical, empirical, and moral inquiry differ, and given that truth and inquiry are internally related, should we not follow Wright and say that there are different notions of truth in play?[20] Peirce's answer to this question is 'no'. What all the truth-oriented discourses have in common is that we expect that experience and argument will lead to 'some definite established conclusion'—and of course, that kind of indefeasible belief is the truth for Peirce. But he sees that he needs to give this answer while bringing on board the idea that there are significant differences between the kind of warrant required for empirical, mathematical, and moral judgements. Peirce wants to say some general things about truth: it is what we aim at in our various inquiries; it is a property of beliefs which could not be improved upon; etc. Then he needs to look at the differences between various inquiries and say something about how statements in each area show themselves to be indefeasible.[21]

Wright says that if pragmatism 'seems to distort our thinking about truth in particular regions of discourse . . . that . . . will be a measure of the local unnaturalness of pragmatism itself' (2001: 781). But Peirce's pragmatism, with its allowances for the variety in our ways of thinking, exploring, and deliberating, is not going to be unnatural in some discourses. For the nature of the discourse itself will determine the texture of the indefeasibility in question. Our practice of inquiry is not a monolith—it is not, for instance, all about the active testing of hypotheses or about arriving at definitive answers to questions. The Peircean will be concerned with articulating some general and important thoughts about the liaisons between truth and inquiry, but in order to begin to do justice to the richness and the texture of a particular kind of inquiry, such as morals, mathematics, or science, a full-length treatment of each is required.[22]

If indefeasibility turns out to be something we can't sensibly aim at in a kind of inquiry, then the judgements that arise from that kind of 'inquiry' are not truth-apt. It is here that the realism/anti-realism debate resides.

For a discourse in which it does make sense to aim at indefeasible beliefs, then when we turn our attention to what makes for indefeasibilty

---

[20] Natasha McCarthy put the question to me in this way.
[21] For an account of how he does this, see Misak 2004: ch. 5.
[22] I have started to do that for moral inquiry in Misak 2000 and for scientific inquiry in Misak 1991, 2004.

in that discourse, pragmatism will not appear so unnatural. A belief is true if it would fully satisfy the requirements and standards of inquiry. In science and mathematics, those requirements and standards are such that a belief that meets them is a belief that has what the pragmatist's opponent has always sought.

It might turn out that what makes scientific statements indefeasible is something very strong indeed—a kind of empirical evidence which causally links those statements to the physical world. And we will think, no doubt, that what makes moral statements indefeasible will be something quite unlike that. In morals, a belief that meets the standards of moral deliberation will be as objective, for want of a better word, as is possible for a belief about what is right or wrong. It may not turn out that we want to say that we aim at indefeasible beliefs in moral deliberation—it may turn out that such an aim in untenable. But Peirce's account of truth at least makes this debate possible.

Here we have yet another reason for thinking that Peirce's project of getting leverage on the concept of truth by exploring its connections with practice is the project we must engage in. Not only does it give us an account of truth that best makes sense of the full range of our practices concerning assertion, belief, reason giving, and inquiry, but it makes sense of and promises some headway in our long-standing philosophical debates about realism and anti-realism. That is no small achievement.

BIBLIOGRAPHY

Bar-On, D., Horisk, C., and Lycan, W. (2000) 'Deflationism, Meaning and Truth-Conditions'. *Philosophical Studies*, 101(1): 1–28.

Brandom, R. B. (1994) Making it Explicit. Cambridge, Mass.: Harvard University Press.

——(2002) 'Explanatory vs. Expressive Deflationism about Truth'. In R. Shantz (ed.), *What is Truth?*, 103–19. Berlin: De Gruyter.

David, M. (1994) *Correspondence and Disquotation*. Oxford: Oxford University Press.

Davidson, D. (1996) 'The Folly of Trying to Define Truth'. *Journal of Philosophy*, 87: 263–78.

Devitt, M. (2001) 'The Metaphysics of Truth'. In M. Lynch (ed.), *The Nature of Truth*, 579–612. Cambridge, Mass.: MIT Press.

Dummett, M. (1978) 'Truth'. In *Truth and Other Enigmas*, 248–68. Cambridge, Mass.: Harvard University Press.

——(2002) 'The Two Faces of the Concept of Truth'. In R. Shantz (ed.), *What is Truth?*, 249–63. Berlin: De Gruyter.

Fine, A. (1986) 'Unnatural Attitudes: Realist and Instrumentalist Attachments to Science'. *Mind*, 95: 149–79.

_____ (2001) 'The Scientific Image Twenty Years Later'. *Philosophical Studies*, 106: 107–22.

Grover, D. (2001) 'The Prosentential Theory: Further Reflections on Locating Our Interest in Truth'. In M. Lynch (ed.), *The Nature of Truth*, 505–26. Cambridge, Mass.: MIT Press.

_____ (2002) 'On Locating Our Interest in Truth'. In R. Shantz (ed.), *What is Truth?*, 120–32. Berlin: De Gruyter.

Gupta, A. (1993*a*) 'A Critique of Deflationism'. *Philosophical Topics*, 21: 57–81.

_____ (1993*b*) 'Minimalism'. *Philosophical Perspectives*, 7: 359–69.

Hookway, C. (2000) *Truth, Rationality and Pragmatism*. Oxford: Oxford University Press.

Horwich, P. (1990) *Truth*. Oxford: Basil Blackwell.

_____ (2001) 'A Defense of Minimalism'. *Synthese*, 126(1–2): 149–65.

Jackson, F., Oppy, G., and Smith, M. (1994) 'Minimalism and Truth-Aptness'. *Mind*, 103(411): 287–302.

Misak, C. (1991) *Truth and the End of Inquiry: A Peircean Account of Truth*. Oxford: Clarendon Press.

_____ (1992) 'Critical Notice of Brian Ellis: *Truth and Objectivity*'. *Canadian Journal of Philosophy*, 22(3): 365–80.

_____ (1998) 'Deflating Truth: Pragmatism vs. Minimalism'. *The Monist*, 81(3): 407–25.

_____ (2000) *Truth, Politics, Morality: Pragmatism and Deliberation*. London: Routledge.

_____ (2004) *Truth and the End of Inquiry: A Peircean Account of Truth*, 2nd expanded edn. Oxford: Clarendon Press.

O'Leary-Hawthorne, J., and Oppy, G. (1997). 'Minimalism and Truth'. *Nous*, 31(2): 170–96.

Peirce, C. S. *Collected Papers of Charles Sanders Peirce*, i–iv, ed. C. Hartshorne and P. Weiss (1931–5); vii and viii, ed. A. Burks (1958). Cambridge, Mass.: Belknap Press.

_____ *Writings of Charles S. Peirce: A Chronological Edition*, 6 vols. The Peirce Edition Project, ed. M. Fisch, C. Kloesel, and N. Houser. Bloomington, Ind.: Indiana University Press, 1982.

The Charles S. Peirce Papers. Microfilm, Widner Library, Harvard University.

Price, H. (2003) 'Truth as Convenient Friction'. *Journal of Philosophy*, 100: 167–90.

Sellars, W. (1962) 'Truth and Correspondence'. *Journal of Philosophy*, 59: 29–56.

Shapiro, S. (1998) 'Proof and Truth: Through Thick and Thin'. *Journal of Philosophy*, 95: 493–521.

Cheryl Misak

Soames, S. (1997) 'The Truth about Deflationism'. In E. Villanueva (ed.), *Philosophical Issues*, viii. 1–44. Atascadero, Calif.: Ridgeview.

Wiggins, D. (2002) 'Marks of Truth: An Indefinibilist cum Normative View'. In R. Shantz (ed.), *What is Truth?*, 316–32. Berlin: De Gruyter.

Wright, C. (1992) *Truth and Objectivity*. Cambridge, Mass.: Harvard University Press.

_____ (1996) 'Response to Commentators'. *Philosophy and Phenomenological Research*, 56(4): 863–8.

_____ (1999) 'Truth: A Traditional Debate Reviewed'. In C. Misak (ed.), *Pragmatism, Canadian Journal of Philosophy*, Suppl. vol. 24: 31–74.

_____ (2001) 'Minimalism, Deflationism, Pragmatism, Pluralism'. In M. Lynch (ed.), *The Nature of Truth*, 751–87. Cambridge, Mass.: MIT Press.

5

Pragmatism, Quasi-realism, and the Global Challenge

David Macarthur and Huw Price

William James said that sometimes detailed philosophical argument is irrelevant. Once a current of thought is really under way,
trying to oppose it with argument is like planting a stick in a
river to try to alter its course: "round your obstacle flows the
water and 'gets there just the same'". He thought pragmatism
was such a river. There is a contemporary river that sometimes
calls itself pragmatism, although other titles are probably better.
At any rate it is the denial of differences, the celebration of
the seamless web of language, the soothing away of distinctions,
whether of primary *versus* secondary, fact *versus* value, description
versus expression, or of any other significant kind. What is left is a
smooth, undifferentiated view of language, sometimes a nuanced
kind of anthropomorphism or "internal" realism, sometimes the
view that no view is possible: minimalism, deflationism, quietism.
Wittgenstein is often admired as a high priest of the movement.
Planting a stick in this water is probably futile, but having done
it before I shall do it again, and—who knows?—enough sticks
may make a dam, and the waters of error may subside. (Blackburn
1998*b*: 157)

So begins Simon Blackburn's contribution to a symposium with Crispin
Wright on 'Realism and Truth'. In opposing this 'smooth, undifferentiated view of language', Blackburn takes issue, in particular, with
Wright's view of the implications for expressivism of minimalism about
truth. Wright is a leading advocate of a widespread view that semantic
minimalism provides a straightforward argument for cognitivism, and
hence against expressivism. For his part, of course, Blackburn is the

principal proponent of a rather subtle version of expressivism, quasi-realism, which he takes to provide the most plausible treatment of a range of philosophical topics: moral, aesthetic, conditional, causal, and probabilistic judgements, for example. Quasi-realism depends on noting *differences* between discourses; yet Blackburn himself is very sympathetic to semantic minimalism—hence his desire to resist the claim that minimalism is incompatible with expressivism, and to oppose the 'undifferentiated view' in general.

For our part, we have considerable sympathy with quasi-realism and with Blackburn's campaign against this homogeneous view of language. We also agree with Blackburn that the latter view is not well described as 'pragmatism'. Indeed, we are going to be calling attention to some respects in which it is quasi-realism that counts as a kind of pragmatism. However, we also want to identify a respect in which quasi-realism differs from pragmatism—a respect which turns on the fact that the quasi-realist view of language remains *too* differentiated, in a sense we'll explain. Among other things, we maintain, this leaves quasi-realism vulnerable to the argument mentioned above, premissed on semantic minimalism, in a way in which more ambitious forms of expressivism (or pragmatism) are not. Indeed, we'll be arguing that the usual version of the argument (as advocated, for example, by Wright) gets the implications of semantic minimalism precisely backwards: semantic minimalism provides almost a knock-down argument *for* a strong or global kind of expressivism, not a knock-down argument against it.

This strong kind of expressivism is also a kind of pragmatism. It is an important and appealing position, in our view, but it remains surprisingly invisible in contemporary philosophy.[1] Our main objective here is to try to make it more visible. Blackburn's paper, and the dialectic of the quasi-realist's struggle with minimalism, provides a useful contrastive background. As just noted, we'll be arguing that minimalism turns out to provide a global argument *for* expressivism. So the news is mixed, from a quasi-realist perspective: good news for the

---

[1] Surprisingly so for two reasons, in our view: first, because the position in question is close in motivation and methodology to familiar views, such as quasi-realism itself; and second, as we'll explain, because the unfamiliar view in question is actually the proper end-point of a familiar line of argument from popular premisses. In both cases, we think, the pragmatist option has been obscured by a dogmatic attachment to an assumption about language with which it conflicts. The assumption in question is often called 'representationalism', and our point may be put like this: it is surprising that representationalism itself hasn't been more widely challenged, given that the means and motive for doing so have been popular currency for the better part of two decades.

expressivist project, but bad news for any merely *local* form of it, such as quasi-realism itself. The stable view is our form of pragmatism.[2] The paper goes like this. In the first section we introduce the variety of pragmatism we have in mind as a particular kind of response to a familiar philosophical puzzle. We then take some care to distinguish it, first, from its neighbours 'on the right': from various metaphysical approaches to similar philosophical puzzles. As we'll explain, a key distinguishing feature of pragmatism, in our sense, is that it is metaphysically *quietist.*

Next, we note the position's relation to its neighbours 'on the left'—to various familiar forms of expressivism, including quasi-realism. There are certainly affinities, but a major difference is that these familiar views are typically local in scope, intended to apply to some topics or vocabularies, but not to others; whereas our kind of pragmatism is necessarily a global view, in the relevant respects. Again, the point turns on quietism. Unlike more familiar forms of expressivism, our pragmatism is quietist (in a sense we'll explain) about the representational character of various vocabularies. As a result, it provides a natural and stable response to the challenge from minimalism, mentioned above. And it retains the best aspects of the differentiation offered by quasi-realism—while avoiding, via representational quietism, a more problematic kind of differentiation.

1. PRAGMATISM AND THE PLACEMENT PROBLEM

Our first task is to bring our target variety of pragmatism into view, by contrasting it with some metaphysical views, on one side, and some more familiar expressivist views, on the other. Both contrasts are best drawn against the background of a familiar kind of philosophical puzzle—a puzzle that often presents itself as a metaphysical issue about the nature, or essence, of some thing or property: What is mind? What is causation? What is goodness? What is truth? Often, what gives such questions their distinctive flavour is that the thing or property in question seems hard

---

[2] As we note in sect. 8 below, Blackburn himself has entertained this global view in some of his more recent work, and indeed has declared himself 'agnostic' (1998a: 318) about the issue that separates it from the older and better-known local version of quasi-realism. Until sect. 8, for ease of exposition, we take our notional Blackburnian opponent to be the original local kind of quasi-realist. If we think of our true opponent as the real (present-day) Simon Blackburn, it is more accurate to say that our message is that he should come off the fence, and opt for the global version of the view.

to 'place' in the kind of world described by science. In this form, these 'placement problems' stem from a presupposition about the ontological scope of science—roughly, the naturalist assumption that all there is, is the world as studied by science.[3]

The pragmatist we have in mind wants to dismiss or demote such metaphysical puzzles in favour of more practical questions, about the roles and functions of the matters in question in human life.[4] But what are these 'matters', precisely? Not the metaphysician's objects or properties themselves, presumably, but the words, concepts, and thoughts in terms of which (as we ordinarily put it) we talk and think *about* such things and properties. In other words, a pragmatist about causation asks not about the role of causation itself in human life, but about the role and genealogy of the notion, term, or concept 'causation'. (The former question may be an interesting one, from some philosophical or scientific standpoints, but it isn't the pragmatist's question.)

Pragmatism thus has a second-order, or 'linguistic' focus. We acknowledge that the term 'linguistic' isn't entirely happy in this context. If we don't want to beg important questions about the relative priority of thought and language, it might seem better to say that pragmatism begins with a focus on *representations*—leaving it open whether the fundamental representations are mental or linguistic in nature. But this terminology has a countervailing disadvantage. The term 'representation' equivocates between two meanings that a pragmatist, of all people, needs to distinguish. In one sense, the term refers to a quasi-syntactical item on the page, or in the head, as it were—e.g. to the sentence or term, in the strictly linguistic case.[5] In the other sense, it characterizes the (supposed) function of that item (i.e. that it represents). As we'll see, a pragmatist has a strong reason to reject characterizations of this kind—standard representationalist accounts of the functions of the psychological or linguistic items in question. Even if intended

[3] This 'naturalist' assumption implies that anything with a good claim 'to be real' must in some sense—perhaps under some other description, for example—be the kind of thing recognized in scientific theory. Naturalism of this kind is enormously influential in contemporary philosophy. Here, what we want to stress is its role as a motivation for metaphysics.

[4] These questions can be naturalistic, too, of course, but in the sense that they involve a naturalistic reflection on aspects of human behaviour. See Price 2004*b* for more on the distinction between these two kinds of naturalism.

[5] This will admit of further differentiation, depending on whether we think of symbols as mere marks, or as something like 'symbols-in-a-language'. These issues are important, but not immediately relevant to the distinctions we're drawing here.

only as a label for the meaning-bearing items in question, the term 'representation' thus provides an uncomfortable vehicle for a view of this kind.

Accordingly, choosing the lesser of terminological evils, we'll say that pragmatism begins with questions about the functions and genealogy of certain *linguistic* items—emphasizing that unless we stipulate otherwise, we're always assuming that these items may be mental, as well as strictly linguistic (in the ordinary sense).

Pragmatism thus begins with *linguistic* explananda rather than *material* explananda; with phenomena concerning the *use* of certain terms and concepts, rather than with things or properties of a non-linguistic nature. It begins with linguistic behaviour, and asks broadly anthropological questions: How are we to understand the roles and functions of the behaviour in question, in the lives of the creatures concerned? What is its practical significance? Whence its genealogy?

In philosophically interesting cases, such as the ones thought to give rise to placement problems, pragmatists will be looking for answers that explain the distinctive character of the topics in question—that account for the distinctive character of evaluative concepts, for example. Their aim is to dissolve the apparent puzzle of these cases, by accounting for the linguistic phenomena at the heart of the puzzle. And their guiding intuition is that if we can explain how natural creatures in our circumstances naturally come to speak in these ways, there is no further puzzle about the place of the topics concerned, in the kind of world described by science.

This intuition isn't self-supporting, however. It needs to be backed up by a case for rejecting a train of thought that otherwise allows the placement problem to re-emerge in metaphysical guise, as puzzling as before. As we are about to see, metaphysicians, too, can ask questions about the functions of the relevant parts of language. For a pragmatist, the crucial thing is to resist the invitation to answer these questions in a way which leads back to metaphysics.

2. TWO WAYS OF STARTING WITH LANGUAGE

At first sight, it might seem that the linguistic focus is itself sufficient to distinguish pragmatism from metaphysical approaches to the placement puzzles. After all, doesn't metaphysics presuppose a material focus? Isn't its interest necessarily in the objects and properties—goodness, causation, mind, or whatever—rather than in the use of the corresponding terms?

But things are not so simple. Let's grant that it is definitive of metaphysics, according to its own self-image, that it has its eyes on the world at large, and not on language specifically. Nevertheless, as the contemporary literature demonstrates, a surprising amount of metaphysical business can be conducted at a linguistic level. Thus contemporary writers interested in the nature of causation, say, or mental states will often take themselves to be investigating the 'truthmakers' of causal claims, or the 'referents' of terms such as 'belief'. They thus characterize their metaphysical targets in *semantic* terms, as the objects, properties, or states of affairs at the 'far end' of some semantic relation. The item at the 'near end' is a term or a sentence, a concept or a proposition, a thought or a belief—in other words (in the broad sense we're presently assuming), something linguistic.[6] In one sense, then, metaphysics of this kind begins with a linguistic focus.[7]

Thus a metaphysician, too, may begin her inquiry with a more or less anthropological concern to account for certain aspects of human linguistic behaviour. If we took that concern to be constitutive of the kind of pragmatism we have in mind, the upshot would be that

[6] We're blurring a distinction here between the case in which the linguistic item in question is something concrete, such as a linguistic token, and the case in which it is something abstract, such as a proposition. A metaphysics that begins with abstract propositions doesn't overlap with pragmatism in the sense we have in mind here, of course. But in practice, the case for believing in propositions is likely to rest on linguistic practices, so that such a view becomes linguistically grounded, in the present sense, after all.

[7] This route to metaphysics needs to be distinguished from a kind of pseudo-linguistic mode permitted by semantic ascent, in Quine's sense. For Quine, talking about the *referent* of the term 'X', or the *truth* of the sentence 'X is F', is just another way of talking about the *object*, X. (As he himself puts it, 'By calling the sentence ["Snow is white"] true, we call snow white. The truth predicate is a device of disquotation.' (1970: 12).) Quine's deflationary semantic notions are therefore too thin for a genuinely linguistically grounded metaphysical programme—too thin to provide the substantial issues *about language* with which such a programme needs to begin (viz. substantial issues about referents and truthmakers). See Price 2004b for more on this point. Blackburn often makes a similar point about semantic ascent construed *à la* Ramsey. Noting that 'Ramsey's ladder' doesn't take us to a new theoretical level, Blackburn remarks that there are 'philosophies that take advantage of the horizontal nature of Ramsey's ladder to climb it, and then announce a better view from the top' (1998a: 78 n. 25). In our terms, the philosophers that Blackburn has in mind are those who fail to see that the fashionable linguistic methods—talk of truthmakers, truth conditions, referents, and the like—add precisely nothing to the repertoire or prospects of metaphysics, unless the semantic notions in question are more robust than those of Ramsey and Quine.

there is an overlap, in principle, between pragmatism (in this sense) and metaphysics. The choice is terminological, but our interest is in highlighting the view that begins with such an anthropological concern, without treating it as a stepping-stone to metaphysics. Since the stepping-stone is provided by semantic or representationalist assumptions, we'll reserve the term 'pragmatism' for the view that rejects such assumptions.[8]

So it isn't a linguistic starting-point alone that distinguishes pragmatism from metaphysics. Rather, it is a combination of such a starting-point and a rejection of the semantic or 'representationalist' presuppositions which otherwise lead our theoretical gaze from language to the world—which turn an anthropological concern into a metaphysical concern, in effect. Diagramatically:

Pragmatism = Linguistic Priority without
Representationalism.

It is easy to miss the possibility of beginning where pragmatism begins (viz. with an interest in understanding our *use* of terms such as 'good', 'cause', and 'true'), without feeling the pull of the metaphysical questions—without wanting to ask what we are talking *about.* Unless the role of the representationalist assumption is made explicit, it is liable to remain part of the implicit geography of our thought about these matters, a pathway that cannot help but lead us from one place to the other. Once it is properly mapped, however, the presupposition can be challenged. We pragmatists can maintain that our predecessors' mistake was precisely to follow that representationalist path, into the cul-de-sac of metaphysics.

3. THREE WAYS OF REJECTING METAPHYSICS

Our next task is to be clear about the ways in which pragmatism (in our sense) differs from its metaphysical neighbours. It rejects metaphysics, but in a specific sense, which we need to distinguish from two weaker ways of rejecting traditional metaphysical concerns.

---

[8] Our choice has a long and excellent pedigree in the pragmatist tradition, of course. Menand (2001: 361) notes that already in 1905, Dewey writes that pragmatism will 'give the *coup de grace* to *representationalism*'. In fact, as we'll see later, it turns out to be important to distinguish two different ways of rejecting representationalism. This will be crucial to our disagreement with Blackburn.

3.1 No Metaphysics versus Anti-realist Metaphysics

Consider the familiar view that moral values are a useful fiction. This view shares with pragmatism an interest in the role and genealogy of moral concepts in human life. But it retains a metaphysical face: it maintains that, literally speaking, there are no moral values. Clearly, this is an ontological claim. (Similarly for fictionalism about other contentious topics, such as possible worlds, or truth itself.)

There are some senses in which fictionalism does reject metaphysics, of course. Moral fictionalists reject metaphysical inquiries into the nature of moral values. Since there are no such things as moral values, according to the fictionalist, there is no nature to discover (except 'within the fiction', as it were). The negative, anti-realist, metaphysical thesis thus disallows a certain kind of positive metaphysical inquiry.

But contrast this anti-realist metaphysics to views which reject metaphysics altogether. Famously, there are global versions of anti-metaphysical theses of this kind, such as that of Carnap's 'Empiricism, Semantic and Ontology' (1950), and (at least arguably) Quine's 'On What There Is' (1948). There are also local versions, often based on the claim that the metaphysical inquiry, in some area, presupposes a mistaken view of the function of the language in which it is couched. As we note below, quasi-realism provides a particularly explicit version of the latter kind of view.

Either way, globally or locally, the relevant contrast is between views which reject the metaphysical issues altogether and views which allow anti-realist, existence-denying metaphysics. Orthodox fictionalism is the latter view, the pragmatism we have in mind is the former. Pragmatism in our sense is thus a no-metaphysics view rather than an anti-realist view, in the metaphysical sense. Pragmatists are metaphysical *quietists*.[9]

3.2 No Metaphysics versus Subjectivist Metaphysics

The second contrast we need turns on the fact that there is a way of answering the 'what is' question which blurs the contrast with pragmatism, by offering an answer to some degree subjectivist. What is causation, or truth, or value? Not something as objective as we might have thought at first sight, according to this proposal, but something

---

[9] Such a quietist may well agree with fictionalists about the *genealogy* of moral terms, of course. More on this below.

that involves us—something partly psychological in nature, perhaps, or something with an implicit relational aspect. In the contemporary literature, the neo-Lockean notion of response-dependence offers a popular model for views of this kind: to be red, for example, is to be such as to produce a certain response in (normal) human observers, under appropriate conditions. So colours are treated as real properties, fit objects for metaphysical scrutiny, but more subjective (or subject-involving) than we might have supposed.

These views are hybrids. They are metaphysical, in that they take seriously the 'what is' questions. But they give the objects or properties or states of affairs a human face, or human foundations—even foundations cast explicitly in terms of use. Again, it is to some extent a terminological matter whether we call these views pragmatist.[10] But whatever term we use, one sharp way of marking the contrast with what we're here calling pragmatism is to note that these subjectivists are not quietists about semantic or representationalist matters. On the contrary, they think that questions about the truthmakers, or truth-conditions, of sentences, statements, or beliefs, or the referents of terms or concepts, have determinate answers—answers that it is the task of philosophy to uncover. (Their distinctive message is that these things turn out to lie closer to home than we thought.)

Thus subjectivism is best viewed as a form of metaphysics. It takes on board the material questions and the representational conception of language which leads to them. In particular, therefore, it is not a quietist view, either about the representational status of the language in question or about associated ontological matters.

3.3 No Metaphysics—Pragmatists as Metaphysical Quietists

Thus, by pragmatism, henceforth, we mean a view that contrasts both with this kind of subjectivist metaphysics and with the anti-realist metaphysics of fictionalism and error theories. Our pragmatists are (normally[11]) happy to stand with the folk, and to affirm the first-order truths of the domains in question—to affirm that there are beliefs, and

---

[10] Johnston (1993) treats response-dependence as a variety of pragmatism—as does Price (1998), at least for dialectical purposes, in arguing that the kind of use-based pragmatism we are defending here provides a better home than response-dependence for Johnston's 'pragmatist' intuitions.

[11] The exceptions are the cases in which the pragmatists are *mere* anthropologists, reflecting on a discourse in which they themselves do not participate.

values, and causes, and ways things might have been, and so on. What they reject is any distinctively metaphysical theoretical perspective from which to say more about these matters—that they do or do not *really* exist, that they are *really* something subjective, or whatever.

This contrast between metaphysical quietism, on the one side, and fictionalism and subjectivism, on the other, echoes an observation made by David Lewis in one of his last papers (2004). There, Lewis's main claim is that quasi-realism is effectively a form of fictionalism. Lewis notes that fictionalism and quasi-realism both endorse the first-order folk claims of a target discourse, but then offer us what amounts to a second-order qualification. In the case of modal fictionalism, for example, it goes like this: 'There are ways things could have been'—that's the first-order claim—'but only in the modal fiction in which we all participate'—that's the fictionalist rider. Lewis seems to suggest that fictionalism and quasi-realism are therefore inferior to the view which accepts such statements without qualification—i.e., as he interprets the unqualified view, to realism.

Let's set aside for the moment the question as to whether Lewis is right to interpret quasi-realism as a form of fictionalism, and focus on the nature of this unqualified alternative, to which Lewis contrasts fictionalism and quasi-realism. What is this unqualified 'realism'? Is it the view that *just* says, with the folk, 'There are ways things might have been'? Or is it the view that says 'There REALLY ARE ways things might have been'—where the capital letters mark some distinctively philosophical claim? If there's a difference between these two possibilities, and if it's the unqualified position Lewis is looking for—in order to claim a comparative advantage over fictionalism and quasi-realism—then it must be the weaker position. Why? Because the stronger also requires an additional qualification, though this time of a positive rather than a negative kind. (The folk don't add the capital letters, if adding the capital letters adds philosophical theory.)

What if there isn't any difference between the weaker and stronger views? That would imply that—as Carnap (1950) thought, for example—there isn't any distinctively theoretical viewpoint that philosophy can bring to such matters of ontology. In other words, it implies that there isn't any distinct stronger position. Again, then, the unqualified position is the weaker position.

However, this weaker position is effectively our metaphysical quietism. Thus—still bracketing the question as to whether Lewis is right to identify quasi-realism with fictionalism—the distinction that Lewis identifies, between unqualified and qualified ways of speaking with the folk, is essentially the distinction that we need, between pragmatism and its metaphysical neighbours.

So our pragmatists are metaphysical quietists. But note that they are not philosophical quietists *tout court*, if there could be such a view. On the contrary, they take some relevant theoretical matters very seriously indeed: in particular, some broadly anthropological issues about the roles and genealogy of various aspects of human linguistic behaviour. It is arguable that these issues are compulsory questions, necessarily addressed, at least implicitly, by all the views we have considered so far. (We return to this issue in section 11.) What distinguishes pragmatism is its commitment to addressing them without the resources of a representationalist model of language. As we are about to see, this is a commitment that pragmatism shares, at least locally, with quasi-realism.

4. QUASI-REALISM AS LOCAL PRAGMATISM?

We said earlier that we intended to outline a variety of pragmatism according to which quasi-realism counts as a pragmatist view, in significant respects. What we meant by that claim should now be apparent. Consider, say, a quasi-realist view of evaluative discourse. Such a view is certainly anthropological, or genealogical, in the sense outlined above. And it rejects what we called the representationalist assumption with respect to evaluative discourse. In other words, crucially, it rejects the assumption that otherwise leads from a linguistic conception of the original puzzle about evaluative discourse to metaphysical issues about the nature of value.

So far, of course, quasi-realism keeps company with orthodox non-cognitivism or expressivism on these matters. (Like those views, in particular, it should not be confused for some version of metaphysical subjectivism. It does not say that in claiming that X is good, we *report* our approval of X, or *describe* X as being disposed to elicit our approval.) Where quasi-realism begins to part company with some cruder forms of non-cognitivism is at the choice point between metaphysical anti-realism and metaphysical quietism. Does non-cognitivism about evaluative concepts imply that, literally speaking, there are no values (thus agreeing with fictionalists and error theorists)? Some non-cognitivists seem to have thought so, but Blackburn is not one of them. As he himself often stresses, quasi-realism is not an error theory: on the contrary, as he puts it, 'quasi-realism is most easily thought of as the enterprise of showing why projectivism needs no truck with an error theory' (1998*b*: 175). Elsewhere, responding to this question—'Aren't you really trying to defend our right to talk "as if" there were moral truths, although in your view *there aren't any really?*'—his answer is emphatic: 'No, no, no' (1998*a*: 319).

Thus Blackburn's view is (i) that when we speak with the folk, we are fully (and literally) entitled to say that there are values, and (ii) that no other legitimate standpoint is available to philosophy, from which we can properly retract such a claim. In our terminology, this amounts to saying that quasi-realism is metaphysically quietist. *Pace* Lewis, in fact, it is precisely this point that distinguishes quasi-realism from fictionalism. Unlike a fictionalist, a quasi-realist who stands with the folk in affirming that there are values (say), does not then proceed to add a negative qualification. (At worst, he merely withholds some further accolade or emphasis or capital letters, to which he takes our 'non-quasi' commitments to be entitled. But this means that if it is the extra qualification which is objectionable, as Lewis suggests, then quasi-realism stays on the side of virtue, in the 'quasi' cases.)

This reading of Blackburn might seem in tension with his own description of quasi-realism as a variety of anti-realism, and especially with an account of the place and nature of quasi-realism he offers (Blackburn 1993*a*). In that context, he contrasts quasi-realism with what he calls 'immanent realism':

Immanent realism is the position that the forms of ordinary discourse in the area form the only data, and themselves impose realism. . . . External realism would be a conjunction of the view that (a) there is a further external, metaphysical issue over whether the right theory of the area is realistic, and (b) the answer to this issue is that it is. Immanent realism entails the denial of (a); quasi-realism agrees with (a), but denies (b). (1993*a*: 368)

Isn't agreeing with (a) incompatible with being a metaphysical quietist? Indeed, isn't it the immanent realist, in Blackburn's sense, who better counts as such a quietist?

No, in our view, although this is perhaps a matter on which Blackburn could usefully have been clearer. For consider the external issue allowed by (a), as seen from the perspective of a quasi-realist. The first external question that arises is not metaphysical, but linguistic. It is the question: 'Is the right theory of this area of commitment a theory that treats it as genuinely descriptive?' If the answer is that the area is genuinely descriptive, the orthodox metaphysical questions are thereby deemed appropriate: Is the area in question in good shape, is there really anything (and if so, what) to which its claims answer, and so on? But if the answer to the initial question is that the best theory in this case is not genuinely descriptive, then the quasi-realist regards these metaphysical inquiries as inappropriate—a kind of category mistake, in effect.

In the latter case, moreover, the quasi-realist is an anti-realist not in the sense of endorsing negative, existence-denying metaphysical claims, but only in the sense of not endorsing positive, capital-R Realist, existence-affirming metaphysical claims. (Compare the difference between an anti-theist who denies the existence of God and an anti-theist who simply rejects the issue altogether, refusing to take sides—or even to label herself as an agnostic—on an issue she regards as in some way ill-founded.)

Thus, once we distinguish these two kinds of anti-realism, and recognize that the kind of external question properly allowed by a quasi-realist is not itself metaphysical—rather, it is the linguistically grounded meta-metaphysical question whether metaphysics is in order, in the domain in question—we can see how it is indeed true, as we claimed, that a quasi-realist is a metaphysical quietist, about those domains he takes to require the quasi-realist treatment.

Quasi-realism thus appears to have all the marks of our species of anthropological pragmatism. In reading quasi-realism in this way, however, we need to stress once more that it is a local pragmatism. It adopts the pragmatist attitude with respect to some areas of discourse, some topics of philosophical puzzlement, but not universally. Elsewhere, as it were, representationalism and metaphysics still reign.[12]

5. THE GLOBAL CHALLENGE

In our view, however, quasi-realism is untenable in this local form. Like other local forms of expressivism, it faces irresistible pressures towards 'globalization'—pressures to concede the field to a view which,

---

[12] Note that there is one important sense in which representationalism still reigns for a quasi-realist, even in the 'quasi' domains. It is still regarded a contentful theoretical question *whether* the domains in question are genuinely descriptive, or representational (the answer being that they are not). As representational quietists, our pragmatists do not admit such a question. More on this distinction later.

approached from this direction, is aptly characterized as *global* quasi-realism, or *global* expressivism. Seen head-on, this new view is the anthropological pragmatism with which we began, in its unrestricted form. Our next task is to explore the sources and consequences of this 'global challenge'.

It turns out that the pressure towards globalization threatens quasi-realism from two distinct directions, one external and one internal. The internal pressure stems from an argument to the effect that unless quasi-realism becomes a global view, it is condemned to be a victim of its own success: roughly, its own success renders redundant any stronger form of realism, of whatever kind a local quasi-realist wants to invoke in the 'non-quasi' cases. We defer this challenge for the time being, however, and turn first to the external challenge.

The external challenge relies on reversing one of the main currents in the river to which Blackburn refers (and which he himself sets out to obstruct) in the passage with which we began. As we noted, semantic minimalism is commonly taken to provide a strong argument against expressivism. In our view, as we said, this gets things precisely backwards. In fact, semantic minimalism provides a global argument in favour of expressivism, and this argument is the external challenge to merely local forms of expressivism, such as Blackburn's quasi-realism.

In turning the familiar appeal to semantic minimalism on its head in this way, we end up agreeing with Blackburn in one sense, but disagreeing with him in another. Blackburn is right, in our view, to deny that semantic minimalism implies an undifferentiated, homogeneous, view of language—on the contrary, as Blackburn argues, the important differentiation most characteristic of pragmatism and expressivism remains firmly in place. On the other hand, we want to argue that minimalism does sweep away the kind of bifurcation that distinguishes Blackburn's quasi-realism—as a local form of pragmatism—from a more global version of the same kind of view.

6. THE MINIMALIST CHALLENGE

In its simplest form, the conventional argument that minimalism about truth is an enemy of non-cognitivism and expressivism goes something like this.[13] If there is nothing more to truth than the equivalence schema,

---

[13] This section draws heavily on material from Price 2006.

then any meaningful sentence 'P' whose syntax permits it to be embedded in the form 'P is true' immediately possesses truth conditions, in the only sense available: viz. 'P' is true if and only if P. Since moral claims, for example, are certainly embeddable in this way, it is immediate that moral claims are truth-conditional, or truth-evaluable, as the cognitivist maintains. In general, then, the thought is that if truth is minimal, it is easy for sentences to be truth-evaluable—and hence implausible for a non-cognitivist to maintain that a superficially truth-conditional statement is not genuinely truth-conditional.[14]

In our view, as we said, this argument is almost completely wrong-headed. The key to seeing this is to note that expressivism normally makes *two* claims about its target discourse, one negative and one positive. The negative claim says that these terms or statements lack some semantic feature: they are non-referential, non-truth apt, non-descriptive, non-factual, or something of the kind. The positive claim offers an alternative, non-semantic account of the functions of the language in question—for example, that it expresses, or projects, evaluative attitudes of the speaker in question. Thus the negative claim is *anti-representational*, the positive claim *expressivist*.

What is the effect on such a combination of views of deflationism about the semantic vocabulary in which the negative claim is couched? If we read the minimalist as claiming, *inter alia*, that the semantic notions have no substantial theoretical role to play, then the consequence is that the negative claim must be abandoned. For it is a substantial theoretical claim, cast (essentially) in semantic vocabulary. But abandoning this claim does not imply that, *qua* theoreticians, we must endorse its negation—i.e. endorse cognitivism. On the contrary, what's thin for the goose is thin for the gander: if semantic terms can't be used in a thick sense, they can't be used on either side of a (thick) dispute as to whether evaluative claims are genuinely representational.

---

[14] An early version of the argument may be found in McDowell 1981, though the point seems to have been in play before that. (It is closely related to some points raised in a filmed discussion between Peter Strawson and Gareth Evans, made for the Open University in 1974.) More recent versions may be found in Boghossian 1990, Wright 1992, and Humberstone 1991. The argument is also endorsed by Jackson, Oppy, and Smith (1994), who propose a response for non-cognitivism, based on the argument that minimalism about *truth* need not imply minimalism about *truth-aptness*, and that it is non-minimalism about truth-aptness that matters for the non-cognitivist's purposes. In our view, non-cognitivism does not need saving: in the important respects, semantic minimalism already represents victory by default.

Consider again the theological analogy. Evolutionary biologists don't think that the species were created by God. Does this mean that they must use the term 'God', in their theoretical voice, in order to deny that the species were created by God? Obviously not—they simply offer an account of the origin of the species in which the term 'God' does not appear. So rejecting the view that God created the species does not require accepting the following claim: God did not create the species. The alternative—the right alternative, obviously, in this case—is a kind of passive rejection: simply avoiding theological vocabulary, in scientific contexts.

As before, the point of the example is that not affirming is not the same as denying, and the lesson carries over to the present case. From a theoretician's point of view, declining to affirm that a linguistic item stands in semantic relations does not entail denying that it does so. One may simply dismiss the issue, as having no relevant theoretical content.

So what is the effect of deflationism on expressivism? It is to deflate the expressivist's (usual) negative claim, *while leaving intact the positive claim*—the expressivist's pragmatic account of the function of the terms in question. Contrary to the received view, then, semantic minimalism is a friend rather an enemy of expressivism. Provided we take it that the core of the expressivist position is what we've called a pragmatic account of the key functions of the judgements in question—an account not cast in representational, 'descriptive', or semantic terms—then deflationism about the key semantic notions is a *global* motivation for expressivism. It is a global reason for thinking that whatever the interesting theoretical view of the functions of a class of judgements turns out to be, it cannot be that they are referential, or truth-conditional. (To repeat: deflationism amounts to a denial that these notions have a substantial theoretical role.[15])

Of course, the difficulty for most expressivists is that they are explicit in wanting their expressivism to be a local view. They want a contrast between the domains in which they offer a non-representational account

---

[15] It might be suggested that the negative claim provides the expressivist's motivation for developing the positive proposal, so that if minimalism deflates the negative claim, expressivism becomes unmotivated. However, this surely underestimates the role of the placement problem, and indeed of the explanatory perspective itself, as motivations for expressivism. The genie of genealogy has long since escaped from the expressivist's lamp, as it were, and can't be contained by the deflationist's thin blanket of syntactical uniformity. (We need some theory at this point, no matter what. Deflationism implies that that theory can't be cast in a semantic key, so expressivism wins by default.)

of the functions of the language in question, and the domains they want to regard as genuinely representational. Even more importantly, as we noted above, they want the question 'Is this domain genuinely representational?' to be in good order, with substantial content, in both kinds of cases. Deflationism disallows this question, and thereby the contrast that depends on it—but it doesn't disallow the expressivist's positive, pragmatic account of what supposedly lies on the non-representational side of the fence. On the contrary, the problem is with what supposedly lies on the representational side (and hence with the existence of the dividing line itself).

Semantic minimalism thus implies global pragmatism, in our sense. Recall our equation above:

PRAGMATISM = *LINGUISTIC PRIORITY* without
REPRESENTATIONALISM.

Semantic minimalism requires that substantial theory about our linguistic behaviour must operate without the semantic categories which underpin representationalism—necessarily without *REPRESENTATIONALISM*, in other words.

Finally, note that this conclusion does not entail a homogeneous, undifferentiated view of language. On the contrary, there's plenty of scope for differentiation, in the pragmatist's functional key. The only differentiation disallowed is that between genuinely and 'quasi' representational discourse. So, as we said, it is good news and bad news, from a quasi-realist's point of view: a cheer for expressivism and genealogy, but a boo for one distinctive aspect of the quasi-realist's version of these ideas, viz. the view that quasi-realism can remain a local doctrine.

7. THE ELEATIC EQUIVOCATION

There are two sides to this conclusion, the general pro-expressivist aspect and the more specific anti- (local) quasi-realist aspect. One reason why both aspects have been overlooked, presumably, is that the representationalist conception of language is so deeply entrenched that it has been hard to see how directly it is challenged by semantic minimalism—hard to see what a radical thesis semantic minimalism is, in this sense. (So much the worse for semantic realism, perhaps—more on this possibility later.)

Another reason has to do with the dialectics of contemporary expressivist positions. Seeing themselves as local views, these theories come to the field with an interest in maintaining the representationalist picture, while reducing its domain. In that context, writers concerned to defend expressivism against the supposed threat of semantic minimalism seem to have confused two tasks. One task is that of arguing that semantic minimalism leaves plenty of room for differentiation in an expressivist key—that it doesn't 'make everything the same'. The other is that of arguing that semantic minimalism leaves room for a particular kind of differentiation: namely, that between genuinely representational and non-representational uses of language. The strength of the expressivist's case for the first point has perhaps obscured the weakness of the argument for the second. The two conclusions haven't been properly distinguished, and the strong argument has tended to shield its weaker sibling.

The most popular argument for the second point—i.e. for the defence of the 'bifurcation thesis' (as it is called by Kraut (1990), following Rorty)—appeals to what we might call the Eleatic Criterion. The central thought goes something like this. We need to appeal to trees to explain our use of the term 'tree', but we don't need to appeal to goodness to explain our use of the term 'good'. So we should interpret talk of trees 'really' realistically, but talk of goodness only quasi-realistically. (See Blackburn 1984: 257; 1998a: 80; Kraut 1990; and Dreier 2004, e.g., for various versions of this suggestion.)

This is an appealing idea, and the Eleatic Criterion may well mark some distinction of interest. However, there are some interesting reasons for doubting whether it draws a line where its proponents would like to draw a line—say, around scientific claims.[16] More importantly for present purposes, semantic minimalism entails that any distinction drawn this way simply can't be a distinction between those utterances which do stand in substantial semantic relations to the world and those that do not. But since that's what it would take to distinguish representational from non-representational uses of language, the Eleatic

---

[16] Briefly, one large issue concerns the status of causal discourse, which is arguably both properly treated in expressivist terms and essential in science. An even deeper issue, perhaps, turns on the status of logical and conceptual generality. Plausibly, the relevant explanations of our use of general terms depends only on the particular instances we and our ancestors happen to have encountered in the past—generality itself seems to play no explanatory role. This point—closely related to the rule-following considerations, apparently—suggests that no interesting part of language really meets the explanatory test. Finally, and in a different vein, it is arguable (see Price 1997) that much of the appeal of the eleatic intuition rests on a kind of perspectival fallacy: of course the ontology invoked in the explanations in question looks privileged, in those contexts; but so it should, for the explanatory perspective is itself scientific!

Criterion can't provide a way of retaining the bifurcation thesis, in the face of semantic minimalism. If the Eleatic Criterion could ground the bifurcation thesis, in other words, that would show that semantic minimalism is simply false—that substantial semantic notions can be built on eleatic considerations.

Thus the Eleatic Criterion can't save expressivists from the following dilemma: either (i) they reject semantic minimalism, building substantial semantic relations on some basis or other (eleatic or otherwise); or (ii) they concede that their expressivism is a global position (albeit one with plenty of scope for distinctions of a non-semantic kind—including some, perhaps, marked by the Eleatic Criterion itself). The latter horn is the one that we recommend—our global anthropological pragmatism, or global expressivism. In a moment, we want to explain why the former horn ought to seem particularly unattractive, from a quasi-realist point of view.

Before we leave the Eleatic Criterion, however, there is another possible move to which we want to call attention. It might be suggested that the proper role of the Eleatic Criterion is to underpin not a *semantic* distinction between genuinely descriptive and quasi-descriptive discourse, but a *metaphysical* distinction, between ontology that deserves our allegiance as realists and ontology that does not.[17] Here, we simply want to point out that this move is out of bounds to a quasi-realist such as Blackburn himself, for at least two reasons. The first is that it would challenge his metaphysical quietism, his insistence in speaking with the folk on the topics to which he applies the quasi realist treatment—his rejection of error theories, for example. The second is that it would mean that quasi-realism was simply tilling the wrong patch of ground, in taking emulation of realism to be a matter of entitlement to the semantic trimmings: to being treated as 'true' and 'false', for example. Quasi-realism would require quasi-causation, not quasi-truth.

8. BLACKBURN AS GLOBAL QUASI-REALIST?

At some points, Blackburn himself comes very close to accepting the latter horn of the above dilemma. Here, for example, is a passage in which he is arguing that Wright is blind to the distinctions permitted

---

17 This is Armstrong's 'Eleatic Principle' (1997: 41).

in Ramsey's and Wittgenstein's view of the matter—and blind, in particular, to the fact that these distinctions are thoroughly compatible with Ramsey's thin notion of truth.

The point is that Ramsey and Wittgenstein do not need to work with a sorted notion of *truth*—robust, upright, hard truth versus some soft and effeminate imitation. They need to work with a sorted notion of a *proposition*, or if we prefer it a sorted notion of *truth-aptitude*. There are propositions properly theorized about in one way, and ones properly theorized about in another. The focus of theory is the nature of the commitment voiced by one adhering to the proposition, and the different functional roles in peoples' lives (or forms of life, or language games) that these different commitments occupy. Indeed, I should say that although a good title for the position might be "non-descriptive functionalism", Wittgenstein could even afford to throw "description" into the minimalist pot. Even if we have to say that all commitments describe their coordinate slices of reality, we can still say that they are to be theorized about in a *distinctive* way. You come at them differently, offering a different theory of their truth-aptitude (again, this ought not to be uncongenial to Wright, since it is only extending the very kind of move he himself makes to rehabilitate versions of the realism debate, in the face of minimalism about truth). You may end up, that is, saying that these assertions describe how things are with values, probability, modality, and the rest. But the way you arrive at this bland result will be distinctive, and it will be the bit that matters. (Blackburn 1998*b*: 166–7)[18]

Indeed, we say; but where this leads is global quasi-realism! It leads to a view in which all the interesting theoretical work, including any contribution from the Eleatic Criterion, is done on the positive, non-representational, side of the expressivist's account. There is sorting, in other words, but no sorting conducted in a representational key—everything is done in pragmatic terms.[19]

9. THE INTERNAL CHALLENGE

To resist this conclusion a (local) quasi-realist needs to take the first horn of the dilemma—in other words, to be non-minimalist about truth

---

[18] Cf. Blackburn 1998*a*: 77–83 for a more detailed discussion of this 'Wittgensteinian' option. Note that Blackburn (1990, 1993*b*) had previously interpreted Wittgenstein as a *local* quasi-realist, so the above view seems to mark a shift.

[19] We suspect that Ramsey, too, never saw this point. Like Blackburn, his expressivism was a kind of half-way house, whose foundations were considerably weakened by his failure to see that he needed to abandon representationalism altogether, in order to cast the view in a stable form. On a related aspect of this instability, see Holton and Price 2003.

and associated semantic notions. As a friend of semantic minimalism, Blackburn himself would find this option highly uncongenial. Indeed, he ought to find it so for a reason more basic than a mere preference for semantic minimalism. This horn of the dilemma is inherently unappealing, from a quasi-realist's point of view, for a reason connected to what we called the internal version of the pressure towards globalization.

To see why, note that what is distinctive and admirable about quasi-realism is that unlike less careful forms of expressivism, it takes seriously the need to explain the representational appearances—the various respects in which the target discourses 'behave like' genuinely representational parts of language. But this exposes it to a familiar challenge, which might be formulated like this:

> Suppose you (the quasi-realist) succeed in explaining, on expressivist foundations, why non-descriptive claims behave like (what you take to be) genuinely descriptive claims. If these explanations work in the hard cases, such as moral and aesthetic judgements, then it seems likely that they'll work in the easy cases, too—i.e. for scientific judgements. In other words, your 'lite' or quasi-semantic notions will suffice to explain not only why moral judgements are treated as truth-apt, but equally why scientific claims are treated in this way. But then the claim that the easy cases are genuinely descriptive—i.e. have some more substantial kind of semantic property—seems problematic in one of two ways. Either it is an idle cog, not needed to explain the relevant aspects of the use of the statements in question; or, if it is associated with some characteristic of use that the merely quasi-kind of truth cannot emulate, then it shows that quasi-realism is a sleight of hand—it fails to deliver the goods, just where it really matters. If it is really successful by your own standards, in other words, then your quasi-realism inevitably escapes from the box, and becomes a view with global application.

Why, then, is a non-minimalist view of semantic notions necessarily unattractive for a quasi-realist? Because it impales him on the horns of the new dilemma just mentioned: either his own methods render any thick component of his semantic theory an idle cog, unnecessary in accounting for the use of semantic vocabulary; or the failure of his methods to do so reveals a failure to achieve his own professed aims, of explaining how non-descriptive discourse can emulate the real thing.

Thus the option of appealing to a non-minimalist semantic theory, in order to meet the external version of the global challenge—i.e. our argument that semantic minimalism entails global expressivism—is not one that a quasi-realist can easily entertain. And the problem turns on the internal version of the global challenge: on the fact that the more successful the quasi-realist programme is in its own terms, the greater its difficulty in not swallowing everything. Since the current sweeping the quasi-realist towards globalization is driven by his programme's own engines, he cannot invoke substantial semantic notions to stem the flow, without putting a spanner in his own works.

Once again, however, we want to emphasize that there is an attractive alternative close at hand. It is a global solution represented by our brand of pragmatism, or global expressivism. The near-invisibility of this alternative in contemporary philosophy seems due in large part to the enormous inertia of the representationalist orthodoxy. The point we've stressed is that to the extent that semantic minimalism is taken seriously—as it has been, in many hands, in twentieth-century philosophy—it actually sweeps away the foundations of this orthodoxy. But far from sweeping away, with it, the diversity of the things that expressivists want to claim that we do with assertoric language, the effect is to reveal the underlying diversity to the theoretician's gaze, unencrusted with the dogma that it is all just *describing*.

This concludes the main argument of the paper. In the two remaining sections, we want to elaborate two aspects of the picture we have outlined so far. In section 10 we sketch the view of language that this form of pragmatism entails. Crucially, as we'll explain, it combines differentiation at one level with homogeneity at another—a single assertoric tool or template, capable of being put to work in the service of many different projects—with both levels being properly investigated in pragmatic terms. In section 11, finally, we return to the theme of quietism, and offer a taxonomy intended to clarify the analogies and disanalogies between the various positions that have been in play.

10. THE PUZZLE OF MANY IN ONE

We began with Blackburn's attempts to defend the possibility of linguistic diversity, in the face of a flood of homogeneity thought by some to spring from quietism and minimalism. We've agreed with Blackburn on most points, but argued that the flood does sweep away any merely local version of expressivism or quasi-realism. At this point, however, readers may feel that they've been shown a kind of conjuring trick. As we ourselves have emphasized, our view has less diversity than that of a local quasi-realist, because it lacks a distinction between genuine and merely quasi description. It's the same thin or quasi-semantic notions, in our picture, across the entire linguistic landscape. But where, then, is the promised diversity? Are we claiming that these same thin semantic notions have different functions in different areas? Surely they are both too thin and too homogeneous for that to be the case?

This challenge calls attention to a feature of our view which deserves greater emphasis. It is, indeed, highly implausible—especially for a semantic minimalist—that there is not a certain unity to basic applications of semantic predicates, in different domains of discourse. If truth is merely a device for disquotation, it has that same function, surely, no matter what the content of the sentences to which it attaches?

One way to see that this needn't be incompatible with the idea that those sentences themselves might have different functions and genealogies, as a pragmatist maintains, is to examine the corresponding point in a broader context. It is highly plausible that there are certain more-or-less universal features of assertion and judgement—e.g., to borrow Brandom's (1994) way of looking at these matters, a common practice of undertaking commitments, and 'giving and asking for reasons'. In some sense, it seems, there is simply one grand language game in which we do these things. The overarching unity of applications of a disquotational truth predicate might be viewed as one small aspect of the broader unity of this 'Assertion Game'.[20]

What needs to be established is that broad unity at this level is compatible with differentiation at a lower level, of the kind our pragmatism requires. It isn't immediately obvious that this is possible, and indeed the task of showing that it is possible takes rather different forms, depending on whether one is a global or merely a local pragmatist. Blackburn's local quasi-realist will presumably come to the table with some ready-made (Fregean?) theory of how the relevant phenomena are to be explained in the genuinely descriptive domains, where there isn't a need to accommodate underlying functional diversity (at least of the relevant kind). The task is then to show how bits of language

---

[20] However, it is questionable whether the disquotational account of the function of the truth predicate is adequate, in this context. See Price 1988, 2003 for a defence of an alternative version of deflationism, based on the proposal that the truth predicate has a richer, essentially normative, role in discourse.

with different basic functions can then properly emulate the surface characteristics of the genuinely descriptive domains.

Global pragmatism requires a different approach. Since it rejects representationalism altogether, it cannot begin by assuming that there is a class of cases for which the explanation of the surface phenomena is already available, at least in principle. In one sense, however, abandoning this assumption makes things easier. We pragmatists can begin with a clean slate, and look for a unitary account of the roles and genealogy of the Assertion Game. In particular, we can look for an account which leaves room for underlying diversity, of the kind needed to accommodate the intuitions that we share with merely local quasi-realists, that there are important senses in which different bits of language do different jobs.

We don't have space here to make a detailed case that this is possible, but we want to mention a proposal that one of us has outlined elsewhere (Price 1988, 2004*a*), to give some sense of how a case might go. The proposal starts with the thought that many of our proto-linguistic psychological states might be such that it would be advantageous, with respect to those states, that we tend towards conformity across our communities. Assertoric language seems to facilitate and encourage such alignment—within the Assertion Game, we give voice to our psychological dispositions in ways which invite challenges by speakers with contrary dispositions. ('That's false' and 'That's true' are markers of challenge and concession, respectively—cf. Price 1988, 2003.)

As ordinary speakers, of course, we don't understand that this is what assertoric language is for—we just do it, as it were, and from our point of view, seem to be 'saying how things are'. But the function of this practice of 'saying how things are' is the one in the background—the function of altering our behaviourally significant commitments much more rapidly than our individual experience in the environment could do, by giving us access to the corresponding states of our fellows (and much else besides).

The suggestion is thus that 'representational' language is a tool for aligning commitments across a speech community. But though in this sense a single tool, it is a tool with many distinct applications, corresponding to the distinct primary functions of the various kinds of psychological states that take advantage of it—that facilitate their own alignment by expressing themselves in assertoric form. And none of these primary functions is representation as such, in the traditional sense—there are no substantial semantic properties in the picture.

Wittgenstein is well known for the view that the surface uniformity of language masks underlying diversity, and one of the analogies he offers in support of this idea in the *Investigations* fits this two-level functional architecture particularly nicely. Speaking of what we see as we look at the linguistic 'surface', Wittgenstein offers this comparison:

It is like looking into the cabin of a locomotive. We see handles all looking more or less alike. (Naturally, since they are all supposed to be handled.) But one is the handle of a crank which can be moved continuously (it regulates the opening of a valve); another is the handle of a switch, which has only two effective positions, it is either off or on; a third is the handle of a brake-lever, the harder one pulls on it, the harder it brakes; a fourth, the handle of a pump: it has an effect only so long as it is moved to and fro. (1953: §12)

In one sense, as Wittgenstein stresses, the various different handles have very different functions. But they are all 'designed to be handled'. In that sense, then, they are members of a category with a significant functional unity—a unity not possessed by the more assorted tools ('a screw-driver, a rule, a glue-pot, glue . . . ') of another of Wittgenstein's examples.

So here's the proposal, as our pragmatist sees it. Thinking of the function of assertions uniformly as representation misses important functional distinctions—distinctions we can't put back in just by appealing to differences in what is represented. To get the direction of explanation right, we need to begin with pragmatic differences, differences among the kinds of things that the assertions in question *do* (or more accurately, perhaps, differences among the kinds of things that their underlying psychological states *do*, for complex creatures in a complex environment). And to get the unity right, we need to note that, in their different ways, all of these tasks are tasks whose verbal expressions appropriately invoke the kind of multi-purpose tool that assertion in general *is*. To say this, we need to say what kind of tool it is—what general things we do with it that we couldn't do otherwise. If the answer is in part that we expose our commitments to criticism by our fellows, then the point will be that this may be a useful thing to do, for commitments with a range of different functional roles (none of them representation as such).

11. VARIETIES OF QUIETISM

We began with Blackburn's remarks about 'a contemporary river that sometimes calls itself pragmatism'. In recommending our own alternative form of pragmatism, we have agreed with Blackburn, in the main, in resisting the 'smooth, undifferentiated view of language' that flows from the river in question. Yet, as Blackburn notes, the philosophers who ride this river often call themselves minimalists, deflationists, or quietists. We, too, have claimed these labels, at various points—as does Blackburn himself, in certain respects. How, then, do we (and he) avoid being swept downstream?

The trick is to distinguish several different matters with respect to which it is possible to be a philosophical quietist. In this final section, we want to sketch a taxonomy of this kind. This will make it obvious how quietism in one key can be compatible with non-quietism in another—and hence, how there is room for the kind of stance that we and Blackburn wish to adopt, in opposition to the homogenizing river. As we'll see, it also provides a sharp way of distinguishing our kind of pragmatism from local quasi-realism.

For present purposes, quietism about a particular vocabulary amounts to a rejection of that vocabulary for the purposes of philosophical theory. This may or may not involve a rejection of the vocabulary in question for other purposes. Thus, to return to our theological example, a theological quietist is not merely agnostic about the issues that divide theists from atheists. She rejects theological discourse altogether, at least as a vocabulary for theoretical investigation. She may reject it for all purposes, simply declining to play that language game at all; or she may regard it as playable with some other point. In the latter case, her attitude is analogous to that of a typical semantic deflationist, who wants not to abandon the truth predicate altogether, but merely to insist that it has no independent role to play in marking a legitimate topic of theoretical investigation.

Concerning the issues we have been discussing, there are three main topics or vocabularies, with respect to which quietism is a possibility. The first involves metaphysical issues, the second semantic and representational issues, and the third the broadly anthropological issues about language emphasized by our kind of explanatory pragmatist. In principle, perhaps, one might be a quietist about any combination of these three topics, giving eight possible variations. In practice, the five options listed in table 5.1 seem particularly significant.

Option A is the position occupied by many contemporary metaphysicians.[21] It accepts that there is a legitimate metaphysical or

---

[21] Jackson 1998 provides a particularly good example.

Table 5.1. Options for quietism

	Metaphysical quietism	Representational quietism	Use-explanatory quietism
A	No	No	No
B	No	Yes	No
C	Yes	No	No
D	Yes	Yes	No
E	Yes	Yes	Yes

ontological standpoint for philosophy, and also a non-minimalist view of semantic notions such as truth and reference. It also recognizes as a well-founded theoretical inquiry the project of explaining various aspects of linguistic usage—our use of causal or moral terms, for example. It is likely to regard these three areas of theoretical investigation as closely connected, of course. It might regard metaphysics as a search for truthmakers, for example, thus connecting (at least) the first and the second investigations.

Option B represents a different kind of metaphysics, a view that rejects the linguistic methods of contemporary metaphysics on the grounds that the semantic notions are too thin to bear the weight. Stephen Stich (1996) defends a position somewhat like this, arguing that it is a mistake to think of the issue as to whether there are beliefs and desires as the question as to whether the terms 'belief' and 'desire' actually refer to anything. Stich's case rests not so much on semantic minimalism as such, as on an argument that there is no prospect of a theory of reference that would adequately decide the issue, one way or the other. But semantic minimalism has the same effect.

Option C corresponds to the attitude of local quasi-realism towards the domains it takes to involve 'quasi' commitments. Concerning moral discourse, for example, we saw that (the original, non-global) Blackburn was not a quietist about the question whether moral commitments are genuinely descriptive—on the contrary, he regarded it as a substantial theoretical discovery that they are not. Having reached that conclusion, he then regards the metaphysical issues as mute, *for that case.* So he is a metaphysical quietist about the topic in question, but no other kind of quietist: there was the substantial issue just mentioned in the second column, and Blackburn is certainly not a quietist in the third column—on the contrary, that's where he takes the really interesting theoretical work to be.

Option D is our kind of pragmatism. The table helps to make clear what's right and what's wrong about characterizing our view as global quasi-realism, or describing quasi-realism as a local variety of pragmatism. What's right about the characterization is that our view does globally what quasi-realism does locally, *in columns 1 and 3*—viz. it combines metaphysical quietism with an interest in the issues which mark a radically non-quietist attitude to the use-explanatory issues in the third column. What's wrong about the characterization is that the two views never agree in column 2. The quasi-realist holds that there is always a substantial issue as to whether a domain of commitment is genuinely descriptive, or representational (and takes quasi-realism to be appropriate when the answer is that it is not); whereas our pragmatism holds that there is never a substantial issue of this kind.

Option E, finally, recommends quietism in all three modes. Some interpreters of Wittgenstein read him in these terms—among them, presumably, the interpreters whom Blackburn has in mind, in the passage with which we began, when he says that Wittgenstein is often admired as a high priest of the crusade to deny differences and celebrate 'the seamless web of language'. In earlier work, noting that this reading flies in the face of the fact that Wittgenstein repeatedly emphasizes that the surface uniformity of linguistic forms masks deep differences in the things we do with language, Blackburn (1990, 1993*b*) had proposed that Wittgenstein should be interpreted as a (local) quasi-realist—albeit one who leaves 'unfinished business' (1993*b*: 589), in failing to address the issue of explaining how we can continue to speak of truth, fact, knowledge, and so forth, in the non-descriptive discourses. This is the task undertaken by the quasi-realist, of course. Hence Wittgenstein is only a proto-quasi-realist, on this reading.

As we have already noted, however, Blackburn's view of Wittgenstein seems to have changed. In the paper with which we began, and in his (1998*a*) of the same year, Blackburn offers Wittgenstein as a model of what we've termed a global quasi-realist, who throws even the term 'description' 'into the minimalist pot'. On this view, then—having thrown the representational notions into the pot—Wittgenstein emerges as our kind of pragmatist, a representational quietist, and belongs in row D.

We close by noting that there is another possible reading, which does locate Wittgenstein in row E—a philosophical quietist in all modes—without ignoring his insistence that language is not a 'seamless web'. The key is to read Wittgenstein as interested in *description*, rather than *explanation*. He calls our attention to the differences, according to this reading of his project, but doesn't regard it as part of the task of philosophy to try to explain them. In particular, he doesn't regard the sideways, third-person stance of our anthropological pragmatists as an available *philosophical* stance.

At this point, there are two possibilities. One takes Wittgenstein to acknowledge that there are significant questions of the kind the pragmatist wants to ask, but to regard them as scientific issues, rather than philosophical issues. The other is more radical, taking Wittgenstein to maintain that there is no legitimate theoretical stance of this kind at all, philosophical or scientific. The former possibility is no challenge to our kind of pragmatism as such, but only to its right to call itself philosophy. We have no strong views on this matter. (If pressed, we could always follow Peirce's famous lead, inventing a new name for the enterprise.)

The second possibility is more serious, and connects with deep and interesting issues about the nature and possibility of theorizing about language. These are issues for another time, however. Our task here has been to distinguish our kind of pragmatism from its less quietist neighbours, and especially from quasi-realism. Pragmatism agrees with quasi-realism that the use-explanatory issues in the third column of the table are no place for quietism—on the contrary, they are some of the most interesting issues in philosophy, and worthy of much noise indeed. But the pragmatist insists that the noise should be that of a single voice, singing only in the key that these issues themselves demand, and resisting the temptation to mix its melody with the familiar but discredited themes of metaphysics and representationalism.

For our part, we've urged, in particular, that minimalism about truth and reference leads to this kind of pragmatism. Whistled down the years by such distinguished lips as Wittgenstein, Ramsey, and Quine, semantic minimalism has long been a melody that everybody in philosophy has in their head. What's surprising, in our view, is that so few people have realized how it finishes: with the last quiet gasp of representationalism itself, as pragmatism prepares to sing.

BIBLIOGRAPHY

Armstrong, D. (1997) *A World of States of Affairs*. Cambridge: Cambridge University Press.
Blackburn, S. (1984) *Spreading the Word*. Oxford: Oxford University Press.

120   *David Macarthur and Huw Price*

Blackburn, S. (1990) 'Wittgenstein's Irrealism'. In R. Haller and J. Brandl (eds.), *Wittgenstein: Eine Neubewertung*, 13–26. Vienna: Hölder-Pichler-Tempsky.

—— (1993*a*) 'Realism, Quasi, or Queasy?' In J. Haldane and C. Wright (eds.), *Reality, Representation, and Projection*, 365–83. Oxford: Oxford University Press.

—— (1993*b*) Review of Paul Johnston, *Wittgenstein and Moral Philosophy*. *Ethics*, 103: 588–90.

—— (1998*a*) *Ruling Passions: A Theory of Practical Reasoning*. Oxford: Oxford University Press.

—— (1998*b*) 'Wittgenstein, Wright, Rorty and Minimalism'. *Mind*, 107: 157–82.

Boghossian, P. (1990) 'The Status of Content'. *Philosophical Review*, 99: 157–84.

Brandom, R. (1994) *Making it Explicit*. Cambridge, Mass.: Harvard University Press.

Carnap, Rudolf (1950) 'Empiricism, Semantics and Ontology'. *Revue Internationale de Philosophie*, 4: 20–40.

Dreier, J. (2004) 'Meta-Ethics and the Problem of Creeping Minimalism'. *Philosophical Perspectives: Ethics*, 18: 23–44.

Haldane, J., and Wright, C. (1993) (eds.), *Reality, Representation, and Projection*. Oxford: Oxford University Press.

Holton, R., and Price, H. (2003) 'Ramsey on Saying and Whistling: A Discordant Note'. *Noûs*, 37(2): 325–41.

Humberstone, L. (1991) 'Critical Notice of F. Jackson, *Conditionals*'. *Philosophy and Phenomenological Research*, 51: 227–34.

Jackson, F. (1998) *From Metaphysics to Ethics*. Oxford: Clarendon Press.

—— Oppy, Graham, and Smith, Michael (1994) 'Minimalism and Truth Aptness'. *Mind*, 103: 287–302.

Johnston, M. (1993) 'Objectivity Refigured: Pragmatism without Verificationism'. In J. Haldane and C. Wright (eds.), *Reality, Representation, and Projection*, 85–130. Oxford: Oxford University Press.

Kraut, R. (1990) 'Varieties of Pragmatism'. *Mind*, 99: 157–83.

Lewis, D. (2004) 'Quasi-realism as Fictionalism'. In Mark Kalderon (eds.), *Fictionalist Approaches to Metaphysics*, 314–21. Oxford: Oxford University Press.

McDowell, J. (1981) 'Anti-realism and the Epistemology of Understanding'. In J. Bouveresse and H. Parret (eds.), *Meaning and Understanding*, 225–48. Berlin: W. de Gruyter.

Menand, L. (2001) *The Metaphysical Club: A Story of Ideas in America*. New York: Farrar, Strauss and Giroux.

Price, H. (1988) *Facts and the Function of Truth*. Oxford: Basil Blackwell.

—— (1997) 'Naturalism and the Fate of the M-Worlds, I'. *Proceedings of the Aristotelian Society*, suppl. vol. 71: 247–67.

_____ (1998) 'Two Paths to Pragmatism, II'. *European Review of Philosophy*, 3: 109–47.

_____ (2003) 'Truth as Convenient Friction'. *Journal of Philosophy*, 100: 167–90.

_____ (2004*a*) 'Immodesty without Mirrors—Making Sense of Wittgenstein's Linguistic Pluralism'. In M. Kölbel and B. Weiss (eds.), *Wittgenstein's Lasting Significance*, 179–205. Boston: Routledge & Kegan Paul.

_____ (2004*b*) 'Naturalism without Representationalism'. In D. Macarthur and M. de Caro (eds.), *Naturalism in Question*, 71–88. Cambridge, Mass.: Harvard University Press.

_____ (2006) 'The Semantic Foundations of Metaphysics'. Forthcoming in I. Ravenscroft (eds.), *Minds, Worlds and Conditionals: Essays in Honour of Frank Jackson*. Oxford: Oxford University Press.

Quine, W. V. O. (1948) 'On What There Is'. *Review of Metaphysics*, 2: 21–38.

_____ (1970) *Philosophy of Logic*. Englewood Cliffs, NJ: Prentice-Hall.

Stich, S. (1996) *Deconstructing the Mind*. New York: Oxford University Press.

Wittgenstein, L. (1953) *Philosophical Investigations*, 3rd English edn. Oxford: Basil Blackwell.

Wright, C. (1992) *Truth and Objectivity*. Cambridge, Mass.: Harvard University Press.

6

Pragmatism and Ethical Particularism

David Bakhurst

1. Ethical particularism is the view that sound moral judgement issues from the exercise of a sensibility that transcends codification into rules or principles. Accordingly, rationality and consistency in ethical practice cannot be explained—or fully explained—in terms of adherence to principles, and the acquisition of a moral point of view cannot be seen—or cannot primarily be seen—as a matter of grasping a set of moral rules. Moral judgement demands sensitivity to the salient moral dimensions of particular cases, and this cannot be properly anticipated by moral principles.

Particularism is a relative newcomer on the philosophical scene. Its primary exponent is Jonathan Dancy, who introduced the position in the early 1980s (Dancy 1981, 1983). Particularism was later defended by David McNaughton in his influential *Moral Vision* (1987), and has recently been the topic of a growing literature that includes Hooker and Little's impressive collection *Moral Particularism* (2000) and Dancy's own book-length exposition of his position, *Ethics without Principles* (2004). Dancy, McNaughton, and Little are all influenced by John McDowell, who is often counted as a particularist, though he does not describe himself as one.

A version of this paper was presented at a symposium on Dewey and ethical particularism at the Western American Philosophical Association meeting in Pasadena, 2004, and at the Queen's Philosophy Colloquium in Autumn 2005. I am grateful to John Fritzman for convening the Pasadena symposium and to my fellow panellists Margaret Little and Raymond Boisvert. I thank Brad Hooker, Rosalind Hursthouse, Christine Swanton, and Jennifer Welchman for their contributions to the discussion at that session. Scott Johnston read an insightful response to the paper at the Queen's colloquium, and my colleagues in Philosophy at Queen's made many helpful criticisms. I am also especially indebted to Jonathan Dancy and John McDowell for their comments and suggestions.

Though the roots of particularism lie in British philosophy, there appears to be an affinity between the position and certain ethical views advanced by American pragmatists. For example, in *John Dewey and Moral Imagination* (2003), Steven Fesmire argues that pragmatism seeks to replace the idea of 'objectivist rationality' with 'imaginative situational intelligence' (p. 28). Since reason is 'ineliminatively temporal, aesthetic, evolving, embodied, practical, and contextual' (p. 52), moral philosophy should abandon 'the quest for univocal principles and systematic rules' in favour of 'a rich, textured account of moral inquiry' (p. 3). The irreducible plurality of moral goods and the uniqueness of moral situations means that we 'cannot *unproblematically* apply a rule to the same situation twice' (p. 58; Fesmire's emphasis), and moral judgement must rest on imaginative attention to 'situational exigencies' (p. 3). Dewey, Fesmire maintains, shows us how to liberate moral philosophy from 'the idolatrous worship of systematized rules' and the 'misguided quest for a grand "one size fits all" [ethical] theory' (p. 3).

This sounds like music to particularist ears, but some might suspect that the affinity is merely superficial. Dancy often writes as if we should abandon moral rules altogether and make moral decisions case by case 'without the comforting support or awkward demands' of moral principles (1983: 530). Fesmire, in contrast, claims that it would be 'preposterous to deny a role in moral judgement for the guidance of general principles, or a role in moral theory for critical reflection on rules' (2003: 58). For him, moral principles represent 'a baby in the bathwater' of traditional ethical theorizing (p. 3). Though they cannot determine how we must act, principles can nonetheless play the indispensable secondary role of 'guiding' ethical inquiry. He therefore concludes that principles 'supplement' rather than constitute philosophical ethics (p. 3).[1] However, though Fesmire's position seems less radical than Dancy's, it is consistent with the views of some other particularists, who now admit the implausibility of eliminativism about moral principles

---

[1] Another Deweyan, Todd Lekan, takes a similar view, casting pragmatist ethics as a 'superior middle way between the view that moral judgement is based on universal principles and that of radical particularists who think of moral judgement in terms of case-by-case intuitive responses' (Lekan 2003: 86). And so does Cheryl Misak, whose pragmatist ethics are informed by Peirce rather than Dewey. She cites Dancy, McNaughton, and myself as extreme particularists from whom she wishes to keep her distance (Misak 2000: 122). (I discuss the relation of Peircian pragmatism and moral realism in Bakhurst 1999.)

and seek to accord them some substantive role in moral thinking (McNaughton and Rawling 2000; Little 2000). It may be that the grimy water of principled ethics contains nothing so pleasing as a baby, but there's something in there worth fishing out. So the pragmatist's insistence on rehabilitating moral principles in a subsidiary role is not in itself at odds with the views of prominent particularists.

I propose to forgo further comparison of their respective pronouncements about principles and explore the supposed affinity between particularist and pragmatist ethics by examining the compatibility of the theoretical conceptions on which the two views rest. In what follows, I argue that there is a profound tension between the principal ideas that inform particularism and central tenets of the pragmatist tradition, as it is often understood. These are, however, principally features of the tradition that 'new pragmatists', among others, want to reject (Stout, Ch.1 above). Moreover, I argue that there is a way of reading Dewey—the pragmatist with the most to say about ethics—that is congenial to the particularist.[2] I conclude that there is a genuine prospect of a fruitful alliance between particularism and pragmatism, and briefly consider three areas where pragmatist insights are relevant to the defence and development of particularism.

2. I begin with McDowell.[3] In a number of influential papers (collected in McDowell 1998), McDowell argues that moral requirements are

---

[2] William James is the most radical particularist among the classical pragmatists, but his subjectivist view of value sets much of what he says at odds with contemporary particularism. James nonetheless provides a number of choice quotes, e.g.:

[T]he intuitional moralists deserve credit for keeping most clearly to the psychological facts. They do much to spoil this merit on the whole, however, by mixing with it that dogmatic temper which, by absolute distinctions and unconditional 'thou shalt nots,' changes a growing, elastic, and continuous life into a superstitious system of relics and dead bones. In point of fact, there are no absolute evils, and there are no non-moral goods; and the *highest* ethical life—however few may be called to bear its burdens—consists at all times in the breaking of rules which have grown too narrow for the actual case. There is but one unconditional commandment, which is that we should seek incessantly, with fear and trembling, so to vote and to act as to bring about the very largest total universe of good which we can see. Abstract rules can indeed help; but they help the less in proportion as our intuitions are more piercing, and our vocation is the stronger for the moral life. For every real dilemma is in literal strictness a unique situation; and the exact combination of ideals realized and ideals disappointed which each decision creates is always a universe without a precedent, and for which no adequate previous rule exists. The philosopher, then, *qua* philosopher, is no better able to determine the best universe in the concrete emergency than other men. (James 1984: 304–5)

[3] This section is a condensed version of Bakhurst 2000: 60–5.

genuine constituents of the world, there to be discovered. Moral properties are nonetheless anthropocentric in character, in that the requirements
they generate may be perceived only by beings that possess the requisite
concepts and sensibilities. The space of moral reasons is real, but it can
be inhabited only by beings that can occupy the moral point of view.
Inspired by Aristotle, McDowell argues that the ability to discern moral
reasons is a form of practical wisdom (*phronēis*). This he portrays as 'a
sort of a perceptual capacity' that cannot be codified (McDowell 1998:
51). It is, he attests, 'quite implausible that any reasonably adult moral
outlook admits of any such codification' (pp. 57–8). Thus he concludes
that 'occasion by occasion, one knows what to do, if one does, not by
applying universal principles but by being a certain kind of person: one
who sees situations in a certain distinctive way' (p. 73).

McDowell complements this particularist view of moral judgement
with a conception of the relation of the moral and the non-moral that
challenges a familiar non-cognitivist account of moral principles. For
many non-cognitivists, the most to which moral criticism can aspire is
to show that a wrongdoer's attitudes are inconsistent. It is natural for
the non-cognitivist to argue that an agent's ethical practice is consistent
just in case she follows rules that pair sets of non-moral properties
with certain moral attitudes, rules that ensure that she responds to
relevantly similar sets of non-moral properties (which are the only
genuine features of the world to respond to) with the same moral
judgement. McDowell, in contrast, holds that the moral is 'shapeless'
with respect to the non-moral; that is, events that warrant description
with the same moral predicate will not necessarily exhibit a pattern of
similarity perspicuous in non-moral terms. There is thus no prospect of
formulating substantive principles that state sufficient conditions for the
application of moral concepts in non-moral terms. One has to be within
morality to appreciate how the natural features of situations are morally
significant. To understand a virtuous person's conception of how to
live, and to see how their various actions constitute manifestations of
virtue, is 'to comprehend, essentially from within, the virtuous person's
distinctive way of viewing particular situations' (p. 71). Such ways
of seeing are aspects of our 'second nature'; we acquire them not by
grasping rules but by enculturation into certain ways of perceiving,
thinking, and feeling (McDowell 1994: 78–84).[4]

---

[4] It is an interesting question whether McDowell's adherence to the non-codifiability
of the virtuous person's conception commits him to full-blooded particularism. For an

Dancy follows McDowell in arguing that moral competence should be understood as a perceptual capacity to respond to the specific configuration of morally relevant properties presented by particular cases. The properties of a situation have a certain 'profile' or 'shape', and to grasp which features are salient and why is to understand how one is required to act. Dancy, however, goes further, overtly attacking prominent accounts of moral principles, including R. M. Hare's doctrine of universalizability and W. D. Ross's notion of prima facie duties.

It is sometimes suggested that particularism is a purely negative doctrine that one adopts when one despairs of finding plausible moral principles (Tännsjö 1995: 573). It is crucial, however, that what underlies Dancy's critique is a distinctive account of the metaphysics of moral reasons. Dancy is a pluralist and a holist about moral relevance; that is, he argues that there is an irreducible plurality of features potentially relevant to the moral assessment of actions and to the constitution of moral reasons, and that which properties are morally relevant in some case, and how they are so, is determined holistically by the interplay of the various features of the case. A property that is morally relevant in one situation may be morally irrelevant in another, or may even change its 'polarity' or 'valence' (e.g. a right-making characteristic in situation *A* may be a wrong-making consideration in situation *B*). Hare's argument that an agent who holds that an action is right is committed to holding that any relevantly similar action is right promises to establish workable principles only on the assumption—which the holist denies—that the cluster of features that make a moral difference in one case make the same difference wherever they appear. And Ross's famous prima facie principles make a similar assumption, each principle identifying a property that is taken to be morally relevant in the same way wherever it occurs. For Ross, properties like a telling of a lie or a breaking of a promise are 'wrong-making characteristics': actions are always the worse for bearing such a property, even if they are right overall in virtue of further properties. Dancy's holism is at odds with this view and with *any* conception of moral principles based on such a generalist view of moral relevance.

Particularists are divided about whether holism applies to all properties, including 'thick' ethical concepts, such as cruelty or kindness. Radical particularists, like Dancy, suppose that it does; modest particularists,

interesting, if elusive, discussion of the role of rules in a McDowellian framework, see Lovibond 2002: 50–1.

like Little, argue that it does not. Little therefore allows moral generalities cast in terms of such properties (e.g. Promote kind acts!; Eschew cruelty!), denying only that there are robust principles that relate moral properties to non-moral properties.[5]

3. Now for the tension I discern between particularism and popular versions of pragmatism. For McDowell and Dancy, moral deliberation is a matter of striving to discern those features of situations that constitute reasons for action. For them, moral thought and action are accountable to moral reality.[6] Moral reasons represent requirements on thought and action, defining what we ought to think or do, what we ought to want, or how we should feel. We can thus think of them as having a certain kind of normative force or authority. Some philosophers hold that we require a general explanation of how it is possible that the considerations we cite as moral reasons have the normative authority we ascribe to them. McDowell, however, does not think that this question deserves an answer. In *Mind and World*, he writes that 'the fact that the demands [of morality] bear on us is just, irreducibly, itself' (McDowell 1994: 83). From within the moral point of view, we can ask of any consideration whether it is significant and why. What we cannot do is step outside ethical thought and life, view our practices 'sideways-on', and provide an account that constructs the normative authority of moral reasons from factors intelligible in non-moral terms. But this, McDowell holds, is of little consequence. Moral reasons are not in need of something standing behind them from which to derive their normative force; hence no philosophical explanation of the sources of their normativity is necessary.

Dancy has more to say about the nature of moral reasons than McDowell (Dancy 1993, 2000), but his view of their normative force

---

[5] Little has recently gone further, arguing that there can be explanatory or lawlike generalizations between moral and non-moral properties, notwithstanding the shapelessness thesis. She maintains that we can grant the truth of generalities like 'lying is usually wrong-making'—and hence accept suitably couched principles—so long as we hold that such generalities simply reflect 'something about the epistemic context one contingently occupies' and do not suppose that natural properties, like telling an intentional falsehood, have an intrinsic 'metaphysically grounded moral nature' (see Little 2000: 302–3). Many particularists will feel that this concedes too much, and moreover casts holism as the rejection of a metaphysical position that no credible generalist defends.

[6] For this reason, they are sometimes called 'moral realists' (e.g. by McNaughton 1987), though this is another term that McDowell avoids, preferring to call himself an 'anti-non-cognitivist'.

is no less austere. For Dancy, reasons for action are, or are constituted by, considerations like *that it might cause her pain*, or *its being a surprise*, or *its being no longer possible to meet next Tuesday*. Reasons are not psychological states (like desires or beliefs); they are features of a reality that is essentially practical. This fact requires philosophical elucidation, but it does not need to be underwritten by a story about how such mundane features are invested with normative authority. We might say, then, that both McDowell and Dancy are committed to the autonomy of moral reasons: their normative force is non-derivative and intelligible only from within the terms of our ethical life.

Many contemporary pragmatists will recoil from this vision. Indeed, they look to pragmatism precisely to emancipate us from the idea of such 'accountability to reality', a notion that Richard Rorty portrays as a kind of secular counterpart to the idea of answerability to the deity. Rorty argues that if humanity is to attain full maturity, we must recognize that we are accountable to no one and to nothing but ourselves (see e.g. Rorty 1982: p. xlii, and the discussion in Stout (Ch. 1 above)). This requires us to reject the idea that reasons can have the kind of autonomy with which McDowell credits them; it is transactions between human beings that constitute the sources of normativity. According to Robert Brandom, Rorty's 'master idea' is that there is no need, in ethics or epistemology, 'to appeal to any sort of authority apart from that manifested in social practices' (Brandom 2000: p. xii). For Rorty, the contemporary relevance of pragmatism is precisely that it shows us how to abandon the idea of ' "the world" as a nonhuman authority to whom we owe some sort of respect' (Rorty 1998: 150).

This is obviously the tip of an iceberg. Rorty does not see himself, of course, as advancing a philosophical story to underwrite normativity, but as getting out from under such metaphysical preoccupations. It is tempting to argue, however, that his thirst to replace objectivity with solidarity is motivated by the implicit influence of a scientism that finds the idea of the objectivity of reasons intolerably spooky and aspires to resolve them into something suitably mundane, such as human agreement. Fortunately, we can avoid the iceberg, at least temporarily. My claim here is only that if Rorty is right that a strongly anthropocentric view of the sources of normativity is essential to the spirit of pragmatism, then pragmatism is irreconcilable with the particularism of Dancy and McDowell.[7]

4. Not everyone, however, shares Rorty's vision of pragmatism.[8] Nicholas Rescher, for example, portrays 'the defining project of the pragmatic tradition' as 'the search for objective and impersonal standards' of inquiry, where 'the rational validity of intellectual artefacts' is taken 'to reside in their capacity to provide effective guidance toward the effective conduct of our extratheoretical affairs—in matters of prediction, planning, successful intervention in the course of nature, and like aspects of the conduct of our practical activities' (Rescher 1993: 737). Nothing here suggests that we should embrace a radically anthropocentric account of reasons or dissolve objectivity into solidarity.

On such a view, a pragmatist approach to ethics will presumably elucidate moral concepts by a detailed exploration of their role in our lives. The task will be to examine what is actually going on when people engage in moral evaluation, deliberate about what to do, justify their

---

[7] Couldn't the point be made more simply by saying that particularists are realists and pragmatists are not? The difficulty of casting the matter in terms of realism, or such concepts as truth, objectivity, etc., is that there is such controversy over their interpretation—even within the pragmatist tradition, let alone beyond it—and so many ways of 'finessing' them that it is hard to keep the central issues clearly in view. Hence my preference for posing the conflict as one over the idea of 'accountability to reality'.

My argument does prompt a further difficult question. Although an anthropocentric account of normativity is at odds with Dancy and McDowell, could such an account be made consistent with holism about moral reasons and the shapelessness thesis? It is clear, I think, that many projectivist accounts, and constructivist views of morality as an institution of social co-operation, would find it hard to embrace holism because the mechanisms of projection and construction will involve the association of appetitive states with discrete parcels of properties explicable in non-moral terms. But it is not obvious that *no* view of the authority of moral reasons as residing, ultimately, in relations between persons could embrace holism and shapelessness in some form.

[8] Neither Fesmire nor Misak has much good to say about Rorty (see e.g. Fesmire 2003: 42, 50, 63; Misak 2000: 12–18). McDowell himself famously has a love–hate relationship with Rorty's work. McDowell sympathizes with Rorty's quest 'to rid ourselves of the illusory intellectual obligations of traditional philosophy' (McDowell 1994: 146; 2000), but argues that Rorty ultimately fails to reveal their unreality and ends up simply 'plugging his ears'. Since McDowell does not cast his disagreement with Rorty as one about the proper interpretation of pragmatism, he sometimes uses the term negatively, as when he complains about 'social pragmatist' misconstruals of meaning (1994: 93), and sometimes positively, as when he chides Rorty for advancing a pragmatism that is 'half-baked', suggesting that a more thoroughly cooked version would meet McDowell's approval (1994: 155).

decisions, praise and blame others, and so on. The pragmatist will seek
to place morality in the context of our other practices, as part of a
compelling conception of humanity's place in nature, and in order to
illuminate and guide practice with a view to 'getting things right'.

Such a conception of ethics is also available to representatives of the
'new pragmatism', who deny that a pragmatist understanding of our
cognitive practices and conceptual norms is incompatible with the idea
that inquiry is accountable to an independent reality. Nothing prevents
the new pragmatist from holding that, though they be fashioned for
our purposes and practices, we deploy our tools of ethical inquiry to
discover moral reasons rather than to construct or invent them.[9]

Moreover, notwithstanding Rorty's affection for Dewey, the latter's
moral writings can be fruitfully read in this light. We can see Dewey as
offering us a perceptive description of our practices of moral evaluation,
designed to reveal something profound about the nature and objectives
of moral inquiry, something that discloses to us where the good lies. Like
all classical pragmatists, Dewey portrays thought as aspiring to interpret
and control experience; on his view, the problems that experience poses
and the strategies we adopt to solve them are always informed by
values. Experience is perceived as recalcitrant relative to the ends of
the experiencer, and what counts as accommodating such experience
depends on our theoretical and practical objectives (though the latter
may themselves be revised under pressure from experience). Human
beings acquire a multiplicity of values through socialization into habits
of thought and behaviour, and they attain independence in so far as
they become aware of those habits, reflect upon and modify them, and
thereby act intelligently. This vision of our epistemic situation applies
smoothly to ethical inquiry. Dewey argues that reflection on moral
experience reveals an irreducible plurality of values. We encounter

---

[9] A new pragmatist may of course believe that morality is a distinctively subjective
domain, in contrast to other modes of inquiry. My point is that it is open to her not to
do so.

When it comes to the compatibility of a particularist construal of reasons and new
pragmatist conceptions of inquiry, everything depends on how the new pragmatist
proposes to reconcile a pragmatist view of norms with the idea that thought answers
to reality. One possibility, which McDowell and Dancy would not favour, is to offer
an anthropocentric account of the construction of normativity and then somehow to
'rehabilitate' objectivity. A preferable strategy is to treat the notion of normativity as
somehow primitive and argue that the idea of thought's accountability to reality does not
stand in need of philosophical legitimation (though it may be illuminated by reference
to the distinctive character of our practices). Where new pragmatists stand, or ought to
stand, on such contentious issues may become more perspicuous in time.

situations of conflict between moral values, and between moral and other values (Dewey 1981–90: v. 279–88). These tensions cannot be resolved from the standpoint of abstract reason, but require the exercise of a situational intelligence, of the kind Fesmire commends. Thus Dewey's description of ethical inquiry quickly introduces something akin to the non-codifiability thesis. But it also reveals the importance of democratic conditions of inquiry. Dewey stresses that experience poses moral problems not to isolated individuals, but to social beings who can solve them only by working in consort. It is not just that successful moral agents are alive to a multiplicity of perspectives; solutions to moral problems often require transformation in social institutions. Dewey's account also brings out the dynamism of moral inquiry. Our ends continuously evolve as we learn from reflection on the fruits of our moral practice. Thus meaningful moral ideals will fix, not upon the realization of some final end, but on a process, such as the personal growth of individuals in pursuit of an expanding common good.

Nothing here is incompatible with McDowell's or Dancy's approach. Indeed, much should be congenial to them. Admittedly, Dewey speaks of the 'construction' of value, but his is not the kind of account that McDowell despises: namely, one that tries to show how values get into an otherwise disenchanted reality (Dewey 1981–90: iv. 203–14). For Dewey, the possibility of value does not stand in need of vindication because he conceives of the world as a problem-space for action rather than a motivationally inert mechanism. His denial that values are just 'there to be discovered' is premissed not upon non-cognitivism, but on the idea that what is worth caring about emerges from our active engagement with reality. He insists that, given that engagement, we can distinguish between what is desired and what is actually desirable (p. 207). Thus there appears to be no obstacle to reconciling Dewey's basic framework with the idea that we are accountable to what is objectively valuable. Indeed, one salutary feature of Dewey's approach is that it is less prone than McDowell's or Dancy's to provoke familiar Mackiean objections about the weirdness of objectively existing, normatively efficacious properties.

5. A McDowellian may nonetheless fear that Dewey's description of ethical inquiry remains a 'sideways-on' account in a problematic sense. At least sometimes, Dewey seems to prescind from the moral point of view in search of a rationale for our evaluative practices that might be grasped by a being that did not share in our participant perspective.

Consider Fesmire's rendition. He speaks of beliefs as 'consequences of and materials for the struggle to establish stability' (2003: 30) and inquiry as a struggle to 'guide our actions so as to satisfy our desires' (p. 32). He proceeds to assert that we sanction 'one disposition, action, or institution rather than another because one is judged (by reference to its interactions and connections) to serve or ameliorate experience. Something is estimated good, and thus to be perpetuated and made secure, only in proportion to its contribution to this amelioration' (p. 97). He then suggests that since human beings 'rely on their sociocultural environment for physical sustenance, for basic resources, and most importantly for meaning', we can establish 'a social criterion for moral appraisal' according to which, as Dewey himself puts it, 'the effect of acts upon the common welfare, the general well-being, is the criterion for judging moral worth of personal acts and dispositions [as well as social institutions and plans for social change]' (Fesmire 2003: 100, citing Dewey 1981–90: vii. 344–5).[10]

This kind of talk is anathema to McDowell, for whom moral inquiry, first-order or meta-ethical, must proceed from within the evaluative viewpoint that informs our practices. What morality is all about is only perspicuous from there, so there is no point seeking a rationale for our moral practices by feigning the perspective of an alien anthropologist. Since McDowell's insistence on the internal perspective follows from his embracing the shapelessness thesis, which is a crucial premiss of particularism, the Deweyan approach will not recommend itself to particularists.

But is Dewey's a 'sideways-on' account in the problematic sense? He certainly sometimes invites such a reading. As Jennifer Welchman argues, Dewey was enamoured of the belief that ethics could be elevated to the status of 'a practical science of cooperation under conditions of moderate scarcity and limited generosity, for enhancing human flourishing' (Welchman 1995: 1), so it is hardly surprising that he should be caught describing morality sideways-on. Moreover, when Dewey writes that way, he comes across as a committed generalist

---

[10] Welchman (1995: 164–5) notes that Arthur Lovejoy was scathingly critical of Dewey's efforts to link individual and communal well-being. Lovejoy comments: 'The crucial transition in the argument seems to depend upon the observation that the individual's real good or happiness demands social well-being because the self is essentially a social self . . . —a characteristically abstract, loose, and shifty piece of neo-Hegelian phraseology that is susceptible of several senses and is, in some of its senses, decidedly open to question' (1909: 143).

advancing a suite of stable values. Thus Gouinlock claims that Dewey's is 'a "principled" philosophy in that certain enduring values (such as the democratic virtues) are proposed to guide conduct in all situations' (Gouinlock 1994: p. xxv).

Dewey can, however, be read rather differently. In much of his work, he writes primarily as a moralist who articulates and defends his cherished ideals—of growth, intelligence, shared experience, democracy, freedom—as part of an immanent critique of our moral ends, albeit one that aims to throw our moral practices into relief by casting them as activities of natural beings interacting with one another and the world. Thus, it might be argued, Dewey does not delineate ends of moral inquiry intelligible without the deployment of thick moral concepts, for, as he himself puts it, 'what sense is there in increased external control except to increase the intrinsic significance of living?' (Dewey 1976–83: xiv. 183). Accordingly, his famous view of the reciprocality of means and ends may be read not as a merely causal thesis, but as invoking the Aristotelian idea of practices with internal goods, where the ends of a practice are not intelligible independently of the perspective internal to the practice itself and where the means deployed by those who engage in the practice are partly constitutive of its ends (see MacIntyre 1981: ch. 14). A sympathetic reader might, therefore, conclude that when Dewey appears to look at morality sideways-on, he is simply in search of critical distance from our practices in order to engage in the sort of reflection upon them that McDowell describes as a constituent of free, rational thinking. This is consistent with his seeing moral theory 'as the reflective clarification of practices that are already underway, or as a map of the terrain of ethics for those already in it', as Matthew Festenstein perceptively characterizes Dewey's project (1997: 26).[11]

---

[11] Dewey's writings do not make it easy to decide between the two readings. It is important to note, however, that much that looks like a sideways-on account turns out, on closer inspection, to be rather different. Consider the following passage:

The point at issue in a theory of educational value is then the unity or integrity of experience. How shall it be full and varied without losing unity of spirit? How shall it be one and not yet narrow and monotonous in its unity? Ultimately, the question of values and a standard of values is the moral question of the organization of the interests of life. Educationally, the question concerns that organization of schools, materials, and methods which will operate to achieve breadth and richness of experience. How shall we secure breadth of outlook without sacrificing efficiency of execution? How shall we secure diversity of interests, without paying the price of isolation? How shall the individual be rendered executive *in* his intelligence rather than at the cost of his intelligence? How shall art, science, and politics reinforce one another in an enriched temper of mind instead of

6. I conclude that Dewey's legacy, at least when read with due sympathy, contains much for the particularist to admire. To what degree, however, can Dewey's ideas prove a genuine resource for the particularist? In what follows, I consider how Deweyan insights might illuminate three issues that particularists need to say more about: (i) the acquisition of the moral point of view; (ii) the role of moral generalities, (iii) the analogy between the moral and aesthetic.

(i) *Bildung*   Following Aristotle, McDowell argues that children are initiated into the moral point of view in the course of their upbringing, or '*Bildung*'. In this process, we acquire the capacities that enable us to perceive moral requirements. McDowell treats these capacities as conceptual in character, and he strongly associates their acquisition with the acquisition of language. He understands initiation into language, however, as a matter of enculturation into traditions of thought and discourse, and perhaps also into modes of feeling and response, rather than as the attainment of certain technical-linguistic skills. *Bildung* is a central concept in McDowell's philosophy as a whole, since he casts an Aristotelian view of ethical upbringing as a model for the acquisition of *all* conceptual capacities (1994: 78–86, 125–6).[12] *Bildung* is our way into the space of reasons in its entirety; the *Bildungsprozess* marks a transition from pre-rational being to rational, self-conscious agency.

   Notwithstanding the importance of the notion, McDowell's account of *Bildung* is characteristically austere.[13] To whom might we turn for illumination? Here Dewey would seem an obvious candidate. Like McDowell, Dewey represents moral discernment as 'a socialized capacity' (Fesmire 2003: 5), and he portrays upbringing—moral and otherwise—as initiation into socially entrenched habits of thought and action. Again like McDowell, Dewey represents upbringing as having a profound influence; the habits we acquire are 'so intimately a part of

constituting ends pursued at one another's expense? How can the interests of life and the studies which enforce them enrich the common experience of men instead of dividing men from one another? (Dewey 1976–83: ix. 257)

Though the passage begins with what seems to be a classic sideways-on claim, the answers to his many questions that Dewey is calling for could only be expressed from a morally engaged perspective on education, and Dewey seems to appreciate this.

[12] McDowell writes: 'Now it is not even clearly intelligible to suppose a creature might be born at home in the space of reasons. Human beings are not: they are born mere animals, and they are transformed into thinkers and intentional agents in the course of coming to maturity' (1994: 125).

[13] So too is Dancy's; see his 1993: 64.

ourselves' that they constitute the self and 'rule our thoughts' (Dewey 1976–83: xiv. 21–2). If we are not to be unthinkingly controlled by these routines, we must bring them to awareness and cultivate only those that are beneficial. As Fesmire puts it, our task is to move 'from customary morals automated by habits to reflective morals mediated by intelligence' (2003: 27).

This picture seems to complement McDowell's, but Dewey and his followers sometimes develop it in ways with which McDowell would not be sympathetic. They become preoccupied with causal questions about habit formation and change. Thus Fesmire's controversy with Gouinlock about the morality of welfare programmes concerns whether such programmes inculcate deleterious habits of dependence by rewarding people for not working, and whether habit change is constrained by innate dispositions of character (see Fesmire 2003: 25–6). This tired exchange seems remote from McDowell's vision of moral education. For him, a self-conscious agent is one capable of critical reflection upon her beliefs, concerns, and commitments, and upon the conceptual structures that articulate those states. So the idea of mature human beings as vehicles of habituated behaviour is one-dimensional, whether that behaviour is portrayed as unthinkingly or 'intelligently' habituated.

Moreover, even if *Bildung* is the transition from pre-rational to rational agency, it does not follow that children are first initiated into unthinking behavioural routines that only later become objects of reflective scrutiny. All concept acquisition involves the child's coming to appreciate the distinctive perspective from which the concept's pattern of use is discernible. From the very outset, the child's deployment of developing concepts is always subject to contestation. This is especially true of moral notions. To represent children as drilled into ways of thinking and speaking only later to question them is to deploy a notion of learning at home in a Victorian schoolroom, but at odds with the realities of child development. If they are conceptual capacities that *Bildung* gifts us, the possibility of judgement and critical reflection is implicit in them from the start. I fear, however, that there are few resources in Dewey's treatment of habits to assist the development of these embryonic ideas.[14]

---

[14] Todd Lekan would certainly disagree with my diagnosis. He places Dewey's notion of habit at the centre of his reconstruction of pragmatist ethics. Lekan develops an account of habits as historically transmitted, social, shared practices that can embody the 'deep-seated commitments of the self' constitutive of character (Lekan 2003: 30). But the notion is asked to carry such an explanatory burden (habits are variously identified with 'complex social functions' (p. 30), 'will' (p. 56), 'norms' (pp. 51, 61), and are said to be

McDowell argues that critical reflection is central to our autonomy. Our beliefs, and many of our actions, are rationally necessitated: we believe what we see we must believe, and do what we see we are required to do. Yet he maintains, with Kant, that rational necessitation is constitutive of freedom (1994: 5). Though these beliefs and actions are necessitated, they are nonetheless free, and this because our powers of critical reflection enable us to endorse them as our own, and act in light of that endorsement. The space of reasons, which *Bildung* enables us to enter, is also the 'realm of freedom' (McDowell 1994: 5). This is a difficult position to understand. Do Dewey's impressive writings on freedom offer any help (see Dewey 1981–90: iii. 92 ff.)? Dewey offers a form of compatibilism that carefully treads a path between what later became known as 'negative' and 'positive' conceptions of freedom. He persuasively argues that the ability to pursue freely chosen ends without hindrance from others is indeed a crucial constituent of freedom, but he recognizes that the ability to make informed choices requires significant social pre-conditions, such as education and resources. There is much here that a McDowellian will find salutary, though again there is little to help with the really hard question of the precise nature of the constitutive relation between freedom and rational necessitation.

(ii) *Principles*   As noted in Section 1, many particularists now accord some role to principles. Little, for example, argues that 'moral generalities play an indispensable role beyond admittedly important heuristic and pedagogic functions', and asserts that '[t]here are aspects of our moral lives that necessarily look beyond the particular to invoke moral patterns, indeed law-like patterns, to carry justificatory weight' (Little 2000: 278). How to reconcile these claims with particularism is, of course, controversial. Here it might be thought useful to consult the Deweyan pragmatist, who, as we saw, also aspires to preserve a key role for principles while stressing the centrality of 'situational intelligence'.

'constituted out of ongoing more or less organized energy of an organism' (pp. 55–6)), that it is hard to see this as an advance over Aristotelian conceptions of second nature as perceptively reconstructed by, e.g., Myles Burnyeat (1980), whom McDowell cites with approval (1994: 84 n.).

   G. H. Mead offers another pragmatist approach to *Bildung*, though his 'social behaviourism' is friendly to the sideways-on perspective. The richest resources are, I believe, to be found in the Russian cultural-historical tradition of Vygotsky and Ilyenkov (see Bakhurst 1997, 2005*b*). For a discussion of the bearing of this tradition on ethical particularism see Bakhurst 1985. Glock (1986) explores connections between Vygotsky and Mead.

Particularist attempts to accommodate principles often focus on the issue of their predictive power. If holism is true, principles cannot fully anticipate the overall moral status of particular cases, but, some particularists concede, principles can assist in making weaker predictions about the features that might matter in some situation. Pragmatists make the same move. In inquiry, we formulate principles or laws to help us anticipate experience. So it is in science, in everyday perception, and in ethics. Moral principles are generalizations from past experience that serve as guiding hypotheses about what can matter and how. They do not determine what matters in any particular case, so they cannot substitute for inquiry, intelligence, and judgement. But they are indispensable if we are to orientate ourselves in experience.

This focus on prediction embodies an exceedingly one-dimensional view of moral principles. When I say to my son, 'Do not tell lies' or 'Breaking promises is wrong', I do not see myself as giving him a bit of predictive wisdom ('Here's a tip, m'boy, most of the acts you'll come across that are lyings or promise breakings will be wrong'uns'); nor am I giving him a piece of practical advice similar to 'If you are lost in the city, ask a policeman for directions' or 'Always check your blind spot before changing lanes', as Todd Lekan implies in his critique of Dancy (Lekan 2003: 96–101). Rather, I am urging him to esteem honesty and fidelity. I am recommending that he be the kind of person that sets himself against some ways of living and endorses others. Moral generalities play a crucial role in this discourse about character; and that role is not, it seems to me, parasitic upon their predictive power. On the contrary, the character traits in question command our respect—indeed, our unqualified respect—notwithstanding the fact that plenty of lies and broken promises do not matter. I have argued elsewhere that particularists need an account of moral generality, consistent with holism, to make sense of moral commitment (Bakhurst 2000, 2005*a*). Without this, we will have no account of the integrity of moral personality. This is less of a problem for Little, who thinks that we can formulate principles in terms of thick moral properties; but it is a concern for more radical particularists. I fear there is not much in the pragmatist position that will be of help. Dewey wrote many wise words about character, but they serve to highlight the problem rather than to solve it.

Particularists could learn a lot, however, from pragmatist ethics' concern with the public sphere. The vision of inquiry as a social process inclines pragmatist ethics towards discussion of moral questions of social concern, and answers to these questions are seen as legitimate

only insofar as they withstand appropriate public scrutiny. Deliberative
democracy is thus often the pragmatist's model for reasonable ethical
inquiry (see Misak 2000). The particularist literature, in contrast, is
almost wholly focused on private morality ('Ought I to visit my ailing
relative when I have promised to help a friend that day?'), a phenomenon
that intensifies the suspicion that particularism's contempt for principles
leaves it with nothing to say about public policy and the law, and that
this is a fatal ineptness.

(iii) *The Moral and the Aesthetic*   Particularists frequently invoke
aesthetic phenomena to illuminate their position. McDowell likens
convincing someone of the relevance of certain features of a moral
situation to teaching someone to appreciate a piece of jazz (McDowell
1998: 85). Dancy portrays moral justification as narrative in structure
(1993: 118). Little, citing McNaughton, argues that aesthetic properties
exhibit the same holism that we find in the moral domain (2000: 280).
So far, however, discussion of the relation between the moral and the
aesthetic has remained at the level of occasional examples, and it remains
unclear how seriously we are to take the parallel.

Here again Deweyan pragmatism is a potential source of insight.
Dewey gave a central role in ethical judgement to imagination, and
he portrayed art as one of the primary vehicles of imagination. While
Dewey himself was often concerned with the influence of artistic
practice upon morality, seeing a vibrant artistic culture as a stimulus
to moral innovation, Fesmire proposes to treat artistic creation as 'a
rich model for understanding the sort of social imagination that is
essential to moral deliberation' (2003: 108). His emphasis on the role
of emphatic projection, dramatic rehearsal, and narrative construction
in moral deliberation should be congenial to McDowell and Dancy. At
the same time, the pragmatist focus on morality as a constructive, social
process inclines Fesmire to stress artistic creation in its social dimensions.
Thus, where McDowell's analogy is between moral perception and an
individual listener's appreciation of jazz (McDowell 1998: 85), Fesmire
takes improvisation by a jazz ensemble as a model of moral life,
suggesting that morality is a matter of the co-ordination of individuals
around a common project, the ends of which are internally related to
the practice itself.[15]

---

[15] Note that the practitioners respond to properties that are both of their own
collective making *and* there to be discovered, and the quality of their responses requires

This is splendid food for thought. Where Fesmire overreaches, however, is in his enthusiasm to establish art as a metaphor for morality. Inspired by Lakoff and Johnson, Fesmire bemoans how much our moral talk deploys metaphors from accounting and commerce (we speak of 'giving credit', 'being indebted', etc.). The influence of these metaphors, he argues, is, disastrous. He proposes that we speak less of 'what we owe each other' and more (I suppose) of learning to jive with each other. However, while it is undoubtedly important to be cognizant of the metaphors that influence our thinking, Fesmire fails to consider whether the metaphors in question are not themselves parasitic upon antecedent moral notions. Our notion of a contract, for example, is a formalization of pre-legal notions of mutual obligation. Moreover, the language of the virtues, or the thick moral concepts, is not so infected with the metaphors that Fesmire disdains. Thus it is not obvious that our moral thinking is simply in the grip of dubious metaphors that must be set aside in favour of a different suite drawn from a practice more congenial than bookkeeping. This concern distracts from the real issue, which is to deepen our appreciation of the interplay between the moral and the aesthetic. Fesmire applauds the work of those who have sought to do this, notably Nussbaum and MacIntyre, but his own discussion falls short.

7. This paper has explored the affinity between pragmatism and ethical particularism. I hope to have shown that, although there is a profound tension between the philosophical views that inform particularism and the spirit of pragmatism as it manifests itself in Rorty's work, there is much in the pragmatist tradition that ought to be congenial to particularists. This is especially true of Dewey's legacy, if it is read sympathetically. Although the work of a classical pragmatist is central to my argument, I don't think it would be wrong to portray the affinity as one between particularism and the new pragmatism, for, it seems to me, the new pragmatism is just the best of the old pragmatism, undistorted by narcissistic anthropocentrism and developed with contemporary means. In any case, I hope to have convinced my reader that the practitioners of particularist and pragmatist ethics stand to profit from critical engagement with each other's works. There remains, of course, an important difference of temperament between the two schools.

---

sensitivity not just to the objective properties of their common creation, but to their collaborators' modes of perception and response.

140 *David Bakhurst*

Pragmatists are usually motivated by the idea that 'the tools of moral philosophy ought to be used to help the process of social reconstruction', as Lekan puts it (2003: 148). Much particularist writing, in contrast, scorns the transformative pretensions of moral theory and remains firmly in the meta-ethical domain. Yet, though this difference of outlook is bound to frustrate any bold alliance, one can say with confidence, and in true pragmatist fashion, that dialogue between the two schools on theoretical questions of mutual concern promises to open fascinating avenues of inquiry.

BIBLIOGRAPHY

Bakhurst, D. (1985) 'Marxism and Ethical Particularism: A Response to Steven Lukes's *Marxism and Morality*'. *Praxis*, 5(2): 209–23.
—— (1997) 'Meaning, Normativity and the Life of the Mind'. *Language and Communication*, 17(1): 33–51.
—— (1999) 'Pragmatism and Moral Knowledge'. In C. Misak (ed.), *Pragmatism. Canadian Journal of Philosophy*, suppl. vol. 24: 227–52.
—— (2000) 'Ethical Particularism in Context'. In B. Hooker and M. Little (ed.), *Moral Particularism*, 157–77. Oxford: Oxford University Press.
—— (2005*a*) 'Particularism and Moral Education'. *Philosophical Explorations*, 3: 265–79.
—— (2005*b*) 'Strong Culturalism'. In C. Erneling and D. Johnson (eds.), *The Mind as a Scientific Object: Between Brain and Culture*, 413–31. Oxford: Oxford University Press.
Brandom, R. (2000) 'Introduction'. In R. Brandom (ed.), *Rorty and his Critics*, pp. ix–xx. Oxford: Blackwell.
Burnyeat, M. (1980) 'Aristotle on Learning to be Good'. In A. Rorty (ed.), *Essays on Aristotle's Ethics*, 69–92. Berkeley: University of California Press.
Dancy, J. (1981) 'On Moral Properties'. *Mind*, 90: 367–85.
—— (1983) 'Ethical Particularism and Morally Relevant Properties'. *Mind*, 92: 530–47.
—— (1993) *Moral Reasons*. Oxford: Blackwell.
—— (2000) *Practical Reality*. Oxford: Oxford University Press.
—— (2004) *Ethics without Principles*. Oxford: Oxford University Press.
Dewey, J. (1976–83) *The Middle Works: 1899–1924*, 15 vols., ed. J. Boydston. Carbondale, Ill.: Southern Illinois University Press.
—— (1981–90) *The Later Works: 1925–1953*, 17 vols., ed. J. Boydston. Carbondale, Ill.: Southern Illinois University Press.
Fesmire, S. (2003) *John Dewey and Moral Imagination: Pragmatism in Ethics*. Bloomington and Indianapolis: Indiana University Press.
Festenstein, M. (1997) *Pragmatism and Political Theory: From Dewey to Rorty*. Chicago: University of Chicago Press.

Glock, H.-J. (1986) 'Vygotsky and Mead on the Self, Meaning and Internalisation'. *Studies in Soviet Thought*, 31: 131–48.

Gouinlock, J. (1994) 'Introduction'. In J. Gouinlock (ed.), *The Moral Writings of John Dewey*, pp. xix–liv. Amherst, NY: Prometheus Books.

Hooker, B., and Little, O. (2000) (eds.), *Moral Particularism*. Oxford: Oxford University Press.

James, W. (1984) 'The Moral Philosopher and the Moral Life' (1891). In B. W. Wilshire (ed.), *William James: The Essential Writings*, 294–308. Albany, NY: State University of New York Press.

Lekan, T. (2003) *Making Morality: Pragmatist Reconstruction in Ethical Theory*. Nashville: Vanderbilt University Press.

Little, M. (2000) 'Moral Generalities Revisited'. In B. Hooker and M. Little (ed.), *Moral Particularism*, 276–304. Oxford: Oxford University Press.

Lovejoy, A. (1909) Review of Dewey's *Ethics*. *American Journal of Theology*, 13: 140–3.

Lovibond, S. (2002) *Ethical Formation*. Cambridge, Mass.: Harvard University Press.

MacIntyre, A. (1981) *After Virtue*. London: Duckworth.

McDowell, J. (1994) *Mind and World*. Cambridge, Mass.: Harvard University Press.

——(1998) *Mind, Value, and Reality*, Cambridge, Mass.: Harvard University Press.

——(2000) 'Toward Rehabilitating Objectivity'. In R. B. Brandom (ed.), *Rorty and his Critics*, 109–23. Oxford: Blackwell.

McNaughton, D. (1987) *Moral Vision*. Oxford: Blackwell.

—— and Rawling, P. (2000) 'Unprincipled Ethics'. In B. Hooker and M. Little (eds.), *Moral Particularism*, 256–75. Oxford: Oxford University Press.

Misak, C. (2000) *Truth, Politics, Morality: Pragmatism and Deliberation*. London: Routledge.

Rescher, N. (1993) 'American Philosophy Today'. *Review of Metaphysics*, 46: 717–45.

Rorty, R. (1982) *Consequences of Pragmatism*. Cambridge: Cambridge University Press.

——(1998) *Philosophical Papers*, iii: *Truth and Progress*. Cambridge: Cambridge University Press.

Tännsjö, T. (1995) 'In Defence of Theory in Ethics'. *Canadian Journal of Philosophy*, 25: 571–94.

Welchman, J. (1995) *Dewey's Ethical Thought*. Ithaca, NY, and London: Cornell University Press.

7

Was Pragmatism the Successor to Idealism?

Terry Pinkard

Although the story of Hegel's relation to the development of analytical philosophy is well known, the story of the relation between pragmatism and Hegelian idealism is a more ambiguous tale. Bertrand Russell and G. E. Moore staked out their new program in analytical philosophy in firm opposition to what they (mistakenly) thought of as 'Hegelianism'. However, the pragmatists had different reactions. Like Russell, John Dewey began his philosophical career as a Hegelian, but William James apparently despised what he at least understood to be Hegelianism, and C. S. Peirce both reacted against and at the same time developed the themes found in both James and the idealists. Whatever their differences over the value of idealism, however, the pragmatists all agreed that they had gone beyond Hegelian (and Kantian) idealism, having transformed it into something more defensible or having defeated it by virtue of the pragmatist approach to issues of the meaning of experience, truth, and the status of natural science in the theory of knowledge.

Part of Dewey's argument for the superiority of pragmatism had to do with his claim that experience itself had changed in light of the changes in modernity itself, a claim which on its surface bears striking similarity to Hegel's claims in the *Phenomenology* about the way 'experience' changes in history (see Dewey 1948: 83–4). On Dewey's well-known view, once we abandon the idea that there are certain, merely given constraints on our evaluative practices that we apprehend in some spectator-like fashion, we are in a position to see that it is indeed up to us to set the norms ourselves, and that the norms of inquiry, of morals, of religious observance, and even of aesthetic appreciation should be those that satisfied *our* needs and interests. Hegel, of course, also defended various practices such as art, religion, and philosophy in terms of the way they answered to the 'deepest' and 'highest' interests of mankind, our 'highest needs', mankind's 'true interests', and so forth.[1] Dewey even admitted the Hegelian heritage of his own ideas on the subject, noting in 1945, 'I jumped through Hegel, I should say, not just out of him. I took some of the hoop . . . with me, and also carried away considerable of the paper the hoop was filled with' (cited in Westbrook 1991: 14). Continuities, rather than outright rejection, thus color some of the pragmatist reaction to Hegel's thought.

Moreover, there is a general similarity between Hegelian ideas about the historical development of our knowledge and ourselves and the world and the more contemporary pragmatist insistence that knowledge should be conceived as a self-correcting, communal enterprise; for those contemporary pragmatists, the lesson to be learned is that we always begin from where we are, and we correct bits and pieces of the edifice along the way; our criteria for doing so have to do with what satisfies our interests, and our interests themselves change over time as we develop new means of satisfying them. For both Hegel and these pragmatists, understanding what kinds of moral, theoretical, and practical claims we make means taking them developmentally in their historical, social, and epistemic contexts.

However, although both Hegelian idealism and pragmatism are, broadly speaking, 'developmental' in their outlooks, the conception of development at work within both pragmatism and idealism seems, at least on the face of it, to be very different. Hegel notoriously opposed all doctrines of evolution (although in his day it was Lamarckian evolution he rejected in favor of Cuvier's non-evolutionary theory), whereas Dewey was adamant about the close connection between his own developmental conception of experience and Darwinian evolutionary theory, always giving his own views a more or less biological, naturalist interpretation. The basic category of his thought, he says, is the 'interaction of organism and environment', and therefore 'knowledge' 'is relegated to a derived position . . . [it] is involved in the process by which life is sustained and evolved' (Dewey 1948: 87). Thus, Richard Rorty (1998) has suggested that what remains to be kept of Hegel in a modern pragmatism would be a marriage between (Hegelian) historicism and Darwinian evolutionary theory—in other words, something like his own view.

---

[1] Art 'only fulfills its highest vocation . . . when it is simply one way of bringing to our minds and expressing the divine, the deepest interests of mankind, and the most comprehensive truths of spirit' (Hegel 1975: 7; 1971: xiii. 20–1).

In light of that, John McCumber once half-jestingly suggested that perhaps we should therefore see Hegelian idealism not as having died out but simply as having mutated in light of developments in culture since his time; just as some people think that dinosaurs did not become extinct, but instead evolved into smaller, more efficient life forms (namely, birds), perhaps Hegel likewise just mutated into smaller, more efficient philosophical forms, and the Quines, Sellars, and Rortys of our day are only the smaller but more efficiently adapted versions of the old all-encompassing and now extinct tyrannosaur, Hegel himself (McCumber 1993: 28–9).

Here I want to suggest something slightly different: What forms the link between pragmatism and idealism is a set of issues about normative authority. We can see this by noting the metaphor of 'inside' and 'outside' in both Hegel's idealism and Dewey's pragmatism. On the one hand, from the normative point of view, there is no 'outside'; wherever we stand, we are always, to use a Sellarsian turn of phrase, inside the practice of giving and asking for reasons. Yet it is also quite clear that we can take an 'outside' point of view on our own reasons and, still standing within the space of reasons, look at our own and others' claims as the products of class, history, self-deception, as expressions of some kind of depth psychology, and so on.[2] Whereas this seems inevitably to drive us to some kind of realism about reasons, on the one hand (as the space of reasons being that within which we always necessarily find ourselves), on the other hand, both the success of the natural sciences and the influence of historicism coming out of the nineteenth century have driven us to a more situated—even towards a more naturalized—conception of rationality. We are in fact pushed in both directions at once: We must acknowledge the contingency of our norms, and we must recognize the necessity of using those norms (at some level) to justify even the claims that the norms themselves are contingent (which in turn pushes us in the direction of a non-contingent conception of normativity). It is this problem of normative authority to which both pragmatism and idealism responded, both by articulating what can be called a developmental and dynamic conception of normative authority and by trying to anchor normative practice in

---

[2] This metaphor of 'inside' and 'outside' has itself been one of the most misleading guides to idealism, since Hegel's own use of so many 'inside' metaphors have naturally given rise to the thought that his system abolishes not only the thing-in-itself but all ideas of an object independent of thought, which in turn drives one (as it did Royce) to a conception of a great mind that includes natural objects and our own minds within it.

the activities of *life* itself—in Dewey's case, in his attempt to bring the new science of Darwinian evolution to bear on philosophical issues. Nonetheless, there remain some crucial differences between Hegelian idealism and pragmatism which play out, I think, to the advantage of idealism. To do that requires a narrative of what Hegel took to be at stake in this debate.

I KANTIAN PHILOSOPHY AND DIALECTICAL REASON

It was this problem of normative authority for which Hegel's rather infamous dialectical conception of reason was supposed to be the answer, but for many people, even in Hegel's own day, the suspicion has never gone away that there is nothing much more to 'dialectical' thought than its metaphorical power (about 'movement', about taming the power of contradiction, and so on). Indeed, the very difficulty of getting any kind of grip at all on the so-called dialectical character of Hegel's thought is exactly what has prompted people from Bendetto Croce to Ernst Cassirer to Allen Wood to insist that whatever contemporary relevance Hegel's theory is supposed to have will have to be articulated independently of the 'dialectical' form in which Hegel framed his own discussions.[3]

The starting point for Hegel's thoughts on dialectic originate with Kant's conception of the 'fact of reason' in his *Critique of Practical Reason*. The 'fact of reason' is a response to a difficulty that Kant brought on himself in his *Groundwork* in his claim that in practical affairs 'the will is therefore not merely subject to the law, but is so subject that it must be considered as also *giving the law to itself* and precisely on this account as first of all subject to the law (of which it can regard itself as instituting)' (Kant 1964*b*: 98 (AA 431); trans. modified). Taking this literally would be paradoxical: If the will can be obligated only by a self-legislated law, and if it also cannot be obligated by an arbitrarily chosen law (by *Willkür*), then it needs an obligatory law in order for it to legislate a law for itself—which means that it would require a non-self-legislated law that is nonetheless self-legislated. The 'fact of reason' was a way of stating that paradox without completely resolving

---

[3] See Wood 1990 for a very self-conscious statement that Hegel's dialectical logic is dead, but Hegel's political theory is not. Frederick Neuhouser (2003) takes a similar approach.

it; it is the view that we always *find* ourselves within the claims of reason even as we continue to see those claims as arising from ourselves and not as lying in some order of the cosmos already 'out there' independent of our own spontaneous activities (Kant 1956: 31 (AA 31)).[4]

It is of course a long story, but Hegel understood that if one were to take the other Kantian lesson to heart—what, following Sellars, we would call the rejection of the myth of the given—then this problem in Kant's moral philosophy became *the* problem of normative authority in general, which in turn threatened to put us into a condition where the possibility of any normative authority itself seemed either to collapse into some form of unconstrained relativism or to push us back into acceptance of some kind of 'given' in some form or another.

This problem of normative authority—that we can be subject only to those laws of which we can regard ourselves as the authors—was, for Hegel, *the* great philosophical problem *par excellence*. It structures what he calls 'dialectic' (or what he more often calls 'speculative' thought). It appears in various ways throughout his writings. In the *Phenomenology*, it finds expression in the way in which 'consciousness' and *Geist* are said to go outside of themselves only to find that the putatively 'external' norms which they had thought underpinned a whole form of life turn out instead to be self-legislated, so that 'consciousness' and *Geist* are thus 'driven back into themselves' as the sources of such legislation. In the *Logic*, it finds expression in the way that thought is said to become the 'other of itself' (*das Andere seiner selbst*) (Hegel 1969: 561). Indeed, so Hegel thought, this simply is *the* speculative problem, a problem that is inescapable once one has moved beyond the Kantian destruction of all pre-Kantian metaphysics and the myth of normative givenness.[5]

There are, of course, many more twists and turns in the story about how Hegel tried to come to terms with stating this 'Kantian paradox';

---

[4] As Kant put it, 'The consciousness of this fundamental law may be called a fact of reason, since one cannot ferret it out from antecedent data of reason, such as the consciousness of freedom (for this is not antecedently given) and since it forces itself upon us as a synthetic a priori proposition based on no pure or empirical intuition . . . one must note that it is not an empirical fact but the sole fact of pure reason, which by itself proclaims itself as originating law.'

[5] I go into this 'Kantian paradox' and Hegel's acceptance and transformation of it more fully in Pinkard 2002. See also Pippin 2000. Christine Korsgaard (1996) has made the theme of self-determination central to her interpretation of Kant. Lately, in her Locke lectures, she has been arguing for a way out of the paradox by invoking the idea of a 'constitutive standard', an inescapable set of substantive commitments built into the very idea of rational agency itself.

he himself had so much trouble working it out that he invented a whole new (and tangled) jargon for doing so (alas, not an entirely successful achievement on his part). Indeed, even stating the problem is liable to misunderstanding, since it might look as if it is claiming that Kant (or Hegel) is trying to argue that such freedom involves a magical leap from out of a non-normative realm into a normative one, something far from his intentions.[6] Hegel took the key to the solution of this 'Kantian paradox' to be found in Kant's own writings, specifically in the Kantian arguments to the effect that there can be no 'unsynthesized intuitions', and hence that intuition on its own can never constitute a source of knowledge that stands completely apart and uninformed by concepts; this indicated to Hegel that implicit in the Kantian scheme was the view that both intuitions *and* concepts could play their distinctive epistemically normative roles only as parts of (or, in his jargon, as 'moments' of) some larger normative 'whole'; in *classifying* part of our experience as an intuition (or as a representation in general), we are really *ascribing* a normative status to it, which is to say that the 'whole' within which these normative roles have their place is reason itself (as inferentially articulating itself). Philosophical inquiry must therefore start from the *unity* of intuitions and concepts, not from their separation, which is merely derivative from the role they play within this normative 'whole'.[7] Indeed, the usual Anglo-American picture of Hegel as a holist gone mad, who detached concepts so much from experience that he really was just spinning in the void, is far off the mark. His point was not that we should be such detached holists, but that we can neither be content with a 'final dichotomy', a sharp separation of 'thought' and its 'other' (to which thought was supposed to answer) without falling either into pre-Kantian metaphysics or the myth of the given, nor can we simply absorb 'being' into 'thought', something he accused 'subjective idealism' of illicitly doing. It was also clear to him that the original statement of the idea of self-legislation (especially as it was so consistently and insistently worked out by Fichte) could indeed

---

6 See Larmore 2004: 149, where he mistakes the paradox for a claim of such a magical leap from the normative to the non-normative.

7 To this end, he noted in his early 1801 *Differenzschrift* how the transcendental deduction constituted, in his words, 'authentic idealism'. See Hegel 1977: 79; 1971*b*: ii.9. The passage which inspires Hegel to this view is no doubt that in which Kant says, 'The same function which gives unity to the various representations in a judgment also gives unity to the mere synthesis of various representations in an intuition, and this unity, in its most general expression, we entitle the pure concept of the understanding' (Kant 1964, A79 = B105).

only be metaphorical. As Kant realized, it is a mad fantasy to believe that we can start from nowhere: We are always operating within the sphere of the 'fact of reason'. However, so Hegel controversially claimed, just as Kant had publicly accused Fichte of fruitlessly and foolishly trying to spin content out of concepts alone (that is, out of the mere 'logical functions of judgment'), so Kant himself had in effect tried to do the same thing in his moral philosophy.

Such an approach works neither in the theoretical nor in the practical sphere: Like theoretical reason, practical reason requires its 'other' if it is to have any content. As Hegel had argued ever since the appearance of his first real book (the *Differenzschrift*) and had quite explicitly stated in his mature *Logic*, the sharp distinction between the a priori and the a posteriori must be rejected in favor of a unity of concepts and intuitions (a unity mediated by our inferential practices — that is, by reason itself) (Hegel 1969, in 1971: v.62).[8]

For practical reasons, this would have two sides: In order for practical reason to be *at work* in the world (to be actual, *wirklich*, in Hegel's term of art), it both needs some way of generating content for itself and to be itself capable of motivating the agent; for both these conditions to be satisfied, practical reason has to be in a 'unity' with its 'other'. 'Pure practical reason', the Kantian alternative, was, for Hegel as for the pragmatists, not something that could ever be at work; to be at work, to be actual, reason requires its unification with 'life'. What that means, however, differentiates Hegelian idealism from pragmatism.

II REASON *AND* NATURE

If we take 'reason' to demarcate the sphere of the normative, then the 'other' of reason is the non-normative, which, in Hegel's philosophy, takes roughly two forms: That of nature and that of the established,

---

[8] Speaking of some post-Kantian attempts (probably those of J. F. Fries) simply to appropriate the Kantian results without further argument, and in particular to reject Kant's notion of the thing in itself without understanding the deeper philosophical motives behind Kant's use of that conception, Hegel notes that such post-Kantians proceed without asking 'Whether and how they are able to be determination of the thing-in-itself (following the Kantian mode of expression), or rather to be determinations of what is rational', to which he then immediately adds: 'The objective logic is consequently the genuine critique of those determinations — a critique which considers them not in terms of the abstract form of apriority as opposed to the a posteriori, but rather considers them themselves within their particular content.'

merely positive rules of society. Each of these is originally encountered as a version of what Hegel calls 'immediacy', as something non-normative that reason simply 'finds' or 'encounters' and which appears as possessing some type of authoritative status for itself, but which turns out to have that status only by virtue of the kinds of norm-instituting and sustaining activities carried out by rational agents.

It is another long story to explain Hegel's own ideas about the relation between philosophy, the natural sciences, and nature (see Pinkard 2005). For Hegel, the most fundamental feature of nature has to do with the way it is, when seen in light of modern science, fully disenchanted; indeed, this disenchantment was a necessary moment in the development of the modern conception of subjectivity, since it was only over and against a disenchanted, 'spiritless' (*geistlose*) nature that modern subjectivity could define itself. The older idea of things having their own function or purpose in nature (either by virtue of their essence or by having been created for that purpose by a beneficent God) made it look as if it were nature alone that set our norms (or that we correctly set them ourselves only by matching up our norms with those to be found in the cosmos). In modern times, however, *Geist* has come to grasp itself as 'other' than nature, and this is to be taken not in a substantialist sense (as if *Geist*, or the mental, was constituted out of a different substance) but as a historical *achievement*, as a normative and not a metaphysical independence from nature. To understand ourselves as having such a self-instituted liberation from nature, however, required us to understand nature itself as disenchanted, as lacking normative authority on its own.

Hegel thus accepted the approach to nature taken by the natural sciences (although he did not think that they could tell us the whole story about nature), and he saw the problem that his own *Naturphilosophie* was to solve as having to do with the strains that his own dialectical theory imposed on an understanding of the role of the natural sciences. On the one hand, he explicitly rejected the idea that any *Naturphilosophie* could be carried out independently of the findings of the natural sciences, since (again) that would suppose that reason could, untainted by its 'other', spin substantive content out of itself alone. Thus, in an often cited passage, Hegel emphasizes that 'not only must philosophy be in agreement with the experience of nature, but the *origin* and *formation* of philosophical science has empirical physics as its presupposition and condition' (1971: ix. §246). What philosophy contributes to this is a reconstruction not of science but of the concept of nature itself that is really *at work* in the practices of the natural sciences, along with an account of why one should think that natural science is best placed to provide us with a rational account of nature.

It is part of Hegel's own typical way of shifting the question that he proposes that we *not* look at natural science in terms of any kind of subject/object opposition and worry about whether natural science can possibly bridge the so-called gulf that lies between our representations and the world they claim to represent. He took himself to have shown that putting the issue that way already prejudices the matter and sends us off with too much conceptual baggage in tow: 'If we set ourselves to working on how we would leap over this gulf, we are certainly letting ourselves be led astray in thinking of nature by making nature, which is an other to us, into something other than what it is' (1971: ix. §246, *Zusatz*). To get at what nature really is, we must, in Hegel's words, 'step back from natural things, *leaving them as they are* and *directing ourselves to them*', all the while doing this 'directing' in terms of the *practice* of natural science (with its attendant virtues of impartiality, its forms of social organization into research groups, and the like) (1971: ix. §246, *Zusatz*; my italics). Hegel's point again has to do with a rejection of 'immediacy': that is, a rejection of both the romantic idea that an experience untainted by the natural sciences is in a position to get at what nature is really like, and the idea that there is some 'immediate' mode of perceiving nature that would provide a normative bedrock for natural science itself.

Hegel is here, as in so many places, trying to use Kant to get out of Kant—in this case, insisting that we come to understand nature as it must be only when we have fully acknowledged the role of human spontaneity in that enterprise. Nature becomes an 'other' to us only as we historically come to understand ourselves—or, in Hegel's preferred terminology, as *Geist* comes to comprehend itself—as normatively independent of nature. That is, we *make* nature into an 'other', into the non-normative confronting the normative order by virtue of *grasping ourselves* in a different way and thus grasping nature in a different way than we had done heretofore. By seeing nature as devoid of meaning, of having no teleology that aims *at* anything, we fashion an 'Idea' of nature in Hegel's sense (a picture, as it were, of what nature is like in its totality and how it is to be intelligible to us) that we *bring to* the investigation of nature and not that we simply read off nature. The *empirical* research that is the cornerstone of natural science is necessary precisely because we cannot read off individual items of nature how we are to grasp them as 'universals'; or as Hegel pithily phrases it, 'things are individual, and the lion as such does not exist' (1971: ix. §246, *Zusatz*, p. 16). Theoretical reason thus finds its 'unity' with its 'other' only as it has comes to understand the role of this 'Idea' of nature in its more commonsense grasp of nature (the grasp of nature as intelligible as non-normative, *as* 'other', and therefore as 'externality', as appropriately the object of mathematically stated laws, and so forth). Reason, that is, confers a type of normative authority on a certain experience of nature as devoid of meaning that nature, as it were, cannot do on its own; it is not a natural fact about us that we have come to comprehend nature in this way.

On its own, reason, considered in isolation from its 'other', would be merely the 'logical function of judgment'; however, as trying to come to terms with its 'other', with nature *as recalcitrant* to pure reason's attempts to grasp it in its empirical multiplicity, reason constructs (or 'posits', in Hegel's terminology) an inferentially articulated 'whole' of this non-normative 'other'—an 'other' in just the sense that it offers us an overall picture of nature which puts us in the position of being able (to cite Hegel's words again) to 'step back from natural things, *leaving them as they are*', which is neither 'creating' nature, nor constructing an arbitrary way of simply 'counting' or 'classifying' nature under wholly constructed schemes. It is a way of articulating the sense of natural things by showing that we can best and most consistently understand ourselves *and* nature only if we understand nature in that disenchanted manner, a way of understanding nature such that we receive from natural scientific investigation not merely 'our take' on nature but *nature* itself. It thus also avoids any kind of dualism of 'a priori scheme' versus 'empirical content', such that we would have the 'logical functions of judgment' on the one side and empirical content supplied on the other.

III REASON *IN* NATURE

What role, though, can a disenchanted nature play for *practical* reason? If one works within a non-dialectical picture of reason and nature as distinct elements to be combined in an overall account of the efficacy of practical reason—that is, of reason supplying some kind of form with the content coming from elsewhere, or reason providing some kind of calculative function while the actual motivation for the action comes from elsewhere—then one is tempted to despair of there being anything like practical reason at all, which in turn leads one to think that there instead be something like a 'desire' or a 'passion' to function as the motivational springboard to make reason effective or to provide the non-chosen final ends in terms of which the content of maxims is to be deliberatively constructed. It is, for example, as Hume himself noted, notoriously difficult to explain why even something as fundamental as the principle of utility can have any motivational force unless it is the case that we inherently find utility pleasing, so that it can be no mystery why something that may clearly not be a person's self-interest can nonetheless have a motivational grip on him. In more contemporary accounts, it is argued that even 'getting it right' cannot have any motivational force unless one posits another desire to put that principle into play (that is, that we have a basic, non-chosen desire to seek truth) (see Wallace 1999).[9]

In all these cases, it seems that disenchanted nature plays the role of providing a non-chosen basis as the way out of the 'Kantian paradox' of self-legislation, but it does so by making the basis of such legislation non-normative, which in turn cannot provide us with *reasons* for acting. It can at best give us explanations for why we do what we do, not justifications.[10]

Hegel's attempt to shift our picture of the relation between disenchanted nature and practical reason relies heavily on his post-Kantian use of the conception of teleology in nature. At the level of organisms, we have a kind of internal teleology—a functional teleology—that neither requires there to be some designing entity, nor requires there to be anything at which nature can be said to be aiming. To classify something as an organism is already to classify it in terms of the way in which the parts—its organs, such as eyes or hearts—function in terms of sustaining the organism and reproducing it. It is therefore only in speaking of organisms in nature that we can meaningfully speak of things such as disease: For something to count as a disease, it must somehow be impairing the organism's ability to achieve its goals (those

[9] Wallace argues that such views ultimately make agency itself impossible, since they require a commitment to the motivational effects of reasons not being traceable to our deliberative activity, but to the operations of causal forces within us (p. 223). If nothing else, it makes it impossible that one could grasp that one has reason to do X, yet fail to be motivated to do X; in other words, *akrasia* and *accidie* would both be impossible.

[10] Moreover, such a view inevitably sets moral deliberation in an infinite set of puzzle cases, since it always remains unclear why this or that desire or emotional state should be incorporated into our maxims and how that is supposed to function as a reason we can share. (In his lectures, Hegel would mention the lifeboat cases as paradigms.)

necessary for it to carry out its functions). For the concept of disease to be applicable, there must be states of the organism that are *good* (or evil) for the organism. A mountain range, a crystalline structure, a planetary system cannot be said to be diseased, because there is nothing that is *good* (or bad) for them.[11] Their mode of organization is simply factual, non-normative. It is only, that is, with organisms that we can speak of there being *goods in* nature.

The appearance of life on Earth thus marks the appearance of there being *reasons* for action, in that organisms may be said to *have* reasons for their actions or behavior *because* there are things that are good or bad for them. (For Hegel, this is not just a matter of linguistic convention: What is good and bad for an organism is not just a matter of our *speaking* about it, as if those goods were simply relative to our ways of talking; it is good and bad for the organism itself.[12]) In this sense, reasons exist *in* nature, since there are goods and evils (for organisms) *in* nature. However, although organisms may be said to *have* reasons in this sense, and reasons may be said to exist in nature, reason itself is *not really at work* (or at best is at work only indeterminately) in nature. Nature itself cannot organize itself as a whole into any way of being better or worse (indeed, the very concept of being better or worse as a whole cannot even apply to disenchanted nature), and there are clearly conflicting goods running all through nature: What is good for the parasite can be evil for the host; what is good for the predator is usually evil for the prey. Thus, although there are reasons *in* nature, reason is not *at work*, is not *wirklich*, in nature. Nature has no way of making itself better or more rational; nature aims at nothing. (This incapacity of nature to order itself in any way in terms of better or worse is what Hegel colorfully calls the 'impotence', the *Ohnmacht*, of nature.[13])

---

[11] Among the many passages that can be cited in this regard, Hegel 1971: ix. §371 stands out: 'The organism exists then within the opposed forms of being and of the self, and the self is just that which is the negative of itself. The rock cannot become diseased because it perishes in the negative of itself, is chemically dissolved, its form does not endure, it is not the negative of itself that reaches out over its opposite as is the case in illness and self-feeling.'

[12] This distinction finds voice in two very different contemporary accounts of goods in nature: MacIntyre 1999 and Thompson 1995. Thompson explicitly draws on Hegel for some of his otherwise non-Hegelian ideas on life.

[13] There is no natural, or even biological, way of drawing the distinction between functioning properly and conveying the truth, since an organism (e.g. in a strange environment) can be functioning properly (as it is supposed to do) but nonetheless wrongly (as when it takes something for food that is not food for it). This is another way

Humans are, of course, organisms, and thus also have things that are *naturally* good and bad for them, and hence naturally *have* reasons to act in some ways and not in others; but humans also have the capacity to maintain a kind of normative self-relation, a being-for-self (*Fürsichsein*), of which the highest exemplification is self-consciousness, and as a result, they not only *have* reasons, they are *reasoning* beings. Or, to put it in terms of the German, although there may be *Gründe* (reasons) in nature, nature cannot rise to the level of *Vernunft* (reason), which involves linking all the *Gründe* in an inferential set of relationships. This kind of self-relation means that for humans, what it means to be a human is always up for questioning, and that the issue of what it 'means' to be human is to be cashed out in terms of normative conceptions of agency, of deliberation and reflection on what would count as the best exemplification (and thus in Hegel's usage, the *true* conception) of human agency. What it means to be human is thereby itself a normative question all the way down, since it involves our stance towards ourselves and how we are to 'take up' and evaluate even the organic facts about our own lives. There is no non-normative fact that fixes for us the meaning of humanity; even our own organic embodiment can become an object of loathing or an object of celebration, depending on the set of interconnected evaluative stances we bring to it.

The appearance of organisms brings reasons *into* the world, but, to use Hegel's language, only as 'in itself', *an sich*, not in any way in which reason itself can be said to be genuinely *at work*, to be *wirklich*, effectively real. The appearance of *Geist*, of human *agency*, on the planet further complicates that picture, since in taking up reasons in a fully normative manner, agents determine for themselves what is to count as a reason, and thus *Geist* seems, at least at first, to detach reason from nature. Unlike the other organisms, human agents have the capacity to evaluate whether the goods they are in fact aiming at achieving really ought to be the goods after which they seek. Moreover, as agents take on new self-conceptions, new goods appear on the scene for them which are not linked in any obvious way to natural goods, which in turn creates new sets of reasons for these agents. Whereas the existence of reasons in nature is completely dependent on there being the goods for the organisms, for human agents reasons, as favoring one action or belief over another, themselves put those goods into question; even the natural

of saying that 'truth' is not a naturalistic concept, a distinction that has been made in a completely non-Hegelian way by John Haugeland (1998).

reasons which we just *have* by virtue of being organisms are themselves always capable of revaluation in light of some other, non-natural set of reasons or self-conceptions. However, if reason is completely detached from those natural goods or from any 'given' set of facts (either the facts of nature or the given social rules of one's social environment), there can be no effective role for it to play. Thus, reason, both practical and theoretical, seems to be both 'independent' of non-normative facts and at the same time to require some kind of dependence on them if it is to be more than empty spinning in the void, the exercise of mere 'logical functions of judgment'.

But what about Hegel's well-known and clearly stated opposition to evolutionary theory? Hegel's opposition to evolution was, of course, not to Darwin's form (which came much later) but to Lamarckian forms of evolution, which he condemned as being too externally teleological and as offering no real explanation for the origin of new species. Instead, he opted for the views advanced by his French contemporary, Georges Cuvier, to the effect that each organism is an internally structured teleological whole that exists in a close harmony with its environment, and therefore changing any small part of it would throw it out of kilter with its environment and lead to its destruction (thus ruling out the long time frame necessary for evolutionary theory). Hegel's acceptance of Cuvier's hypothesis (widely held among German intellectuals at the time) also colored his view of history, leading him to see the various forms of life of Greece, Rome, and the like as if they were strictly analogous to the self-contained nature of a Cuvierian organism.[14] How central this Cuvier-inspired idea is to Hegel's theory is a large topic that cannot be explored here. Here I can limit myself to the observation that it is not completely implausible that this part of the Hegelian system could be excised without doing much harm to the rest; and if it were, the apparent opposition between Hegelian idealism and Darwinian evolutionary theory would itself dissolve, leaving the field open for a reconsideration of the links between the two.

IV REASON *IN* THE SOCIAL WORLD

The non-orthodox character of Hegel's proposal should now be clear. Because *having* reasons is tied to there being *goods* for organisms, Hegel

---

[14] I discuss the role of Cuvier in the development of idealism in Pinkard 2002.

is, after a fashion, a realist about those goods (and therefore about the *reasons* to which those goods give rise) *in* the natural world, even if most of organic life is unaware of there being such goods, and even if only a very small part of organic life acts in light of those goods. Likewise, for human agents, for *Geist*, there are goods to be found in the natural world (which would include the more ground-level facts about human organic flourishing, such as the kinds of natural goods that are involved in maintaining one's health and in the rearing of children).

Given that, one might expect that Hegel would attempt to do something very similar for the practical world and either look at certain facts about the social world (such as 'we do things this way nowadays') and see which could be universalized or perhaps take a kind of neo-pragmatist turn and see which kinds of desires or interests are at work and how they do or do not cohere with each other.

Hegel, of course, does nothing like that. Simply to import facts into some universalizable form or take interests as in any way 'given' and then test them for mutual compatibility or consistency would beg all the questions that the 'Kantian paradox' (or 'dialectical philosophy') only brings to the fore. It begs, that is, the issue of the normativity of these matters, and, more colloquially expressed, why we should care about them. *That* we care about them might be true; but why we *should* care about them is another issue.

Hegel's proposal is that in effect we need to take Kant's rather bold assertion in the *Grundlegung* that all prior attempts at securing the principles of ethical life had to fail *because of* their failure to see that such principles had to be self-authored and follow that out to its conclusion.[15] In Hegel's hands, that in turn demands a different kind of philosophy, a *developmental, social,* and *historical* account about what is at work in our subjective commitments to these practices, which nonetheless cannot be merely a 'positive' history. It must instead make it intelligible how it is that this *given* set of commitments has *come to be* regarded as authoritative—as our 'own essence'—*by virtue of* prior dissolutions of other sets of commitments, and why that way of coming-to-be counts

---

[15] On the Hegelian telling of the story, it is *Geist's* own historical achievement of normatively detaching itself from nature that fleshes out Kant's bold claim in the *Groundwork*: 'We need not now wonder, when we look back upon all the previous efforts that have been made to discover the principle of morality (*Sittlichkeit*), why they have one and all been bound to fail. Their authors saw man as bound to laws by his duty, but it never occurred to them that he is subject only to his own but nonetheless universal legislation' (Kant 1964: 100 (AA 432).

as rational. Just as in physics, 'phenomenology' is the study of true motion in contrast to apparent motion, so Hegel proposed that we look for a metaphorical *phenomenology* of social shapes of mindedness to distinguish the 'true motion' of that mindedness in history from all the various contingent events that pile up one after another—in short, that we adopt a more historical and practice-oriented approach that eventuates in a comprehensive story about the 'shape of spirit', or whole social form of life in which the commitments in question have come to be *at work* in the lives of the people whose form of life it is. And that, of course, shifts the question: We ask not about the relative coherence of such forms of life, but about how those forms of life are most deeply experienced and 'lived out' by the participants, and about whether some types of ways of life must, so to speak, inevitably collapse under their own weight because they put impossible demands on the people actually living those lives.

Hegel's own developmental story, as it is carried out in works like the *Phenomenology of Spirit*, is, of course, far too complex to summarize adequately here.[16] What it attempts to show, though, is that the 'true motion' of human like-mindedness in history has to do, to put it very generally, with the ways in which the succession of European forms of life from Greece to Rome to the nineteenth century not merely succeeded one another in a temporal order but was each itself the result of the very determinate failures of the kinds of communal commitments undertaken by different forms of life and how those determinate failures each demanded and resulted in successors whose own form of life essentially determined itself in terms of those failures (or as their 'determinate negations').

But even that is too abstract to get at what Hegel was trying to say. We can perhaps get some kind of grip on what Hegel is trying to do by simplifying his claim (and then qualifying our simplification). Just as theoretical reason requires for its success an 'Idea' of nature—a concept of nature as an intelligible whole that we *bring to* our experience and investigation of nature—so practical reason requires for its success a 'practical Idea', a concept of the social whole that we bring to our practical endeavors and in light of which we orient our lives. This 'Idea' of the social whole is, by and large, a set of ideals and goods that are authoritative for that form of life, and it furnishes, to shift back into

---

[16] For a detailed account, see Pinkard 1994; for shorter summaries, see Pinkard 2000: ch. 8, and 2002: ch. 9.

Kantian language, the basic 'laws' by which we legislate other laws for ourselves.

Such a 'practical Idea' is comprised, therefore, of those pre-reflectively grasped set of goods and ideals in terms of which people make commitments and lead their lives within a given form of life. Each of them constitutes what Hegel in his early writings called a *Lebensform*, a form of life (which he shifted to describing as a 'shape of spirit' in the *Phenomenology*, only to return to describing it in his famous 'Preface' to the *Philosophy of Right* as a 'form of life' (*Gestalt des Lebens*)). A 'shape of spirit' forms part of the background, usually implicit understanding possessed by participants in a form of life which involves a fusion of *norms* and *facts*; it is a 'view', that is, of how people *imagine* their social existence, how they see themselves as fitting together with others, their views on what they can reasonably expect to go on among them and their compatriots, how those expectations are to be normally met, and, crucially, a conception of what the *world* is like that makes those norms *realizable* (or not).

What is distinctive about Hegel's view here is (again to put it too abstractly) that the way in which that European past has to be narrated shows that the various attempts to hold onto some kind of non-chosen, 'given' anchor for their practical projects unraveled in light of the ways they imposed incompatible demands on individuals and on the collective form of life as a whole. Those forms of life, or shapes of spirit, in which those conceptions were at work—involving things like the natural perfections of agents, God's law, and the corresponding accounts and reassurances of those kinds of ways of making sense of what we are to do—could not be sustained, in that in holding themselves and each other to account in terms of those given ideals, people experienced a set of commitments that could not themselves be sustained because of contradictory or irrational demands they found themselves rationally required to put on themselves and each other. The story of those kinds of normative and experiential dissolutions is the account of how it came to be a matter of non-chosen requirements that we be subject only to laws of which we could regard ourselves as the authors.

As Hegel saw, there is the rub: Such norms cannot be experienced as *individually* authored; they must be seen as having been *collectively* authored so that they now appear as the background, taken-for-granted goods of a particular (in this case, modern) form of life. The *dialectical* problem of being subject only to those laws of which we could regard ourselves as the authors thus required a solution in terms of *sociality*. *I* cannot be the author of the law to which I am subject, and any kind of non-normative 'other', such as a given set of desires or the mere fact that my society does things in such-and-such a way, cannot therefore be the kind of reason that could successfully underwrite my authoring one law as opposed to another.

The only 'other' that could fulfill that function—that is, could give me a *reason*—would be another rational agent who serves as the 'author' of the 'law' that I follow. This has its first formulation in Hegel's celebrated dialectic of *Herrschaft* and *Knechtschaft*. The problem with all such solutions in terms of mastery and servitude is that it makes the basis of the master's rule itself a non-normative matter that cannot itself be redeemed by reason. The penultimate solution, so Hegel thought, was found in Christian religion, in which a divine person (Jesus) appears to 'give us the law' to which he himself is subject; but, as founding a religion based on the book, Jesus founds a religion that requires a theology, and theology, as submitting itself to reason, ultimately becomes philosophy, and the internal teleology of philosophy's submission to the claims of reason pushes it to its own penultimate position of the Kantian demand for a critique of reason by itself and the 'Kantian paradox' that comes about as a result.

As Hegel realizes, that sets the bar quite high (and with our own inherited contemporary suspicions about the distorting effects of ideology, we are surely inclined to suspect that it sets the bar impossibly high). We must be able to show *not* that our duties follow from a set of principles (in the fashion of old-fashioned European manuals of law) but instead that the set of background, pre-reflective ideals and goods that are accepted as the basis for our everyday practical reasoning themselves can be redeemed as rational—and for 'we moderns' this means that the story to be told has to do with the realization of freedom, the way in which our more everyday *individual* deliberations about the right and the good can be seen to be expressions of a *collectively* authored 'Idea' of a free life in terms of an overall, comprehensive account of the various relationships and dependencies we have to each other such that a set of 'ethical relationships' (another Hegelian term of art) can be redeemed as rational.[17] For an 'ethical relationship' to be experienced as a *demand*,

---

[17] It would be the topic of another paper, but it also illustrates why Hegel is so intent on the 'other' of practical reason being the 'practical Idea'. It might seem, for example, that at the most abstract level the 'other' of practical reason would be simply the 'good' or the 'right'. Although in his *Logic*, he originally makes it the 'good', he tries to argue

as something to which one is required to keep faith, there must be some way in which the individual *identifies* himself with that demand so that it comprises *his own* goods and ideals. In Hegel's own terms, for this to work, the goods and principles of this form of life cannot therefore be '*alien* to the subject' but must be 'his own essence', such that 'the relation between the two is closer to identity than faith or trust are' (1971: vii. §147).

The complete unorthodoxy of Hegel's position should now be even more clear. At various points Hegel looks like a rationalist, a social constructivist, and a realist. Reasons (that is, goods) that favor one action over another are to be *found* in the social and natural worlds, and in that sense Hegel is a rationalist realist about ethics. However, those goods change historically as our self-conceptions change, and in that sense he looks like a constructivist. In fact, he is both: We need an *objective* account of how reasons function in the social world and why certain states of affairs—your being in trouble, or Polyneices' body lying unburied outside the city walls—can favor one action over another, and how those reasons can nonetheless be at work, be *wirklich*, only by being mediated by *subjective* features of agency—by virtue, that is, of their playing a certain role in the pre-reflective background grasp of the social world as a whole, the 'Idea'.[18]

At this point in the story, though, it should not be surprising that Hegel's own view of what it means for freedom to be at work, to be *wirklich*, in the modern world departs from at least standard liberal accounts. For Hegel, freedom cannot be *wholly* a matter of *Willkür*, unencumbered free choice, or 'arbitrariness'. For Hegel, as for Kant, freedom is self-determination, and in light of his 'dialectical' approach, this means that the agent, in *giving* himself the law, must first find

---

that even this abstract conception of 'the good' requires further articulation into the 'Idea'. The *Rechtsphilosophie* follows this schema, beginning with the 'other' of practical reason as *das Recht* (the right), following up with the other in *Moralität* being *das Gute* (the good), with both having their foundation in *Sittlichkeit* (ethical life as the Idea).

[18] It is another issue, but one to which Hegel seems to commit himself, that our understanding of this background and the goods that appear in its horizon is highly particularistic and cannot even be captured in *ceteris paribus* clauses. We have to be able to see what to do, and any attempt at specifying the conditions under which we would, for example, claim we did not have a duty would be potentially infinite. Thus, *ceteris paribus* clauses could not play the role they are supposed to play, since in principle we cannot enumerate all the conditions that have to hold if we are to be able to make such judgments. This forms part of Hegel's Aristotelian inheritance, something he never took pains to hide. See Pinkard 1999.

himself always and already committed to other norms and ideals, which he must be able to understand as expressive of something deep about himself such that he can at the same time *consider* himself *as* having authored them in the sense that they can be regarded as 'having come from him'. The appearance of paradox in both Kant's and Hegel's accounts, with their talk about the 'will willing itself' and the like, has to do with the way in which practical reason finds its content and its motivational force in this 'other'—in the practical cases, in the given social world in which the individual is educated and in which he or she moves. In Hegel's best-known formulation, to be free is said to be 'in one's own sphere in an other' (*in diesem Anderen bei sich selbst*); that is, for an agent's practical reason to get its content and force from an other in which he recognizes himself. It is not, however, to others *as individuals* that we necessarily turn, as if we were always negotiating with others about our maxims. Rather it is to the non-chosen background form of life, and the issue for 'we moderns' is whether that form of life can sustain the kinds of commitments that make up individuality and freedom.[19]

Freedom and individuality are the basic destinies, or *Bestimmungen*, to which modern agents find themselves called. That kind of self-conception is, to appropriate some terms from Charles Taylor, what 'powers' us, serves as the 'source' of moral motivation such that individuals not only find themselves already *committed*, they *commit themselves* to certain projects and other goods so that this calling can be

---

[19]   That this also involves a compatibilist account of freedom that eschews all references to there being any kind of special causality involved in agency—which distinguishes Hegel sharply from Kant—is an important part of this story, which itself requires another paper. For a discussion of these issues, see in particular Pippin 1999. I also discuss this in Pinkard 2002. For Hegel, as opposed to Kant, freedom is not the ability to act according to one's own causality—as it were, to be able to set oneself into motion by pulling some metaphysical lever outside the realm of natural causality—but the ability to act in a way in which one can, as it were, see the action as coming from you, see yourself *in* the action, and therefore for which one can be held responsible (where, again, responsibility itself is not a notion that is determined outside of, or prior to, our practices of praising and blaming). Curiously, Hegel only explicitly stresses this point in his Nuremberg *Propaedeutic*, where he discusses his version of the well-known Kantian 'incorporation' thesis: 'The truth, however, is that I have behaved therein not only passively but also essentially actively, in that my will has *incorporated* these circumstances as motives, has let them count as motives', and, Hegel adds, '*the relation of causality does not occur here*. The circumstances do not comport themselves as cause, and my will is not their effect. . . . As reflection, I can go beyond any determination which is posited by the circumstances. . . . Circumstances or motives have only as much dominance over a person as he lets them . . . for the essence of his will is that nothing can be in it that he himself has not made his own' (Hegel 1971: iv. §15, pp. 222–3; my italics).

realized, can be subjectively experienced as being *at work* in their own lives. The *experience* of this kind of personal commitment is not that of mere 'choice' among competing preferences, but something more akin to what Taylor has called 'strong evaluation', of simply *finding* oneself committed to what is 'other' than mere choice and then *sustaining* that commitment by the course of one's actions (see Taylor 1989). That kind of sustaining, however, is not simply a matter of strength of will, but has to do with the form of life in which such concepts are at work and with whether the non-chosen, non-negotiated commitments required of such agents are themselves rationally sustainable. We can each successfully be modern *individuals* only if others can be such individuals; individuality, as a good, is a historical achievement that requires a form of ethical life for it to be *effectively real*, to be at work in our lives.

V SPIRIT'S INTERESTS

There is therefore a reference to the *interests* that grow out of our like-mindedness and the kind of development it has undergone in its history, and to whether certain types of social and cultural formations best articulate and satisfy those interests: namely, in whether the kinds of mutually established self-relations that shape a form of life can be sustained. In that respect, idealism on the surface looks like a form of (or perhaps a predecessor of) pragmatism.

There are, however, two ways in which this form of idealism differs on the face of it from pragmatism. First, for this idealism, this interest in our own agency is not an interest that we have *prior* to becoming agents. Our interest in agency itself, in leading our life, is more like Kant's 'fact of reason': We have no prior interest in it; rather, the 'fact of reason', our own like-mindedness, *prompts* an interest in us, so that the mere exhibition of the 'fact' is enough to motivate us to seek to realize it—that is, to bind ourselves to its norms. This is an expression of how we are always, from the normative point of view, inside the space of reasons (or, rather, how, from the normative point of view, the 'inside/outside' distinction does not work). The unconditional demands of reason that we put ourselves in the position to justify our claims means that this cannot be simply a 'tool' that we find to satisfy other preexisting desires or interests, since the justification for that claim itself takes us right back into the space of reasons (or, perhaps more accurately, shows us that we were never out of it in the first place).

Second, invoking the 'fact' of reason in this way also does not mean that we must see ourselves as *just being* the kinds of creatures that give and ask for reasons without this 'fact' itself having any further intelligibility. In Hegel's terms, our subjectivity is potentially 'infinite', expressing the 'unboundedness' of the conceptual; that is, our subjectivity is ultimately pushed to become fully intelligible to itself, not of course in the sense that we would ever be in a position to derive every fact about ourselves from some set of a priori principles, but in the sense that our justifications for why we take things to be the way they are cannot finally end in some kind of 'given', or unintelligible 'positivity' beyond which there are no further justifications. As we might otherwise put it, our fundamental interest has to do with the *meaning* of our other interests for us in the course of our conception of what it is to lead our own lives. It is not that we author all the facts about ourselves—we obviously do not—but that we determine what significance those facts have for us, and that the non-normative facts themselves severely underdetermine the meaning that they can have for us.

This is another way of saying that spirit's fundamental interest has come to be that of freedom, but it also makes the more radical claim that this freedom is a historical achievement, not a metaphysical fact about us or a transcendental condition of our agency. On this kind of developmental story, it is not as if there has always been some metaphysical capacity on our part that we have overlooked, or that because of our own 'immaturity' we have failed to exercise; it is instead a story about how we came to rely less and less on natural facts (or what were taken to be natural facts) as normatively authoritative for us in determining what it *meant* to lead our own lives.

VI HEGEL THE PRAGMATIST?

Was Hegel thus a pragmatist *avant la lettre*, whose insights were to be brought to fruition by Dewey, James, and Peirce and by those who now carry on what they began? To be sure, agency, or spirit, has its 'interests': namely, in coming to an understanding of what it is to lead a human life and what it means to be a human being, and its interests lie its ultimate norms being evaluated in terms of what truthfully counts as answering those questions. This is not, however, a matter of taking some pre-given set of interests and then looking for tools to satisfy the desires stemming from them. It is more a matter of recognizing the role that reason plays as an outgrowth of natural powers already there in organic life but which nonetheless cannot be given a naturalistic explanation (without at the same time itself being committed to any further kind of metaphysical supernaturalism). And, to be sure, Hegel was the first to stress the social character of knowledge (a pragmatist theme).

This kind of normative reading of the Hegelian conception of the absolute has its counterpart in Robert Brandom's widely influential inferentialist semantics.[20] Indeed, on Brandom's account, Hegel is very much the pragmatist *avant la lettre*, and Brandom characterizes his own work as broadly Hegelian. The obvious question is: How does this view of Hegel stack up against Brandom's own finely nuanced and insightful interpretation of Hegel? Answering that question would require another essay, but a couple of short remarks (which, because they are so short, must also be unsatisfactory) may at least help to highlight the differences and similarities.[21]

In many ways, Brandom's own version of Hegelianism has more in common with the historical figure of Fichte than it does with Hegel. Like Brandom, Fichte argued that if the whole notion of a norm could not be derived from a *fact* of any kind at all—that had been the fundamental error in interpreting Kant made by Fichte's predecessor at Jena, Karl Leonhard Reinhold—then it had in some way to be the result of some kind of *self-authorization*. No natural or mental fact (even Reinhold's celebrated 'fact of consciousness') could *authorize* anybody to do anything. Moreover, since modern conceptions of nature had also completely undermined all attempts at resuscitating a conception of the cosmos as containing natural purposes within itself that could therefore authorize humans to do certain things, no attempt at specifying a *natural* human telos would suffice to do that. Such norms would have to be *instituted*, not discovered, and most basically, they seem to involve the issuing of inference licenses (to use Gilbert Ryle's term), permission to infer from A to B. (This is not so anachronistic as it might seem: Fichte interpreted even the law of identity, 'A = A', as an inference license, as, 'from A, you may infer A'.) Moreover, as Fichte also quite clearly saw,

---

[20] See Brandom 1994. Brandom has laid out the outlines of how he would interpret Hegel in light of them in his 1999.

[21] The most in-depth account of the issues about how Hegelian Brandom's Hegel really is are to be found in Pippin 2005. The main point of Pippin's objection has to do with how he sees Brandom as ultimately substituting a conception of 'social positivism' for Hegel's more robust conception of normativity.

understanding norms as instituted and as involving inference licenses only raised the question of who-or-what *authorized* who-or-what to perform such an act of instituting. Fichte famously concluded that it could only be the 'I' (or the 'absolute I'), which was itself to be seen as a kind of *Tathandlung*, a 'deed-act', signifying the way in which the semantical function of norms incorporates elements of both of declarative and imperative sentences.[22] The 'I' must simultaneously both *issue* such inference licenses (such as 'If A, then A') and *authorize* itself to issue such licenses. The 'I' as a subject of entitlement and (epistemic and moral) responsibilities is thus not a natural thing, but it is also not a supernatural or 'unnatural' thing. It is in fact not a *thing* in the literal sense at all; it is a normative *status*.

The problem, as Fichte so clearly saw, was that if the story ended there, there would be no account of any rational constraints on such authorizations and licensings, such undertakings of commitments and attributing of entitlements. For that, the subject of such undertakings had to posit that there was something—famously, in Fichte's obscure jargon, a 'Not-I'—that normatively constrained our acts, and by 1796, Fichte was already attributing that function to another subject; such individual subjects then constrained each other via acts of mutual recognition. Indeed, *only* other subjects are capable, Fichte argued, of normatively constraining the authorizations of each other as subjects in acts of mutual attribution of responsibilities and entitlements.

In Hegel's view, Fichte's account still remained impossibly 'subjective' and 'psychological'. We are 'minded' because we authorize ourselves, which we accomplish in acts of mutual recognition; but this makes our own status as 'minded' subjects dependent on the prior individual *attitudes* that others take toward us. Although Fichte clearly came to think that the process of self-authorization was social (and did not come about through some miraculous act of an isolated 'I' positing

---

[22] See Lance and O'Leary-Hawthorne 1997. That is, asserting a norm calls on the agent to accept responsibility for the content of the norm, as is the case with a declarative assertion; and it authorizes himself or another to act, as is the case with an imperative. One of the differences has to do with the nature of imperatives; one cannot issue an imperative to oneself, but one can impose, so it seems, a norm on oneself. This has to do with the social nature of norms; norms can be imposed only to the extent that they are collectively imposed. Individually imposed norms are only norms in an analogical sense, in the same sense as when one says (in English), for example, that one 'makes it a rule' to eat an apple every day. 'Making it a rule' imposes no norm on oneself, nothing binding on oneself. (On this point of the impossibility of issuing imperatives to oneself, my account of sociality departs from Lance's and O'Leary-Hawthorne's.)

itself), by virtue of his model of such sociality he nonetheless could only understand mindedness as a structure of mutual recognition by *individual* agents.[23]

Such 'individualism' in the normative sphere, though, failed to resolve its deepest problem: For the other to be able to have the *authority* to constrain my acts of 'positing'—of issuing inference licenses and authorizing myself to issue such licenses—'I' must bestow that authority on him, and vice versa. Given Fichte's own suppositions, though, that means that in each case, what I *ought* to do is constrained by what the other *actually, factually* does. A normative matter, that is, is ultimately decided, or based on (or derived from) a positive fact; yet, if it really is 'norms all the way down', as Fichte had effectively argued had to be the case, then it also could not be the case that any fact could entail a norm (even if it could offer evidential support for one). Brandom's own strategy for basing normativity in attitudes and using the technique of 'score-keeping' to derive an objective point of view out of the merging of individual acts of score-keeping sounds in this respect much more Fichtean than it does Hegelian; and it sounds as if it reduces normativity to 'positive' socially enforced rules rather than holding fast, as Hegel does, the irreducible normativity (or what Hegel calls 'absolute negativity') of our practices.

But that clearly is not the last word on the matter. So the question again: Is Hegel a pragmatist? Hegel understood himself to be drawing out the implications of Kant's own reliance on the 'fact of reason' as having to do with the *realization* of our own freedom and with the various interests provoked by the demands of what it would mean to put *that* kind of freedom into practice; if that is part of pragmatism, then it makes sense to speak of Hegel as a pragmatist. If not, then perhaps he is not best described as a pragmatist. But about that interest in freedom, Hegel says: 'This absolute end is a content that gives witness to itself and supports itself, and in which everything of interest to man has its hold' (1994: 29).

---

[23] Hegel formulates his criticism of Fichte's individualism in this way: 'In the first place, the I retains as a result the significance of an individual actual self-consciousness, opposed to universal, absolute self-consciousness, that it, to *spirit*, within which it is itself only a moment; for individual self-consciousness is just this: With regard to an other, it stays put off to the side. If for that reason the I became the absolute essence, the result would be scandalous because in fact the I makes its appearance only in the sense of individual self-consciousness, that is, the subject, opposed to the universal' (Hegel 1971: xx. 408).

BIBLIOGRAPHY

Brandom, Robert (1994) *Making It Explicit: Reasoning, Representing, and Discursive Commitment*. Cambridge, Mass.: Harvard University Press.

—— (1999) 'Some Pragmatist Themes in Hegel's Idealism: Negotiation and Administration in Hegel's Account of the Structure and Content of Norms'. *European Journal of Philosophy*, 7(2): 164–89.

Dewey, John (1948) *Reconstruction in Philosophy*. Boston: Beacon Press.

Haugeland, John (1998) 'Truth and Rule-Following', in John Haugeland, *Having Thought: Essays in the Metaphysics of Mind*, 305–61. Cambridge, Mass.: Harvard University Press.

Hegel, G. W. F. (1975) *Aesthetics: Lectures on Fine Art*, trans. T. M. Knox. Oxford: Clarendon Press.

—— (1977) *The Difference between Fichte's and Schelling's Systems of Philosophy*, trans. H. S. Harris and Walter Cerf. Albany, NY: State University of New York Press.

—— (1980) *Lectures on the Philosophy of World History*, trans. Robert Nisbet. Cambridge: Cambridge University Press.

—— (1971*a*) 'Rechts-, Pflichten-, und Religionslehre für die Unterklasse', in *Werke*, iv, §15, pp. 222–3.

—— (1994) *Vorlesungen über die Philosophie der Weltgeschichte: Band 1: Die Vernunft in der Geschichte*, ed. Johannes Hoffmeister. Hamburg: Felix Meiner Verlag.

—— (1971*b*) *Werke in zwanzig Bänden*, ed. Eva Moldenhauer and Karl Markus Michel. Frankfurt am Main: Suhrkamp Verlag, 1971. Abbreviated as *Werke* and volume number.

—— (1969) *Wissenschaft der Logik*. Hamburg: Felix Meiner, 1971. Trans. as *Science of Logic*, by A. V. Miller. Oxford: Oxford University Press.

Kant, Immanuel (1956) *Critique of Practical Reason*, trans. Lewis White Beck. Indianapolis: Bobbs-Merrill, 1956.

—— (1964*a*) *Critique of Pure Reason*, trans. Norman Kemp Smith. London: Macmillan Co.

—— (1964*b*) *Groundwork of the Metaphysics of Morals*, trans. H. J. Paton. New York: Harper & Row.

Korsgaard, Christine (1996) *The Sources of Normativity*. Cambridge: Cambridge University Press.

Lance, Mark, and O'Leary-Hawthorne, John (1997) *The Grammar of Meaning: Normativity and Semantic Discourse*. Cambridge: Cambridge University Press.

Larmore, Charles (2004) *Les Pratiques du Moi*. Paris: Presse Universitaires de France.

MacIntyre, Alasdair (1999) *Dependent Rational Animals: Why Human Beings Need the Virtues*. Chicago and LaSalle, Ill.: Open Court.

McCumber, John (1993) *The Company of Words: Hegel, Language, and Systematic Philosophy*. Evanston, Ill.: Northwestern University Press.

Neuhouser, Frederick (2003) *Foundations of Hegel's Social Theory: Actualizing Freedom*. Cambridge, Mass.: Harvard University Press.

Pinkard, Terry (1994) *Hegel's Phenomenology: The Sociality of Reason*. Cambridge: Cambridge University Press.

—— (1999) 'Virtues, Morality, and *Sittlichkeit*: From Maxims to Practices'. *European Journal of Philosophy*, 7(2): 217–46.

—— (2000) *Hegel: A Biography*. Cambridge: Cambridge University Press.

—— (2002) *German Philosophy 1760–1860: The Legacy of Idealism*. Cambridge: Cambridge University Press.

—— (2005) 'Speculative *Naturphilosophie* and the Development of the Empirical Sciences: Hegel's Perspective', in Gary Gutting (ed.), *Continental Philosophies of Science*, 17–34. Oxford: Blackwell.

Pippin Robert, (1999) 'Naturalness and Mindedness: Hegel's Compatibilism'. *European Journal of Philosophy*, 7(2): 194–212.

—— (2000) 'The Actualization of Freedom', In Karl Ameriks (ed.), *Cambridge Companion to German Idealism*, 180–99. Cambridge: Cambridge University Press.

—— (2005) 'Brandom's Hegel'. *European Journal of Philosophy*, 13(3): 381–408.

Rorty, Richard (1998) 'Dewey between Hegel and Darwin', In *Philosophical Papers*, iii: *Truth and Progress*, 290–306. Cambridge: Cambridge University Press.

Taylor, Charles (1989) *Sources of the Self: The Making of the Modern Identity*. Cambridge, Mass.: Harvard University Press.

Thompson, Michael (1995)'The Representation of Life'. In Rosalind Hursthouse, Gavin Lawrence, and Warren Quinn (eds.), *Virtues and Reasons: Philippa Foot and Moral Theory*. Oxford: Clarendon Press; New York: Oxford University Press.

Wallace, R. Jay (1999) 'Three Conceptions of Agency'. *Ethical Theory and Moral Practice*, 2: 217–42.

Westbrook, Robert B. (1991) *John Dewey and American Democracy*. Ithaca, NY: Cornell University Press.

Wood, Allen (1990) *Hegel's Ethical Thought*. Cambridge: Cambridge University Press.

8

Pragmatism and Objective Truth

Danielle Macbeth

The pragmatist tradition, both classical and contemporary, is oddly divided on the question of the coherence of a robust conception of objective truth. Whereas both Peirce and Sellars take Peirce's conception of meaning, on which the pragmatist tradition is founded, to make an essential contribution to an adequate account of objective truth, other pragmatists (notably James, Dewey, and Rorty) take that same conception to foreclose once and for all the possibility of such an account. There is, I think, real merit to both these wings of the tradition. My aim is not, however, to defend that claim—at least not directly—but instead to achieve a better understanding of the relationship between Peirce's pragmatist maxim and the notion of objective truth by reflecting on the nature and significance of that maxim.[1]

Peirce's conception of meaning is often put in terms of the thesis that the meaning of a proposition lies in its observable, practical consequences. The formulation is misleading insofar as it suggests that even in, say, mathematics and logic the meaning of a proposition lies in its empirically verifiable consequences. Peirce did think that in some

---

[1] Peirce provides two formulations of the maxim in 'Issues of Pragmaticism' (1905):

Pragmaticism was originally enounced [1878] in the form of a maxim, as follows: Consider what effects, which might conceivably have practical bearings, we conceive the object of our conception to have. Then, our conception of those effects is the whole of our conception of the object.

I will restate this in other words . . . as follows: The entire intellectual purport of any symbol consists in the total of all general modes of rational conduct which, conditionally upon all the possible different circumstances and desires, would ensue upon the acceptance of the symbol. (*EP* ii. 246).

In various places Peirce also endorses another, more multi-faceted, conception of the meaning of a term, one that includes also the objects to which the term is correctly applied and something like a definition (see Misak 2004: 12–16). For reasons that will become apparent, I do not think that this broader notion represents his best wisdom.

important sense mathematics and logic are experimental sciences; but he did not think that they are empirical sciences in the sense that physics, for example, is an empirical science. The pragmatist maxim is at once more subtle and more interesting than this standard formulation might suggest. It will help in our explication of it to restrict our attention, at least at first, to the case of mathematics, the case that provides, for Peirce, the paradigm of the insight embodied in his principle.

In his 1871 review of Fraser's edition of Berkeley's works, Peirce argues that the empiricist conception of the meaning of mathematical concepts in terms of our sensory experience of things must be rejected. Were Berkeley, or any other empiricist, right in holding that all our conceptions are mere reproductions of sensations and so themselves images—whether visual, aural, gustatory, tactile, or olfactory—it would be unintelligible that we might come to grasp many familiar concepts in mathematics, concepts such as those of 'negative quantities, the square root of *minus*, and infinitesimals . . . on the grounds that we can form no idea of such things' (*EP* i. 102). We can have no sensory experience of such entities, and yet, it would seem, we can understand such things, an understanding that is demonstrated in our consistent and fruitful employment of such concepts in actual mathematical practice. As Peirce argues, a difference—such as that between concepts instances of which can be given in sensory experience and concepts instances of which cannot—that makes no difference in practice, is (as James would put it) no difference at all. Peirce writes:

Do things fulfill the same function practically? Then let them be signified by the same word. Do they not? Then let them be distinguished. If I have learned a formula in gibberish which in any way jogs my memory so as to enable me in each single case to act as though I had a general idea, what possible utility is there in distinguishing between such gibberish and a formula and an idea? Why use the term *a general idea* in such a sense as to separate things which, for all experiential purposes, are the same? (*EP* i. 102)

Though we have sensible symbols for them in the language of mathematics, we can form no sensible image either of negative or of irrational or of complex numbers, and yet we use the signs for such numbers in consistent and fruitful ways, both in mathematics and in the other exact sciences. What practical reason, then, is there to deny that we have the relevant concepts?

Interestingly enough, Frege, who could hardly be described as a pragmatist, would emphasize exactly this point just over a decade later in his *Grundlagen der Arithmetik* (1884).[2] Taking as one of the three guiding principles of that work the principle 'never to ask for the meaning of a word in isolation, but only in the context of a proposition', Frege argues (1980: p. x) that contravening that principle leads one ineluctably 'to take as the meanings of words mental pictures or acts of the individual mind', and thereby to collapse the distinction between the psychological and the logical. As he argues later in the work (§. 60), 'that we can form no idea of its content is . . . no reason for denying all meaning to a word, or for excluding it from our vocabulary', and it is not a reason because 'time and time again we are led by our thought beyond the scope of our imagination, without thereby forfeiting the support we need for our inferences'. An illustrative example is provided in §. 104:

Have we really no right to speak of $1000^{1000^{1000}}$ until such time as that many objects have been given to us in intuition? Is it, till then, an empty symbol? Not at all. It has a perfectly definite sense . . . To convince ourselves of this, we have only to show, introducing the symbol a^n for the nth power of a, that for positive integral a and n this expression always refers to one and only one positive whole number.

We know how to use the sign '$1000^{1000^{1000}}$', how to 'go on' with it in actual mathematical practice. That we can form no sensory intuition of that many things is simply irrelevant to the question of the meaning of such a sign. And the same holds for other mathematical concepts that cannot be exhibited in any intuition.

There is no practical distinction to be drawn in mathematics between concepts (such as that of a sphere, or that of three things in a collection) that can be exhibited in sensory intuition and concepts (such as that of a negative or complex number, or of a number so large that a collection that size could never be met with in sensory experience) that cannot be so exhibited. The next step is to recognize that intuition more generally conceived so as to include pure, or a priori, as well as empirical intuition must also be banished from our account of the contents of mathematical concepts and thereby from our account of the truth of mathematical judgments. The a priori method, whether in its Cartesian or its Kantian guise, is, as Peirce put it in the 1877 essay 'The Fixation of Belief', in essence 'to think as one is inclined to think' (*EP*

---

[2] A useful discussion of Frege's 'pragmatic rationalism' is to be found in Burge 2005. See also the Introduction to that collection.

i. 121). It is, then, no more likely than, say, the method of authority to yield true beliefs. Though Kant and his followers had assumed that fundamental mathematical concepts are clearly known in virtue of their constructibility in pure intuition, in reality (as developments in mathematics early in the nineteenth century, especially in higher analysis, had made abundantly clearly), many fundamental concepts in mathematics are not well understood at all. As Peirce (as well as, for instance, Bolzano[3]) argues, what is needed in place of the a priori method in mathematics is a postulational or conjectural method according to which one proposes, hypothetically, that things are thus and so in order to derive consequences. The constituents of mathematical concepts are to be conjectured rather than discovered a priori, and an account of such concepts is shown to be adequate not by its intuitive appeal but by its fruitfulness in mathematical practice.

According to Peirce's pragmatist maxim, the meaning of a mathematical concept is to be understood not directly in terms of what is the case if an application of it is correct but instead in terms of what follows from its application, in terms of its consequences in actual mathematical practice. Peirce holds that the same maxim applies also in logic, and again it is worth noting that, contrary to what is often supposed, Frege concurs. According to Frege, we do not know the basic truths of logic indubitably or a priori, but only by following out their consequences. As Frege put the point in the Introduction to *Grundgesetze*, the test of his 'logical convictions' as made explicit in the basic laws of his system lies not in their apparent obviousness to us but instead in their consequences—that is, in the theorems that may be derived from them according to the rules he has laid out; those logical convictions can be refuted only by 'someone's actually demonstrating either that a better, more durable edifice can be erected upon other fundamental convictions, or else that my principles lead to manifestly false conclusions' (1964: 25). As van Heijenoort notes, on Frege's view of logic,

the only question of completeness [and, we can add, consistency] that arises is, to use an expression of Herbrand's, an *experimental* question. As many theorems as possible are derived in the system. Can we exhaust the intuitive modes of reasoning actually used in science?... The two volumes of *Grundgesetze der Arithmetik*... can be regarded as a step in an ever renewed attempt at establishing completeness [and consistency] experimentally. (1967: 327)

[3] See Rusnock 1997.

The test of the truth of one's axioms lies not in whether they seem on the face of it to be true, but in their consequences. It is for just this reason that belief in mathematics and logic is inherently provisional: 'it not only corrects its conclusions, it even corrects its premises' (*RLT* 165).[4]

The pragmatist principle as it applies to concepts in the exact sciences—that is, to concepts in mathematics, logic, and natural sciences such as physics, the concepts of which are one and all mathematically formulable—is that the content of a claim is to be understood not directly in terms of what is the case if it is true (as if we had some special insight into the meaning and truth of such judgments), but indirectly in terms of what follows if it is true. On this view, the only way to assess the truth of the fundamental laws of some science (be it logic, or mathematics, or any other of the exact sciences) is 'experimentally', by deriving theorems. Because (on this view) the meaning of a concept is exhausted by its consequences, by the inferences permitted by an application of it, it follows that such a concept is, as the point might be put, wholly within the purview of the faculty of spontaneity. Quite simply, if concepts are wholly constituted by their inferential relations one to another (as codified, ideally, in a fully axiomatized system), then because all such inferential relations can be refashioned as reason sees fit, it follows that *anything* we think in regard to such concepts can in principle be called into question. No matter how intuitive some inferential relation may seem at some particular point in our intellectual history—to take two familiar examples, that it follows directly from the concept of a number that a greater number cannot be subtracted from a lesser, or that the continuity of a function entails its differentiability—we can nonetheless come to have good reason to think that it fails to hold.

It is worth emphasizing that Frege takes this to be true as well, and that he does so even in logic. As he points out, again in the Introduction to *Grundgesetze*, although we ourselves have no reason to doubt a law of logic such as, say, the law of identity, that $a = a$, although we now, in the particular historical circumstances in which we find ourselves, cannot imagine in the least how such a law could be false, we can nevertheless imagine beings who do doubt it—which just is to say that we can imagine ourselves one day having grounds for doubting the

---

[4] Russell's derivation of a contradiction from Frege's basic laws in *Grundgesetze* is an obvious example of the point. We assume that a logically adequate concept invariably determines an extension or, as Frege would put it, a course of values; but, as Russell's paradox shows, it turns out that we were wrong: that assumption leads to a contradiction. For further discussion of the point see Macbeth 2005, ch. 5.

law of identity (as formulated). As Frege says, 'this impossibility of our rejecting the law in question hinders us not at all in supposing beings who do reject it; where it hinders us is in supposing that these beings are right in so doing, it hinders us in having doubts whether we or they are right' (1964: 15).[5] We think that we *know* that the law of identity as expressed in the sign design '$a = a$' of our symbolic language is true. The insight embodied in the pragmatist principle of meaning is that what we in fact know is only that we (here and now) have absolutely no reason to doubt it. We should for that very reason adopt this law in our practice. (We must begin where we are.) But it would contravene what Peirce thinks of as the first—and in a sense, the only—rule of reason to take this law to be *known* to be true, now and for all time to come. The road of inquiry must not be blocked by *any* 'absolute assertion', neither by an absolute assertion to the effect that things are and must be thus-and-so, nor by an assertion to the effect that something cannot be known, nor by the assertion of some element of a science that it is 'basic, ultimate, independent of aught else, and utterly inexplicable', nor, finally, by the assertion 'that this or that law or truth has found its last and perfect formulation'.[6] Of course we must start our inquiry where we are, with whatever seems, at least for the time being, to be true. It is nonetheless a 'venomous error', Peirce thinks, to fantasize that some at least of what we think we know and understand is immune to criticism in principle.

Although we have focused to this point on mathematical and logical concepts, it is clear that both Peirce and Sellars take the pragmatist insight to be an insight into the meaning of any and all concepts, and not merely logical and mathematical ones. Peirce writes, for instance, in a very familiar passage in 'How to Make our Ideas Clear', that 'our idea of anything *is* our idea of its sensible effects; and if we fancy that we have any other we deceive ourselves, and mistake a mere sensation accompanying the thought for a part of the thought itself... Consider what effects, which might conceivably have practical bearings, we conceive the object of our conception to have. Then, our conception of these effects is the whole of our conception of the object' (*EP* i. 132).[7]

---

[5] Because Frege clearly takes the question whether we or they are right to be a good one, he is not (as he is sometimes taken to be) imagining here a 'hitherto unknown sort of madness' of the kind he discusses in the preceding paragraph.

[6] These are the four common forms of the fundamental mistake that metaphysicians tend to make, according to Peirce. See *RLT* 179–80.

[7] It is perhaps this thought, that the pragmatist principle applies not only to mathematical and logical concepts but to all other sorts of concepts as well, that explains

On Peirce's view, there is no content to any thought that is not subject to the pragmatic maxim; the whole content of every cognition is to be understood in terms of its observable consequences. The cognition itself, in other words, is purely hypothetical in Peirce's sense. We have no power immediately to apprehend an object; every cognition is always already determined by previous cognitions.[8] What then of cognitions of, say, sensory qualities such as red that seem not to be exhausted by their (observable) consequences but immediately to present a particular phenomenal quality? Peirce recognizes that perceptual experiences can have this character, but denies that it has anything to do with cognition: 'that character is not a character of red as a cognition' (*EP* i. 26). It cannot be, he thinks, because this sensory character can be known only by beings like us endowed with the relevant sensory modalities.

> The matter of sensation is altogether accidental; precisely the same information, practically, being capable of communication through different senses. And the catholic consent which constitutes the truth is by no means to be limited to men in this earthly life or to the human race, but extends to the whole communion of minds to which we belong, including some probably whose senses are very different from ours, so that in that consent no predication of a sensible quality can enter, except as an admission that so certain sorts of senses are affected. (*EP* i. 90)

Sellars takes essentially the same view. Although there may seem to be a fundamental difference between concepts such as that of a complex number (not Sellars's example) the conceptual meaning of which is, as Sellars puts it in 'Inference and Meaning', 'entirely constituted by their "logical grammar", that is, by the fact that they are used in accordance with certain syntactical rules', and concepts such as *red* the conceptual meaning of which seems to involve also the way red things look in normal circumstances, in fact there is no such difference. In all cases,

> material transformation rules determine the descriptive meaning of the expressions of a language within the framework established by its logical transformation rules . . . The familiar notion (Kantian in its origin, but present in various disguises in many contemporary systems) that the form of a concept is determined by 'logical rules' while the content is 'derived from experience' embodies a

the fact that Peirce sometimes claims that meaning has not one but three aspects, that it includes also the extension and intension (i.e. connotation or definition) of a term. It will be suggested below that the meanings of terms for e.g. sensory qualities do involve, in a distinctive way, the objects to which the terms are correctly applied.

[8] See EP i. 11–27.

radical misunderstanding of the manner in which the 'manifold of sense' contributes to the shaping of the conceptual apparatus 'applied' to the manifold in the process of cognition. The contribution does not consist in providing plums for Jack Horner. There is nothing to a conceptual apparatus that isn't determined by its rules. (Sellars 1953: 336–7)

Sellars, like Peirce, does think that *somehow* sensory experience must guide empirical judgment. But he also thinks, following Peirce, that there is nothing to a concept, any concept, that is not captured by the pragmatist principle of meaning. As the point might be put, all experience, even the most basic perceptual experience of something as (say) red, is ineluctably and thoroughly theory-laden. It follows, according to Sellars, that the theory/observation distinction itself is merely methodological, a matter of what people can as a matter of fact be trained reliably to respond to. On Sellars's view, though it is obvious 'that at least some of the descriptive predicates of a language must be learned responses to extra-linguistic objects in order for the language to be *applied* . . . not even these predicates ("observation predicates") owe their conceptual meaning to this association' (1953: 334). What we learned with the rise of modern science, then, is that one theory, our everyday sensory understanding of things, is to be replaced, superseded, by another, the scientific world view. And it can be so replaced because the view of things embodied in our everyday understanding is no less theoretical or 'mathematical' (that is, pragmatist) than our most sophisticated theories in physics.

Both Peirce and Sellars take the pragmatist principle to be not merely an insight into the mathematical concepts characteristic of the exact sciences but an insight into meaning in general. Indeed, they seem to think that it is obvious that the principle should be extended in this way, obvious that if we have learned anything in the last 300 years, we have learned that nature is correctly described not in sensory terms but instead in mathematical terms and, correlatively, that all our awareness of things is conceptually mediated. To recognize that the Given is a myth *just is* (on this view) to recognize that there is and can be no content to (any of) our concepts that is not a matter of their (practical) consequences. If that is true, we will see, it is very hard to understand how we might avoid the anti-realist conclusion of pragmatists such as James, Dewey, and Rorty: the conclusion that there is and can be no notion of truth independent of our interests.

Consider, first, a mathematical judgment—for instance, the judgment that the square root of two is irrational (that is, that it cannot be expressed as a ratio, m/n, of whole numbers m and n). On a robust conception of mathematical truth, this judgment is true just in case the number designated by the expression '$\sqrt{2}$' of the formula language of arithmetic has the property of being irrational. According to standard mathematical practice, we can show that this is true by the following chain of reasoning thought to be due to the Pythagorean Hippasus.

Suppose that there were whole numbers m and n such that $\sqrt{2} = m/n$, where m and n have no common factors not already cancelled out. It follows by simple arithmetic that $2 = m^2/n^2$, and so that $2n^2 = m^2$. The number m^2 must, then, be an even number; so m must be even as well. Hence, there is some whole number p such that $2p = m$. Substituting identicals for identicals yields $2n^2 = (2p)^2$ which simplifies to $n^2 = 2p^2$. So n^2, and hence n itself, must be even. But if m and n are both even (as has been shown), they must have a common factor, which contradicts our original supposition. There cannot, then, be whole numbers m and n such that $m/n = \sqrt{2}$; the square root of two is irrational.

Such a proof seems clearly to provide mathematical knowledge. It does so, however, only if we have knowledge of the fundamental mathematical principles on which the proof depends. Since those fundamental principles cannot themselves be proved, on pain of a vicious regress, there would seem to be just two options: either we do know those fundamental principles, in which case our cognitive access to them is different in kind from our access, by way of reasoning, to theorems proved on the basis of them; or we do not, properly speaking, know those fundamental principles, in which case our mathematical knowledge is better conceived as conditional, of the form 'if such and such fundamental principles are true, then various theorems, such as that the square root of two is irrational, are true as well'. Neither option, Benacerraf (1983) has argued, is fully satisfactory.

According to the first option, we do know the fundamental mathematical principles with which our chain of reasoning begins, so can also be correctly described as knowing that, say, the square root of 2 is irrational. The problem is to clarify how we know those principles, given that it is neither by way of proof (as we have seen) nor, given the non-empirical character of the science of mathematics, by way of empirical investigation. To say that our cognitive access to such truths is by way of a special faculty of mathematical intuition (as, for instance, Gödel does) might seem to help, but only if more could be said about how exactly such a faculty affords us cognitive access to the objects of mathematical knowledge. In fact, as we have already seen, to appeal to mathematical intuition is, in essence, 'to think as one is inclined to think' (*EP* i. 121).

The second option is to suppose that mathematical knowledge, insofar as it is knowledge at all, properly speaking, is conditional in form, since all we can know on the basis of the sort of reasoning characteristic of mathematical practice is that a proven theorem is true if the fundamental principles providing the premises of the proof are true. The views that Benacerraf describes in 'Mathematical Truth' (1983) as 'combinatorial' all pursue essentially this strategy. According to it, we deem a mathematical judgment 'true' just in case it is provable on the basis of some privileged set of principles. The problem for the strategy is that (by its own lights) it can give no account of the truth of those principles, and so provides us no reason to take this use of 'true' to have any connection at all with the concept of truth. As Benacerraf puts the point,

> motivated by epistemological considerations, they [i.e. 'combinatorial' accounts] come up with truth conditions whose satisfaction or nonsatisfaction mere mortals can ascertain but the price they pay is their inability to connect those so-called 'truth conditions' with the truth of the propositions for which they are conditions. (1983: 419)

If mathematical truth is understood in terms of provability in some system of fundamental principles, it ceases to be recognizable as a conception of truth.

Pragmatists such as James, Dewey, and Rorty think that a similar sort of argument can be made for the case of empirical inquiry, since in this case too, they argue, nothing can be given as the firm foundation on which to ground our beliefs. As Rorty has put the point, 'if our awareness of things is always a linguistic affair, if Sellars is right that we cannot check our language against our non-linguistic awareness, then philosophy can never be anything more than a discussion of the utility and compatibility of beliefs—and, more particularly, of the various vocabularies in which those beliefs are formulated' (1998: 127). On Rorty's view, Sellars's psychological nominalism 'according to which *all* awareness of *sorts, resemblances, facts,* etc., in short all awareness of abstract entities—indeed, all awareness even of particulars—is a linguistic affair' (Sellars 1996: § 29), leads directly to anti-realism about truth. The argument is simple: either thought is ostensively tied to (and so directly constrained by) the reality on which it aims to bear, or there is no content to the notion of objective truth; but as both Peirce and Sellars hold, the first disjunct is false (because it contravenes the pragmatist maxim), and therefore the second disjunct is true: there is no content to the notion of objective truth. What could be simpler? Yet neither Peirce nor Sellars accepts the conclusion. Because they do reject the first disjunct, that thought is directly constrained by reality, they must, then, reject the disjunction, the either/or. This is just what they do. What they take to be the lesson of the rejection of any given foundation for knowledge is not that there is therefore no coherent notion of objective truth, but instead the more radical thought that there is therefore no *need* for any foundation in a coherent picture of objective truth. The static foundationalist picture in play in the arguments just rehearsed is to be replaced by one that is dynamic, evolutionary, and non-foundationalist, one in which the key notion is that of self-correction. As Sellars says in 'Empiricism and the Philosophy of Mind' (§38), although 'there is clearly *some* point to the picture of human knowledge as resting on a level of propositions—observation reports—which do not rest on other propositions in the same way as other propositions rest on them', this 'metaphor of "foundations" is misleading', and it is misleading '*above all* . . . because of its static character'.

One seems forced to choose [as we saw above] between the picture of an elephant which rests on a tortoise (What supports the tortoise?) and the picture of a great Hegelian serpent of knowledge with its tail in its mouth (Where does it begin?). Neither will do. For empirical knowledge, like its sophisticated extension, science, is rational, not because it has a *foundation* but because it is a self-correcting enterprise which can put *any* claim in jeopardy, though not *all* at once.

But how might a science correct itself, rather than merely change, if all our awareness is postulation? A robust notion of objective truth would seem to require that thought is answerable to things as they are, and this requires in turn that things as they are exert a rational constraint on thinking. But how can there be such constraint if thought is not internally—that is, constitutively—related to things as they are, if there is no 'ostensive tie' between our thought and the reality on which it aims to bear? Though I will not try to defend the claim here, neither Peirce nor Sellars is able to provide a compelling answer.[9] What I will try to do is to pinpoint where I think they go wrong and to outline an alternative based on that diagnosis.

---

[9] See Macbeth 2000 for a discussion of some of the limitations of Sellars's account.

We begin with an idea defended by McDowell in *Mind and World*, that some of our deepest philosophical perplexities are due to our failure properly to understand the lessons of modern science. As McDowell explains the point, 'the modern scientific revolution made possible a newly clear conception of the distinctive kind of intelligibility that the natural sciences allow us to find in things . . . We must sharply distinguish natural-scientific intelligibility from the intelligibility something acquires when we situate it in the logical space of reasons.' But, as he goes on, 'we need not identify the dichotomy of logical spaces with a dichotomy between the *natural* and the normative. We need not equate the very idea of nature with the idea of instantiations of concepts that belong in the logical space—admittedly separate, on this view, from the logical space of reasons—in which the natural-scientific kind of intelligibility is brought to light' (1996: p. xix). Our mistake, McDowell thinks, is to take the scientist's conception of nature in terms of mathematically expressible laws as the whole truth about nature, as, in effect, replacing the pre-modern view of things. What I want to suggest by way of a diagnosis here is a variation on just this theme: that the mistake of pragmatists is to assume that the pragmatist conception of meaning can, and should, be taken to replace—to supplant rather than merely to supplement—a prior and more primitive conception. Though, as we will see, Peirce's maxim does articulate a fundamental insight into the nature of (modern) mathematical concepts, and thereby into a robust conception of objective truth, it is no more an insight into meaning (and truth) *überhaupt* than on McDowell's view the (modern) scientist's insight is an insight into nature *überhaupt*. Our capacity to form the sorts of concepts that fall within the purview of the pragmatist maxim is essentially late, and although that capacity does operate freely within its own sphere, it is nonetheless intelligible only as a modification of a more primitive capacity to form concepts that cannot be comprehended by appeal to Peirce's pragmatist maxim.

I have suggested that we need to distinguish between two essentially different sorts of concepts. Modern mathematical concepts as they came explicitly to be understood by, for instance, Peirce and Frege are a paradigm of one sort of concept, the sort to which the pragmatist maxim obviously can be applied. The content of such a concept is exhausted by its consequences, by what follows from its application, either immediately or together with the application of other concepts in the theory relative to which the concept first acquires its meaning. A paradigm of the second sort of concept is that of a sensory quality such as red, the content of which is not exhausted by its inference potential but includes also reference to how red things look in suitable circumstances to appropriately placed perceivers of the relevant sort. As McDowell puts the point, the concept of such a sensory quality 'cannot be understood in abstraction from the subjective character of experience. What it is for something to be red, say, is not intelligible unless packaged with an understanding of what it is for something to look red' (1996: 29). Clearly, then, someone lacking the relevant sensory capacities (for example, someone blind from birth in the case of a quality such as red) could not acquire a concept of this sort. Now the pragmatist will deny that there are any such concepts. He may, as for instance Rorty does, take this denial (as it makes its appearance in Sellars's 'Empiricism and the Philosophy of Mind' (1996)) to be 'pretty much the last word philosophers ever need to utter about perception' (Rorty 2000*a*: 126). But even Rorty recognizes that such an attitude must be treated with care. As he himself says in another context, 'to say "I'll try to defend this against all comers" is often, depending on the circumstances, a commendable attitude. But to say "I can successfully defend this against all comers" is silly. Maybe you can, but you are no more in a position to claim that you can than the village champion is to claim that he can beat the world champion' (2000*b*: 6). To think otherwise is just the venomous error Peirce finds in the writings of many metaphysicians. We must ask, then, whether the pragmatist maxim applies across the board to all our concepts, as pragmatists assume, or whether it instead applies only to distinctively mathematical concepts—that is, to mathematical concepts as they first came to be understood in the seventeenth century.

The pragmatist assumes that the consequentialist conception of meaning, which seems clearly applicable to the case of mathematical concepts and even (though perhaps less obviously) to the case of logical concepts, applies to all concepts. Even a concept of a sensory quality such as red is to be understood solely in terms of its inference potential, in terms of what follows from its application. Any and all concepts the content of which might seem to involve not merely inference potential but also how various objects appear to creatures like us (concepts such as that of red, say) are to be completely purged of non-inferential content. But why exactly? What reason is there for this surprising move? The answer implicit in pragmatist writings seems to be that because nature is, as we have learned, the realm of law, and correlatively, the Given a myth, it follows that although it might seem that we have sensory as well as mathematical concepts (in the broad sense intended here), what we have learned with the rise of modern science and modern philosophy is that there are and can be no such concepts. But how exactly is this inference to go?

Peirce argues, we have seen, that mathematical concepts cannot be understood on the model of sensory concepts; they cannot be taken to derive any of their content from experience, whether from sensory intuition, as the empiricist thinks, or from pure intuition, as the Cartesian or Kantian thinks. The contents of mathematical concepts are exhausted by their inference potential as articulated (ideally) in a theory, an axiomatic system setting out their inferential relations one to another. But we have also seen that Peirce also thinks that this is true of any concept, that *concepts* are inherently mathematical (in our sense). It is hard to see on the basis of the pragmatist insight into mathematical concepts alone why we should think this. If we consider *only* the pragmatist insight as it is an insight into (modern) mathematical concepts, it is perfectly coherent to suppose that we have and deploy both sorts of concepts, both those in terms of which the world shows up in our experience of it and those we have learned to deploy in modern mathematics and modern science. But if that is right, then the pragmatist principle does not in and of itself show that all concepts are mathematical in our sense, their contents exhausted by their consequences. Indeed, if the notion of a concept constitutively involves the notion of truth, of how things are independent of how they seem to one to be, then it begins to seem that the pragmatist principle could not possibly be an insight into concepts *überhaupt*; for what it would seem to show in that case (as the work of pragmatists such as James, Dewey, and Rorty makes clear) is that there are no concepts answerable to the norm of truth at all.

The pragmatist principle taken alone does not seem to show that all concepts are to be understood solely in terms of their consequences. Do the findings of modern science show this? What the findings of modern science show is that, conceived independent of any particular sensory perspective on it, the world is correctly described in mathematical terms. From the perspective of science, the world is the realm of law, and as we will see, there is a perfectly intelligible sense in which that perspective is privileged, that it reveals things as they are, as contrasted with things as they appear from this or that essentially sensory perspective. But that is consistent with claiming that our sensory perspective provides us nonetheless with *a* view of the world, not a view of it as it is in itself, the same for all rational beings, but a view of it nonetheless. It is manifest that were we to have very different sensory modalities from those we in fact have, we would have a very different (sensory) view of things; the world would in that case show up for us in radically different (and, for us here and now, literally unimaginable) ways. But it does not follow from that manifest truth that our 'view' is not really any sort of a view at all. What needs to be shown is that, given that things as they are, are mathematically described, it follows that sensory experience is not *experience* of things at all. We do not claim that nature conceived as the realm of law can somehow figure in our experience of it. That, as the pragmatist sees, would be incoherent. As mathematically understood, the world is not an object of experience but instead an object of thought. But again, it does not follow from this fact that our sensory experience is not revelatory of the world as it appears to creatures like us. We did learn, with the rise of modern science, to distinguish between the world as it appears to us and that same world as it is in itself, the same for all rational beings, but (so it would seem) we could learn that only because our experience provides *a* view of the world. The perspective of the scientist, the view from nowhere, would not be a view at all were it not grounded in the view from here as its evidential base. Modern science posits how things are *based on how they appear to us*; and if things do not in fact *appear* to us, show up in our experience, then it is incoherent to claim that science is an investigation into how things are. The findings of modern science cannot show that our everyday view of things is not really any kind of a view at all.

That mathematical concepts do not derive any of their content from sensory experience does not show that even sensory concepts have no content that is not inferential. That nature as it comes into view in modern science is exhaustively described in mathematical terms does not entail that our everyday sensory perspective is not actually a perspective on the world at all. What, then, of the Myth of the Given? Does the fact that the Given is a myth show that all concepts are to be understood solely in terms of their consequences in practice? According to McDowell, what the critique of the Given shows is only that all awareness is inferentially articulated and essentially learned. If McDowell is right, and it will be argued below that he is, that the Given is a myth cannot by itself reveal the incoherence of the idea that some at least of our concepts constitutively involve reference to how things in fact show up for us in our experience. Again, were nature merely the realm of law, then the idea of such concepts would be incoherent. And again, were it constitutive of something's being a concept at all that it be exhaustively characterized by its inference potential, then it would follow that no concept could be inherently sensory—that is, unintelligible in abstraction from the subjective character of experience. But we have seen that neither counterfactual condition is met. If it is to ground the pragmatist's assumption that all concepts are to be understood on the model of mathematical concepts, the insight that the Given is a myth must do so on its own merits, and that, it will be argued, it cannot do. All that the critique of the Given can show is that our sensory view of things is, as McDowell has taught us to think of it, second-natural, an essentially acquired, essentially holistic, view.

Although (as we will see) the view from nowhere is privileged as the view of things as they are anyway, the same for all rational beings, it does not follow that our everyday sensory perspective is not also a view of the world. Indeed, it would seem to be clearly incoherent to suppose that the view from nowhere is the only view we enjoy of the world; taken on its own, we have seen, the view from nowhere is not intelligible as a view of anything. If we can achieve the perspective of modern science, we can do so only because we have already a perspective on the world in our sensory experience of it. If, on the other hand, all we had or could in principle achieve was the view from here, if we were somehow constitutively incapable of achieving the perspective of modern science, incapable of grasping modern mathematical concepts, then it would be wrong, I think, to describe that 'view' (that is, the 'view from here') as a view of the world. For in that case, experience could not be understood to be revelatory of things as they are. Experience is revelatory (whether directly, or indirectly by way of providing the data for our theories to explain) of things as they are because it serves (more exactly, can come to serve, has the potential to serve) as the evidential basis for our scientific theories. The ancient view of the world is correctly described as a view of the world for just that reason. Nor does it seem to be merely a fortuitous accident that we can achieve the modern view, as if there could be creatures otherwise just like our ancestors who could not achieve the perspective of modern science. The view from here—that is, from the perspective afforded to us by our biological and cultural inheritance—is inherently unstable as a view of the world, and it is unstable because it is not fully intelligible on its own terms. That we experience the world as we do is a kind of accident of nature and of culture; there is, and can be, no reason to think that the world as it is in itself, the same for all rational beings, should be just as we experience it to be. Reason demands, then, that we do not rest with the view from here, that we learn to form new sorts of concepts, mathematical concepts that are fully intelligible—that is, the same for all rational beings. And we can learn to do this because, as we will see in more detail below, even our everyday awareness is, and must be, inferentially articulated. Having an everyday view of things—in our case, a view that we share in all essentials with all human beings whether ancient or modern—is not only necessary but sufficient for achieving the modern scientific view.

McDowell argues that the Myth of the Given shows not that there is no content to a concept that is not a matter of its inferential relations to other concepts but only that awareness of the sort we enjoy, self-conscious awareness as it contrasts with the merely conscious awareness of mere animals, is essentially second-natural—that is, acquired in the course of our acculturation. Much as an ethical upbringing opens one's eyes to the justice or injustice of an action, to courage as a virtue of character, and so on, so, more generally, an upbringing opens one's eyes to the color, feel, shape, and so on, of things. One acquires the capacity to *see* that, say, grass is green and snow white; one becomes capable of taking in manifest facts. Will it be objected that grass is not *really* green, that where we think we see something green there is really only some physical object reflecting wave/particles of light? We have already seen that such an objection has no independent motivation. *As green* is exactly how grass shows up for creatures like us; that *is* how grass appears to us, how grass *is* in our sensory experience of it. That grass would not be so characterized from the scientist's perspective must not be taken to imply that we do not, in everyday experience, take in, *see*, the color of grass.

In the course of one's acculturation, on McDowell's view, one acquires a view of the world, and thereby the capacity to take a stand on how things are—that is, the capacity to judge that things are thus-and-so. It is essential, on this account, both that the view *be* a view of the world (and not merely of a part of it as it shows up in this or that circumstance) and that it be a view that is acquired in the course of one's upbringing. The first requirement can be clarified by way of a contrast between our experience of the world and a mere animal's responsiveness to its immediate environment. Mere animals do not act for reasons, but nor can their behavior be understood as merely lawful; an animal can respond to its environment not merely mechanically but intelligently. An animal can learn, for instance, how to get around in some reasonably large portion of the terrain; it can come to know various paths through it, how to get from one landmark to another. What a mere animal does

not do is synthesize the information implicitly contained in the totality
of paths it is able to traverse into a unified whole as if seen, as we say,
from a bird's-eye view. We do exactly that. We come to have a view of
the whole—that is, of the relative locations of all the various landmarks
with which we are familiar; and it is precisely because we come to such
a view that we can be said to have a view of the world at all. A mature
human being, by contrast with a mere animal, 'conceives the present
environment as the region of the world within one's present sensory
and practical reach: as where one happens to be, in contrast with other
places one might be' (McDowell 1996: 118–19). And having in this
way a view of the world, rather than merely perceptual sensitivity to
the environment in which one finds oneself, is essential to knowing,
because only someone with such a view can entertain the possibility that
things may not be as they appear to be in one's current circumstances. It
may look to me, here and now, as though one landmark is further away
than another, but I may nonetheless know in light of my conception of
the layout of the land as a whole that this is merely an appearance. As
McDowell puts the point for the case of our capacity to see colors, as
that capacity contrasts with the perceptual sensitivity of a mere animal,

no subject could be recognized as having experiences of colour except against
a background understanding that makes it possible for judgements endorsing
such experiences to fit into her view of the world. She must be equipped
with such things as the concept of visible surfaces of objects, and the concept
of suitable conditions for telling what something's colour is by looking at it.
(1996: 30)

Perceptual sensitivity is a necessary condition of having a view of the
world, but it is not sufficient. One needs also a conception of the
whole, spatially, of the locations of things each relative to all the other,
and more generally, of the inferential relations, the putatively rational
linkages among concepts that are constitutive of our view of the whole.
As McDowell emphasizes, 'natural language, the sort of language into
which human beings are first initiated, serves as a repository of tradition,
a store of historically accumulated wisdom about what is a reason for
what' (1996: 126). Because it provides in this way a view of how each
thing hangs together with everything else, natural language embodies
a view of the world. And to acquire such a language is to acquire a
view of the world, as it were, a bird's-eye view relative to which one
can distinguish at least in principle between things as they appear to
one here and now and things as they are. That such a view must be

acquired—that is, be second-natural rather than something one might be born with—follows directly from the fact that only so could one be capable of second thoughts. Because (and insofar as) the habits of thought of a mature human being are just that, habits, they can be refashioned as reason dictates. Such a critically reflective capacity for self-correction would be unintelligible if our view of the whole were (somehow) a natural (as opposed to cultural) endowment. A view of the whole such as we enjoy is the essentially acquired, essentially late, culmination of our piecemeal acquisition of this and that path through the world.

But, although having the world in view in this way is an actualization of ourselves as knowers, it is in another way merely a potential, a potential that was fully realized only with the rise of modern science, and in particular with our newly founded capacity for properly mathematical thought. Of course the ancients did have mathematics, but their mathematical concepts were essentially sensory; they were not mathematical in our sense—that is, wholly constituted by their inference potential.[10] Whereas the proper sensibles (that is, sensory properties such as colors, tastes, sounds, and so on) are perceptible only by one sense modality, what Aristotle thinks of as the commonsensibles (that is, 'mathematical' properties such as shape and number) are distinctive in being perceptible by more than one sense modality. A commonsensible such as (say) the property of being spherical is no more intelligible independent of an understanding of what it is for something to look and feel spherical, on Aristotle's view, than a proper sensible such as red is intelligible independent of what it is for something to look red. Just as the color red is to be understood, at least in part, in terms of its characteristic look (to normal perceivers in standard circumstances), so a shape such as a sphere or a number such as seven (that is, a collection of units) is to be understood in terms of its characteristic look and feel. On the ancient conception, 'mathematical' properties such as shape and number are to be understood on the model of sensory qualities such as red. Though the ancients had achieved what we have described as a bird's-eye view of the world, they did not yet have the view characteristic of modern mathematical science. What such a view involves can be illustrated by appeal, again, to the concept of space.

---

[10] This may seem surprising. If it does, that is due to our deplorable tendency to read our modern mathematical understanding back into pre-modern texts. Jacob Klein (1968) provides a first step towards correcting this tendency.

Though we cannot in any single perceptual experience of it take in the whole layout of some large expanse of land, we nonetheless can acquire a view of the whole, a view that can be exhibited in a map showing the relative locations of things as if seen from above. Space, on this conception, is understood 'bottom-up': one begins with objects, landmarks given in one's perceptual experience, and one learns to conceive the relevant layout of the land as an integrated whole, each of the landmarks located relative to all the others. What is depicted in a map so conceived is the relative locations of objects as if seen from above. Such a conception, I have suggested, is essentially pre-modern. But, given such a conception, the modern conception can be achieved through a radical and thoroughgoing transformation, a kind of gestalt shift the upshot of which is that we learn to conceive the map not as a bird's-eye view of things—that is, bottom-up—but instead top-down, as a presentation of space abstractly conceived as an antecedently given and essentially unitary whole within which landmarks are directly located, each independent of all the others. Instead of beginning with objects in their relative locations, one now begins with the whole of space itself laid out like a grid within which objects can be, but need not be, placed. What is presented in a map on this modern conception is not how things *look* at all. What is presented is space as a given whole of possible positions together with information about the locations of things in that space—in effect, their Cartesian coordinates. Whereas on the sensory conception the parts are prior to the whole, on this new, essentially late conception, the whole is prior to its parts, space to spaces, just as Kant argues in the Transcendental Aesthetic of the first *Critique*.[11] It is in light of just such a conception that we can understand a sphere not as the ancients did, as a three-dimensional object with a characteristic look and feel, but instead abstractly, mathematically, as a two-dimensional surface all the points of which are equidistant from a center, and can understand a number not as the pre-moderns did, as a collection of units (which is why even negative numbers were unintelligible to them), but more abstractly, as a node in the antecedently given whole of computational space. The idea that a concept might be exhausted by its inference potential, by its consequences in actual practice, that it might be wholly characterized by the axioms of some theory conceived

---

[11] Interestingly enough, Kant nevertheless does not have the modern conception of mathematical concepts. According to him, as already noted, mathematical concepts must be exhibited in (pure) intuition.

as an antecedently given and irreducible whole, is in this way essentially modern, possible only through a radical transformation of our already achieved view of the world.[12] But if that is right, then the pragmatist insight into the meaning of (modern) mathematical concepts is not and cannot be an insight into the meanings of concepts *überhaupt*.

I have suggested that we need to acknowledge the distinctive and indeed privileged status of modern mathematical concepts *without* taking them to provide the model for all concepts, thereby undermining the (essentially sensory) ground on the basis of which our grasp of mathematical concepts is first made possible. *Pace* the pragmatist, modern mathematical concepts are not the only sorts of concepts there are.[13] Nevertheless, they are distinctive and, in a way, privileged. This distinction and privilege has at least two related aspects, one subjective and one objective. Subjectively, mathematical concepts contrast with sensory ones in being, if only potentially prior to the full axiomatization of the relevant theory, fully transparent to thought. Unlike a sensory concept such as that of red, which ineluctably involves something brute—namely, the look of red things (in standard circumstances) to creatures like us—a mathematical concept is, or can become in an axiomatized theory, fully intelligible. Though one may be mistaken as to its cogency, one can know (at least in one important sense) *exactly* what one thinks by means of a mathematical concept; though one cannot know all its consequences, one can set out in an axiomatization that from which all those consequences follow. One can in this way take *full* responsibility for such concepts. The objective privilege of mathematical concepts is, correlatively, that insofar as the contents of such concepts are utterly independent of the particular sensory experience of things that is our biological and cultural inheritance, they are concepts of just the right sort to describe things as they are anyway, independent of the knowing subject. We cannot expect radically different sorts of beings, beings with very different sense modalities and very different forms of life, to understand the world as it shows up for us in our sensory experience.

[12] This fundamental transformation in our understanding is traced in more detail in Macbeth 2004. See also Macbeth 1994.

[13] Of course, the pragmatist would not put the point this way. What I have described as an insight into distinctively (modern) mathematical concepts is taken by the pragmatist to be a point about meaning and concepts generally. It does not so much as occur to him that the principle might apply only to (modern) mathematical concepts. On our account, the emphasis on interest-relativity of pragmatists such as James, Dewey, and Rorty is only a consequence of the assumption that the contents of all concepts are exhausted by their consequences.

We cannot expect them to understand our poetry, our history, our codes of conduct. What we can expect them to understand (as the rational beings they are), at least in principle, is our logic, our mathematics, and our physics. As we have seen, inferential articulation, even of our sensory concepts, is a necessary condition of their being concepts at all. In the case of mathematical concepts, such articulation is also sufficient (though only against the backdrop of a sensory view of the world). It follows that, though they would perhaps begin with a radically different sensory view of the world from our own, other rational creatures could in principle come to just the mathematical conceptions we come to. The mathematical conception of reality is correctly described as 'the view from nowhere' for just this reason, and for that same reason it is privileged as the view of how things are anyway, however they show up in the perceptual experience of this or that rational creature. But, I have argued, such a view is intelligible *only* as an essentially late modification of, as it were, the view from here—that is, the view from some particular biologically and culturally articulated perspective, whether our own or that of another sort of rational creature. We must *begin* with our sensory, perspectival view of the world, *and* we must learn to transcend that view, to form concepts that are exhausted by their consequences and thereby to take the view from nowhere.

Neither Peirce nor Sellars seems ever to have doubted that the pragmatist maxim constitutes an essential contribution to an adequate account of objective truth. And according to both, the key to understanding how it can constitute such a contribution lies in our rational capacity for self-correction. There is nothing brute to our mathematical concepts, nothing in them that is merely given (as, say, the sensory character of redness is given in our experience of red objects). The whole content of such concepts is available to rational scrutiny and subject to revision as reason demands. But rational scrutiny requires rational constraint by what is the case, and (although I have not tried to show it here) neither Peirce nor Sellars can provide an account of such constraint. What I *have* argued is that they cannot, because they mistakenly assume that the pragmatist maxim applies to all concepts. The pragmatist maxim, while it is indeed an insight into meaning, is not an insight into meaning *überhaupt*. It is an insight into the meaning only of distinctively modern mathematical concepts; and such concepts, I have argued, are intelligible only as an essentially late fruit of our ongoing sensory experience of the world as we first find it.

BIBLIOGRAPHY

Benacerraf, P. (1983) 'Mathematical Truth'. In P. Benacerraf and H. Putnam (eds.), *Philosophy of Mathematics: Selected Readings*, 2nd edn., 403–20. New York: Cambridge University Press.

Burge, T. (2005) 'Frege on Knowing the Foundation'. In *Truth, Thought, Reason: Essays on Frege*, 317–55. Oxford: Clarendon Press.

Frege, G. (1964) *The Basic Laws of Arithmetic: Exposition of the System*, trans. M. Furth. Berkeley and Los Angeles: University of California Press.

_____ (1980) *The Foundations of Arithmetic*, trans. J. L. Austin. Evanston, Ill.: Northwestern University Press.

Klein, J. (1968) *Greek Mathematical Thought and the Origin of Algebra*, trans. Eva Braun. Cambridge, Mass.: MIT Press.

Macbeth, D. (1994) 'The Coin of the Intentional Realm'. *Journal for the Theory of Social Behavior*, 24: 143–66.

_____ (2000) 'Empirical Knowledge: Kantian Themes and Sellarsian Variations'. *Philosophical Studies*, 101: 113–42.

_____ (2004) 'Viète, Descartes, and the Emergence of Modern Mathematics'. *Graduate Faculty Philosophy Journal*, 52: 87–117.

_____ (2005) *Frege's Logic*. Cambridge, Mass.: Harvard University Press.

McDowell, J. (1996) *Mind and World*. Cambridge, Mass.: Harvard University Press.

Misak, C. J. (2004) *Truth and the End of Inquiry*. Oxford: Clarendon Press.

Peirce, C. S. (1992) *The Essential Peirce: Selected Philosophical Writings*, i: *1867–1893*, ed. N. Houser and C. Kloesel. Bloomington and Indianapolis: Indiana University Press. Referred to as *EP* i.

_____ (1992) *Reasoning and the Logic of Things: The Cambridge Conference Lectures of 1898*, ed. Kenneth Laine Ketner. Cambridge, Mass.: Harvard University Press. Referred to as *RLT*.

_____ (1998) *The Essential Peirce: Selected Philosophical Writings*, ii: *1893–1913*, ed. N. Houser and C. Kloesel. Bloomington and Indianapolis: Indiana University Press. Referred to as *EP* ii.

Rorty, R. (1998) 'Robert Brandom on Social Practices and Representations', *Philosophical Papers*, iii: *Truth and Progress*, 122–37.

_____ (2000*a*) 'Reply to McDowell'. In R. B. Brandom (ed.), *Rorty and his Critics*, 123–8. Oxford: Blackwell.

_____ (2000*b*) 'Universality and Truth'. In R. B. Brandom (ed.), *Rorty and his Critics*, 1–30. Oxford: Blackwell.

Rusnock, P. (1997) 'Bolzano and the Traditions of Analysis'. In W. Künne, M. Siebel, and M. Textor (eds.), *Bolzano and Analytic Philosophy*, Grazer Philosophische Studien, 53: 61–85.

Sellars, W. (1953) 'Inference and Meaning'. *Mind*, 62: 313–38.

—— (1996) 'Empiricism and the Philosophy of Mind'. In *Empiricism and the Philosophy of Mind*. Cambridge, Mass.: Harvard University Press.

van Heijenoort, J. (1967) 'Logic as Calculus and Logic as Language'. *Synthese*, 17: 324–30.

Index